Herb Gardening

THE COUNTRYMAN PRESS
A division of W. W. Norton & Company
Independent Publishers Since 1923

Herb Gardening

MELISSA
MELTON
SNYDER

How to Prepare Soil, Choose
Your Plants, and Care For,
Harvest, and Use Your Herbs

For information about special discounts for bulk
purchases, please contact W. W. Norton Special Sales
at specialsales@wwnorton.com or 800-233-4830

Book design by Nick Caruso
Manufacturing by RR Donnelley, Shenzhen

Library of Congress Cataloging-in-Publication Data

Snyder, Melissa Melton, author.
Herb gardening : how to prepare the soil, choose your
plants, and care for, harvest, and use your herbs /
Melissa Melton Snyder.
pages cm.—(Countryman know-how)
Includes bibliographical references and index.
ISBN 978-1-58157-312-1 (pbk.)
1. Herb gardening. 2. Herbs. I. Title. II. Series:
Countryman know how.
SB351.H5S765 2016
635'.7—dc23
                          2015030291

THE COUNTRYMAN PRESS

www.countrymanpress.com

A division of W. W. Norton & Company
500 Fifth Avenue, New York, NY 10110
www.wwnorton.com

10 9 8 7 6 5 4 3 2 1

Photo Credits

Page 6: © Morrison/Shutterstock.com; 8: Jozef Sowa/Shutterstock.com;
10: © Christian Sabau/Shutterstock.com; 20: © globalfolkart/iStockphoto.com;
28: © Africa Studio/Shutterstock.com; 31: © Marta Jonina/Shutterstock.com;
38: © Imfoto/Shutterstock.com; 40: © Alzbeta/Shutterstock.com; 46: © oticki/
Shutterstock.com; 52: © Natalia bulatova/Shutterstock.com; 60: © Victoria
Field/Shutterstock.com; 64: © Jeanette Dieti/Shutterstock.com; 70: © estike/
Shutterstock.com; 72: © Toa55/Shutterstock.com; 74: © Jamie Hooper/
Shutterstock.com; 83: © jopelka/Shutterstock.com; 84: © Lee Snider Photo
Images/Shutterstock.com; 92: © Viacheslav Lopatin/Shutterstock.com;
97: © johnandersonphoto/Shutterstock.com; 101: © Alexander Bark/
Shutterstock.com; 102: © Antigoni Lekka/Shutterstock.com, © Dionisvera/
Shutterstock.com, © Anna Shepulova/Shutterstock.com, © Diana Taliun/
Shutterstock.com, © Dionisvera/Shutterstock.com; 103: © Olha Afanasieva/
Shutterstock.com, © Juta/Shutterstock.com, © Bohbeh/Shutterstock.com,
© teleginatania/Shutterstock.com; 104: © alina_danilova/Shutterstock.com,
© Kennerth Kullman/Shutterstock.com, © Olha Afanasieva/Shutterstock.com;
105: © Malivan_Iulila/Shutterstock.com, © Natalia bulatova/Shutterstock
.com, CGissemann/Shutterstock.com; 106: © GreenArt Photography/
Shutterstock.com, © stockcreations/Shutterstock.com, © Aneta_Gu/
Shutterstock.com; 107: © Zhanna Glinkina/Shutterstock.com, © Shulevskyy
Volodymyr/Shutterstock.com, © Matthew Benoit/Shutterstock.com,
© Lu Mikhaylova/Shutterstock.com; 108: © fotoknips/Shutterstock.com,
© olenaa/Shutterstock.com, © Pitchayarat Chootai/Shutterstock.com,
© EQRoy/Shutterstock.com; 109: © Ijh Images/Shutterstock.com, © membio/
iStockphoto.com; 110: © mtreasure/iStockphoto.com; 111: © Gita Kulinitch
Studio/Shutterstock.com; 112: © deepskenya/iStockphoto.com, © melis/
Shutterstock.com, © Alina Simakova/Shutterstock.com, © Bildagentur Zoonar
GmbH/Shutterstock.com; 113: © Vaclav Mach/Shutterstock.com, © fotokris/
iStockphoto.com, © shihina/Shutterstock.com; 114: © LianeM/Shutterstock
.com, © hichako_t/Shutterstock.com, © jdm.foto/Shutterstock.com;
115: © Bruce Amos/Shutterstock.com, © freya-photographer/Shutterstock
.com, © Imageman/Shutterstock.com, © silviacrisman/iStockphoto.com;
116: © alexsol/Shutterstock.com, © dabjola/Shutterstock.com;
117: © DeSerg/Shutterstock.com, © Greg Kushmerek/Shutterstock.com,
© Katie Hamlin/Shutterstock.com; 118: © Diana Baliuk/Shutterstock.com,
© Izf/Shutterstock.com, © Fotokostic/Shutterstock.com, © grannyogrimm/
iStockphoto.com; 119: © Dirk Richter/iStockphoto.com, © Ruud Morjin
Photographer/Shutterstock.com; 120: © T.W. van Urk/Shutterstock.com;
128: © Westbury/iStockphoto.com; 130: © Madlen/Shutterstock.com;
144: © capecodphoto/iStockphoto.com; 154: © AtomStudios/iStockphoto
.com; 156: © Petegar/iStockphoto.com; 164: © NightAndDayImages/
iStockphoto.com; 170: © AMV_80/Shutterstock.com; 184: © imnoom/
Shutterstock.com; 187: © Elena Elisseeva/Shutterstock.com; 190: © mythja/
iStockphoto.com; 191: © VTT Studio/Shutterstock.com; 196: © Mahathir
Mohd Yasin/Shutterstock.com; 198: © ChaiyonS021/Shutterstock.com;
200: © Fotokostic/Shutterstock.com; 210: © gabczi/Shutterstock.com;
216: © Shalith/Shutterstock.com; 224: © Kletr/Shutterstock.com;
225: © Chaikom/Shutterstock.com; 234: © GoodMood Photo/Shutterstock
.com; 236: © Oliver Hoffmann/iStockphoto.com; 242: © George tsartsianidis/
iStockphoto.com; 244: © Adriana Nikolova/Shutterstock.com

DEDICATION

This book is dedicated to all the women in my life, past and present, who have inspired me with their love of flowers and all things beautiful. Both my grandmothers, Honey and Daisy, taught me much about the elegance of the natural world and the usefulness of plants in all forms; Adelma Grenier Simmons taught me about the five seasons of herb gardening and was my original inspiration for leaving a comfortable life in the city for the dream of living the country life, meandering in an herb garden with a cup of coffee while tamping down the rootlets of a wayward thyme plant. I also want to remember the spirits of those predecessors who once occupied my current home; the hardworking pioneers and farm women who left behind hints of their herb gardens in the bundles of herbs in the attic rafters. They didn't plant herb gardens just for pleasure—the herbs they grew on this land were just as important to the life they led as were their animals and crops. We share their legacy now in some way.

Additionally, I would like to dedicate this book to the memory of Susan Urstadt, the first agent who saw the potential in my husband Steve, helped launch his writing career the same year we moved to Vermont, and was so instrumental in the early days of this amazing journey. I like to think she is smiling on us from above.

CONTENTS

The Basics

1

What's the Difference Between an Herb and a Plant?

That was a real question asked by a grade-schooler who wanted to use herb plants in a science-fair project. How was he to know that herbs *are* plants? Nobody ever told him about this stuff before. This was not an idiotic question. In this chapter we'll start off with some of the more frequent questions about herbs: the basics.

Are you a busy person who wants to try your hand at herb gardening? Have you always loved the idea of herbs in your garden, but felt that herb gardening seemed so difficult, so geometric, so formal? There's so much to learn about herbs, and you'll never figure it all out, right? Wrong! Herbs are among the easiest plants to grow, and they adapt to many different growing conditions—even those caused by beginning gardeners.

Most herbs just want a sunny spot with good drainage. If you've got that, you should have no problem. There are a few exceptions, of course, but we'll get into those in later chapters. Just start with

an idea or two, and build on that. As you gain confidence, you'll soon realize that herb gardening is not the least bit intimidating. And you'll actually *enjoy* it, too! The bottom line is, understanding a few basics about how plants grow—and why they sometimes don't—will help ensure the success of your herb garden-to-be.

Herbs are so accommodating. You can add some dill and basil to your vegetable garden, toss lavender and artemisia into your perennial border, or tuck a little plot of thyme and sage by your kitchen door. One of the best things about gardening with herbs is their diversity; you can choose from kinds with interesting foliage or showy flowers, or you can just stick with the culinary types. And these great little plants are so appealing that you won't be able to resist touching, sniffing, and tasting them every time you pass by.

There are a million reasons why gardening with herbs is not only easy, but enjoyable, too. For instance, there's nothing like being able to reach right out and snip some fresh chives or parsley for cooking, or stroll through the garden on a summer morning picking flowers for potpourri.

If you're feeling ambitious, you can give your little garden a theme, turning it into a colonial garden or a flower-filled cottage garden. If you're interested in dyeing your own fabrics, you could plant a dyer's garden. If you're fascinated with herbal medicine, you could plant an apothecary garden. Believe it or not, it's easy; the only limit is your imagination.

Another gratifying thing about herb gardening is there's not really an "off season" when nothing blooms. The variegated leaves of golden sage or silver thyme look beautiful all year, even when not in bloom. In some cases, the foliage is even more attractive than the blossoms! When other annuals have succumbed to the first frosts, parsley, summer savory, and lavender still hold their beauty, and the hardy little calendula will continue to bloom well into cold weather.

Finally, you don't have to wait for a special time to start using your herbs. As soon as the plants are large enough, you can start taking sprigs for cooking. In fact, pinching the ends off many leafy herbs like basil, rosemary, and tarragon will encourage bushy growth.

Rubbing or touching the leaves and stems of most herbs releases their scent.

With all these plants to choose from, this can all seem intimidating at first. What should you put in your garden? And how do you care for them? What if they get sick and die? But if you take it one step at a time, you'll get a handle on what kind of herb garden you want and which plants to put in it. The rest comes naturally. Before you know it, your neighbors will be coming over and asking who you hired to landscape your yard!

But before we get into those kinds of specifics, let's take a step back and cover a few basics.

What *Are* Herbs?

This is one of the most frequent questions I get at the farm. Many people think of herbs as just a few seasoning plants, but the definition of "herb" can be very broad! The dictionary defines an herb as "a seed-producing annual, biennial, or perennial that does not develop persistent woody tissue but dies down at the end of the season." But that definition would eliminate many plants that are considered herbs, like rosemary and sage. So for the purposes of this book, we'll use a broader definition: an herb is "a plant valued for its medicinal, savory, or aromatic qualities." This covers many more possibilities, including shrubs, trees, and many common flowering annuals and perennials that may already be in your garden, like roses and peonies.

Thousands of plants are considered herbs in this broader definition. In fact, if it's useful . . . it's an herb!

The Different Categories of Herbs

Most people today think of herbs as food seasonings, but a growing number are becoming aware of their medicinal properties. Historically, herbs have been used not just for cooking and medicine, but as dyes, perfumes, cleaners, cosmetics, and insect repellents. To top it off, many plants cross over into several of these categories. For instance, sage does double duty as both a poultry seasoning and a soothing tea for sore throats. Rosemary is beloved for its use in cooking, but it's also used medicinally, in aromatherapy, for potpourri, and as a brunette hair rinse.

Anise, angelica, caraway, dandelion, hops, hyssop, marshmallow, thyme, and nettles are all listed in ancient herbal texts as both medicinal and culinary herbs.

THE WONDERS OF A LITTLE YELLOW FLOWER

The cheerful flowers of calendulas were once used as a saffron substitute, to color butter and cheese, as a yellow dye for wool, and as a hair rinse to bring out highlights in brunette and blonde hair. But perhaps most importantly, in the form of a salve, oil, or tincture, the plant was used as a gentle treatment for chapped skin, bruises, cuts, and rashes. A tea made from the flowers promotes perspiration, and it was used as a folk treatment for jaundice during colonial times. It's generally agreed that the plant has no known side effects, and it's even safe enough to treat diaper rash on babies!

LAVENDER

Lavender is one of the most useful herbs of all. Most people are familiar with lavender's fresh scent, used in perfumes and soaps, but did you know that lavender buds are an ingredient in the seasoning blend *Herbes de Provence*? The flowers are also used in jams and jellies, and can be candied for decorating desserts. *And* lavender has a long history as an antiseptic for freshening sickrooms, is used in aromatherapy to relieve headaches, is added to bathwater to calm irritable children, and is an ingredient in smelling salts. Cosmetically, lavender vinegar is helpful for oily skin and is used in facials.

Lavender's ornamental qualities make it a must for both gardens and crafts, with the wonderful scent lingering for a very long time, even when dry. As an age-old ingredient in potpourri and sachets, it keeps linen closets and drawers spring-time fresh while deterring moths. Who knew one little plant could do all those things?

Weeds or Herbs?

Guess what? Many weeds and wildflowers are considered herbs. Why? Because some of them came over with the colonists, "escaped" from the confines of early herb gardens, and became naturalized. Many a New England farmhouse is still surrounded by the old lilacs that were planted in every dooryard, or a stand of tansy, comfrey, and scentless chamomile. Dame's rocket, maiden pinks, and Alexanders are other examples.

Others such as beebalm, Joe-pye-weed, and witch hazel are native American plants that gained popularity when the colonists learned their uses from the Indians. A huge number of plants are included in this category, purple coneflower, boneset, goldenrod, and meadowsweet among them.

HERBAL *WEEDS*?

Then there are the herbal "weeds." Yes, I said weeds. Old herbals are filled with common plants that were once held in high esteem but are now treated like noxious pests. OK, maybe some of them are, but think about this: Dandelions are more nutritious than spinach, containing both vitamin C and vitamin A. They were so well-respected for generations that one nineteenth-century source gives advice on growing them as a crop! Other healthy herbal "weeds" are plantain, burdock, stinging nettle, purslane, sheep sorrel, and chickweed. Don't get me wrong—I'm not suggesting you plant these in your formal herb garden. But instead of trying to eradicate these from your yard, consider harvesting them!

Some specialty herb catalogs actually sell seeds of "improved" varieties of dandelion, burdock, and purslane.

HERBAL *TREES*?

Yes, there are herbal trees, too. Did you know that the inner bark of the willow tree contains salicylic acid, from which aspirin was developed? Elder flowers yield drinks, cosmetics, and dyes. The ripe fruits of the hawthorn are used to treat heart and circulatory disorders. Linden blossoms make a remedy for nervous tension. We'll cover more of these in later chapters, but for now I just wanted to give you an overview of all the different varieties of useful plants that make up the world of herbs.

What's the Difference Between Herbs and Spices?

This is the second most-asked question I get at the farm. Referring to the dictionary again, herbs are the leaves, stems, and flowers of plants grown in temperate climates like most of the United States. Examples are basil, rosemary, and borage.

Spices are the seeds, roots, barks, and pods of *tropical* plants. Examples of spices are cinnamon, which comes from the bark of a tree; cloves, which are the flower buds of *Syzygium aromaticum*, an evergreen tree in the myrtle family; and vanilla, which is the seed pod of a fifty-foot tropical orchid.

Herbs are usually green and have subtler flavors, while spices tend to be shades of brown, black, or red and have a dramatic, pungent flavor.

Here's one that covers both bases: The fresh or dried green leaves of the coriander plant (*coriandrum sativum*) are called cilantro or Chinese parsley, both *herbs*. But the brown seed of the same plant is known as the *spice* coriander.

Finally, because most spices have also been used for their aromatic and healing qualities, this places them under our broader definition of *herbs*, which, remember, is "a plant valued for its medicinal, savory, or aromatic qualities."

So even though not everyone will be able to grow a fifty-foot orchid in their backyard for a homegrown supply of vanilla, we still consider spices to be herbs.

SOME MORE EXAMPLES OF SPICES

Saffron: The dried stigma of an autumn blooming crocus. The world's most expensive spice, it takes thirty-five thousand flowers to produce one pound of the spice.

Hot peppers: You thought they were veggies, didn't you? Cayenne pepper is valued as a medicinal herb. High in vitamin C and vitamin A, the active component in cayenne pepper is capsaicin, which has stimulant effects on the digestive system, as well as soothing (yes, *soothing!*) qualities. A skin salve made with capsaicin to treat arthritis and shingles is sold over the counter in the US.

Black pepper: The dried fruit of a perennial climbing shrub. The world's most popular spice, black pepper is used both as a condiment and as a food preservative. Medicinally, it's used for constipation, nausea, vertigo, and arthritis.

Ginger: The fresh root of a creeping tropical perennial. Not just for gingerbread and mulled cider, ginger has a long history as an anti-nausea treatment. That's why Mom always used to give you ginger ale when you were feeling queasy.

Cardamom: The seeds of a ten-foot tropical perennial. Used to season beverages, pickles, breads, and coffee, it's also an ingredient in curry powder. Chewing the seeds freshens the breath and relieves flatulence, indigestion, and headaches.

Star anise: The fruit of a thirty-foot flowering tree. The seed is an important spice, and is used as a substitute for aniseed. Medicinally, it's used for indigestion, flatulence, bronchitis, and coughs.

Nutmeg: The fruit of a twenty-five-foot flowering tropical tree. The fruit contains a kernel (nutmeg) surrounded by a red aril (mace). Nutmeg is used to season milk and cheese dishes and beverages.

Coffee: The dried seed of a long-lived perennial evergreen shrub. Never thought of coffee as an herbal beverage? You're not alone. But like the other herbs and spices we've discussed, coffee has multiple uses. In addition to its classic use as a morning pick-me-up, coffee's active ingredient, caffeine, is used with aspirin in some well-known pain relievers to battle headaches and other aches and pains, and has been shown to alleviate asthma attacks.

Your First Few Tries

When I started my first real herb garden, I was so excited just to be planting something in the lead-infested soil of my urban backyard that I ignored every single piece of advice I had heard or read. I stuffed dozens of herbs, flowers, and vegetables into a tiny space that only got two hours of sun a day, not taking into account minor details like their growth habits, the fact that a plant actually needs *sun*, and what the term invasiveness *really* means. I just planted with abandon.

I learned some interesting lessons those first years. Tomatoes from the ground are *much* bigger than those in a grocery-store six-pack; same with cucumbers. Nasturtiums deprived of sunlight will grow foliage the size of dinner plates but hardly any flowers. And the otherwise indestructible lamb's ear will rot away to nothing during a shady, wet summer.

On the other hand, I learned that some of the conventional wisdom was not necessarily etched in stone. Sure, beebalm prefers full sun, but in partial sun I got beautiful, tall blooms that lasted the whole second half of the summer; same with purple coneflower! And rosemary *can* survive outside as far north as northern New Jersey if it's protected during the winter. I experimented a lot; some of my attempts worked, some didn't. One of the best lessons I learned was that experimenting is OK.

Some lessons I just can't seem to get through my head and am still doing "wrong," like putting more than one kind of mint in a bed (without employing the bottomless restraining bucket that everyone recommends). But I really enjoy watching the different varieties duke it out every summer. It makes for a beautiful contrast in the bed, between the variegated leaves of pineapple mint, dark purple stems of peppermint, grayish green applemint, and vivid green spearmint. And when they get out of hand, I can always rip them out and make tea!

An Early Botany Lesson

One of the first things I had to learn was the difference between annuals, biennials, and perennials. I'll go into this in more detail in Chapter 3, but basically, the herb world is made up of all three types. Like most people, I always thought of annuals as just bedding plants like impatiens and petunias, and perennials as large border plants like daylilies and irises. What a revelation to discover that herbs fall not only into both categories, but that many of the perennials that are commonly grown in flower gardens are also considered herbs! Knowing the differences between them will take you a long way toward understanding how to grow them.

A Few Quick Definitions

Annual: A plant that grows, flowers, sets seed, and dies in one season. They're usually fast growing, and many will flower abundantly all summer long. Most annuals are easy to grow, and many can be grown from seed right in your garden. Annuals are broken down into *half-hardy*, meaning they will continue to grow and flower after the first frost until a very hard freeze, and *tender*, meaning they will die at the first hint of a frost.

Biennial: A plant that lives for two years. A biennial grows its leaves the first season, then flowers, sets seed, and dies its second year. Biennials frequently form a rosette of leaves close to the ground their first year and send up a tall flower spike the second.

Perennial: A plant that lives for more than two years. There are long-lived perennials, like mint, tansy, and wormwood, and there are short-lived perennials like foxglove. These usually set lots of seed, and sometimes you won't even notice that the following year's plant is really just the offspring of the original. Perennials are further broken down into groups of *herbaceous*, meaning they die to the ground in winter; and *woody*, meaning the stem gets

HERE ARE SOME POPULAR EXAMPLES

- Annuals: (*half-hardy*) borage, calendula, German chamomile, cilantro, dill; (*tender*) basil, nasturtium, cayenne pepper
- Biennials: angelica, clary, parsley, woad
- Perennials: (*herbaceous*) anise hyssop, beebalm, catnip, comfrey, horehound, lemon balm, mint, oregano, pennyroyal, sorrel, tarragon; (*woody*) germander, hyssop, lavender, sage, santolina, southernwood, roses, willow, eucalyptus; (*tender*) bay laurel, rosemary (in some areas), lemongrass, lemon verbena, scented geraniums, sweet marjoram

woody with age, like a tree, and new growth each year comes from those stems. Some herbs of each group are *tender*, meaning they must be taken inside for the winter in most parts of the United States.

What Herbs Need

It's been said that herbs thrive in poor soil. Well, that's partly true, but very few plants can survive in totally depleted soil. For example, they won't grow in the subsoil left over from construction or under a tree where nothing else will grow. However, many of the better-known herbs come from the Mediterranean, where conditions can be pretty harsh. These herbs have had to withstand brisk winds, sandy and rocky soil, and very hot temperatures, so the conditions in your yard are likely to be somewhat better than where they came from.

In the chapter on soil, we'll talk about easy ways you can make your garden a haven for herbs. But for now, just remember that most herbs need sun, good drainage, and a little compost every spring. Obviously, there are many exceptions (like my urban shade garden), but this is the basic rule of thumb. If you've got these things, you can grow herbs.

Mother Nature Knows Best

In nature, plants get their nutrition from the decomposition of their predecessors seeping back into the soil—and part of the normal cycle of things includes bugs. In a healthy garden, there is a balance between the pests that feed on the plants and the beneficial insects that feed on the pests. Unfortunately, some modern gardening practices have interrupted this process, making bug infestations much more noticeable. In this book we'll explore ways of keeping the natural cycles in balance, from using compost as mulch to learning to control a bug infestation. Healthy herbs are amazingly pest resistant, which is reason enough to grow them. So let's get started, shall we?

CHAPTER 2

A Brief History of Herbs

In this chapter we'll look briefly into the past to gain some perspective on the long and glorious history of herbs. Throughout time, humankind has depended on the usefulness of plants for food, medicine, and raw materials for building, clothing, and ornamentation. In the book of Genesis, life begins in a garden. In the Islamic paradise, a walled garden with shade trees and flowing water nurtures fragrant flowers and exotic fruits. In reality, gardens of the Muslim world contained roses, jasmine, lilies, and fruit and nut trees such as pomegranates, apricots, and almonds hedged with myrtle.

Chinese, Indian, and Egyptian Medicine

The world's oldest healing systems are Chinese, Indian, and Egyptian. Herbalism in China has survived as an unbroken tradition to this day and is accepted as the most thorough and effective herbal healing system in the world.

The first tome of Chinese medical knowledge to be translated into a Western language (1596) was the work of Li Shih-Chen, who detailed more than one thousand plant substances and twelve thousand prescriptions. His work is still valued as a reference in China today.

The oldest Chinese pharmacopoeia is the Pen-ts'ao ("Herbal"), traditionally ascribed to the emperor Shen Nung between 3737–2693 BC (it was probably actually written closer to 1000 BC). The Pen-ts'ao records more than three-hundred herbal concoctions. From the third century BC to the seventh century AD, Chinese herbal medicine was heavily influenced by the Taoist doctrine of prevention that incorporated acupuncture, herbs, proper diet, therapeutic massage, and gentle exercises to correct imbalances in the body.

The Indian healing tradition, much like the one employed in China, strives to maintain health

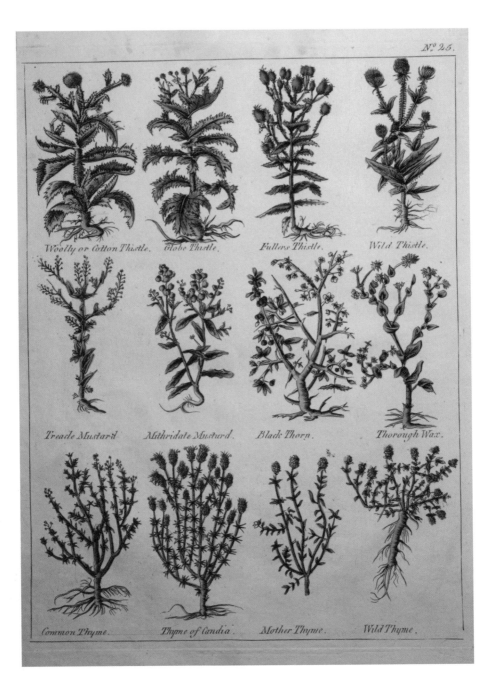

Woolly or Cotton Thistle.   Globe Thistle.   Fullers Thistle.   Wild Thistle.

Treacle Mustard   Mithridate Mustard.   Black Thorn.   Thorough Wax.

Common Thyme.   Thyme of Candia.   Mother Thyme.   Wild Thyme.

and prevent sickness through a healthy diet, exercise, and "yogas" (methods of regulating the body's vital energy). The Indian "Ayurveda" or "science of life" was also highly developed by 1000 BC. In the "Rigveda," an ancient Hindu text, more than a thousand medicinal plants are detailed. References to India's herbal remedies are found in Dioscorides's famous first century herbal.

From what archaeologists and historians have been able to gather, some of the earliest herb gardens appear to have been cultivated in Egypt as much as four thousand years ago. Herbs were linked with temple sites, where various herbs and flowers were needed for daily religious ceremonies. Cornflowers, poppies, and mandrakes are all featured in surviving paintings found on temple walls.

> Embalming used fragrant spices and herbs such as cumin, anise, marjoram, cassia, and cinnamon. Chamomile was the primary herb used in the embalming oil of Ramses II.

The herbal healing tradition of the Egyptians seems to have developed at about the same time as those in China and India. Egyptian medicine, however, also included magic, sacrifice, prayer, and the casting of spells, along with empirical study and even some surgical procedures. Surviving documents have offered modern scholars a surprisingly detailed view of ancient Egyptian medicine.

Papyruses 3,000 to 4,000 years old suggest that even older oral traditions existed before Egyptian medicine began to be put down in writing.

> **TRIVIA THYME:**
>
> One of the greatest finds of Egyptologists came in 1874 when Georg Ebers discovered a 65-foot-long papyrus detailing information about surgery, internal medicine, and hundreds of medicinal drugs, including herbs such as fennel, coriander, fenugreek, caraway, and thyme.

The Greeks and Romans

The ancient geometric gardens influenced the Greeks, who in turn influenced the Romans, who then brought their gardening ethic to Europe. The Greek Theophrastus (371–287 BC), a student of Plato and Aristotle, is called the "father of botany."

> The first known botanical garden was Aristotle's Lyceum in Athens, filled with specimens sent back by his student Alexander the Great.

With their enclosed courtyard gardens, the Romans deserve the credit for what we'd call today the art of European gardening. The Romans incorporated the aquatic and geometric features of the Persians and the container gardening of the Ancient Egyptians. They also developed their own unique inventions like the topiary. Urban homes had roofless garden "rooms." Favorite plants of the Romans were rosemary, bay, and myrtle. Other herbs and flowers were grown as much for their aromatic and visual appeal as for their culinary or medicinal qualities.

The Romans' talent for garden design was most evident, perhaps, in the Roman villa. Precisely geometrical classic villa gardens like those in Pompeii, which included statues, colonnades, and raised beds, have been discovered in places as far away from Rome as England and Portugal.

Our word "baccalaureate" comes from the Latin *bacca laureus*, a garland of bay laurel bestowed upon new doctors in ancient Rome.

Roman medicine was based in the writing of the Greeks Galen (130–200 AD) and Dioscorides (first century AD), who wrote the first true herbal documenting the medicinal plants of the Mediterranean and their proper use. *De Materia Medica* succinctly details about five hundred plants. Galen's writings gave more complete advice on usage.

The legend of the "Hanging Gardens of Babylon" has been borne out by archaeological evidence that a large, elaborately terraced garden structure existed in what is now Iraq.

The Middle Ages and Monasteries

Early Christian monasteries were modeled after the Roman villa, with a covered walkway (called a "cloister") surrounding a central open courtyard. They were also typically designed in a geometric and formal pattern, again like the Roman villa. Few new innovations were made in the Christian monasteries; they primarily kept alive the ancient traditions of Greece, Rome, Egypt, Syria, and Persia, in which valued plants were nurtured in enclosed gardens to shield them from predators (both animal and human).

The Muslim invasion of North Africa resulted

in texts from ancient Greece being translated into Arabic. With the subsequent invasion of Spain by the Moors, these texts were then translated into Latin. Through this indirect route, European medical schools were introduced to extensive lists of healing herbs and to the principle of the garden as a place of restoration that benefited human health through a combination of rest and exercise.

The cultivation of plant life became so firmly engrained in monastic life that when Benedict founded his order at Monte Cassino in Italy in the sixth century, gardening was second in importance only to prayer in the daily routine. In the Benedictine *Regula Monachorum*—the basis of monastic life even today—it is stipulated that vegetables, fruits, grapes, herbs, dye plants, and aromatic plants for incense should be grown. Monasteries were largely self-sufficient, placing special emphasis on herbs to heal the sick. Monks saw the care of the sick as one of their chief duties; through this mission they became well-versed in the classic practices of herbal healing. Aromatic herbs were planted outside windows to sweeten the air, and strewn on the floor to repel insects and cover offensive odors.

The medieval monastery provided a more or less secure and peaceful haven after the fall of the Roman Empire and the onset of the so-called "Dark Ages." Horticulture and medicine, in addition to other forms of learning, were kept alive. Monastic gardens within the cloister were rarely planted with flowers and herbs; instead they were simply a geometric lawn with a water feature, such as a small pond or fountain, in the center. These were meant to be places of quiet contemplation. The functional gardens were usually planted outside the cloister or in a very utilitarian plot.

In addition to the Islamic invasions of Europe, the European invasion and occupation of Palestine during the crusades (1096–1291) opened a whole world of herbs and spices to the West. Now that they controlled many of the old spice-trading routes from the East, the crusaders enthusiastically brought their discoveries back to Europe.

Among the secular community, herb gardening grew more fashionable in the thirteenth century. Most wealthy households grew a large variety of herbs for everyday use, while more modest homes were surrounded by a combination of fruit and nut trees, grasses, and a kitchen garden in which vegetables, herbs, and flowers were grown together.

A castle garden was necessarily small, but these "pleasure gardens," though also centered on a lawn or "flowery mead," were lavishly planted with sweet-smelling herbs and flowers. Often intended as a romantic getaway for ladies and/or their lovers, they often contained fruit and nut trees for shade and chamomile-covered turf seats. These gardens became the focal points for the idealized courtly love and romances of the chivalric age. Tapestries of the era are filled with vast numbers of herbs and flowers, full of symbolism both religious and romantic.

Our concept of cuisine in the Middle Ages (roughly 600–1500 AD in most of Western Europe) is of bland, monotonous gruel and coarse, black

bread. For the peasantry, this may have been more or
less true. But just as the gulf between rich and poor
was great, so were the dietary habits. The cuisine of
the wealthier noble and merchant classes was not
unlike what we think of Indian cuisine today, especially the highly spiced curries. Herbs and spices
such as cumin, basil, ginger, cardamom, coriander,
and black pepper were used extensively in complex
blends. Wintertime would of course bring a more
restricted diet, but in spring, summer, and fall a
wide variety of native herbs, vegetables, and flowers were eaten in salads (sallets), in addition to the
ubiquitous beans, peas, and coleworts (brassicas).

Herbs such as costmary and ground ivy were also
used extensively to brew ale and to make wine more
palatable—wine was often of poor quality, even in
noble households.

The Age of Herbals

The "Great Age of Herbals" began in the 1500s with
the publication of lavishly illustrated herbals by
two of the fathers of German botany: Otto Brunfels
and Leonard Fuchs. Fuchs penned his *De Historia
Stirpium* because of the widespread ignorance about
herbs among his fellow physicians. This collection
of ancient herbal wisdom with discoveries from the
New World, paired with realistic and lush illustra-
tions of plant life, was to remain popular for more
than a century.

An *"herbal"* is a book written for the mass market, describing plants and how they should be
used, with an emphasis on the medicinal. These
books were invaluable in an age where medicine
rested primarily in the hands of the housewife.

Another popular herbalist was Belgian Rembert
Dodoens, whose *Cruydeboeck* was published in 1554,
then revised and republished in Latin as *Stirpium
Historiae* in 1583.

In the sixteenth century, extensive herb gardens

were planted (often in alphabetical order) by universities for teaching botany and medicine—subjects that were inextricably linked until separated by advances in modern science during the eighteenth century. The first "physic garden" was planted at the University of Padua in 1545. By the end of the seventeenth century, there were physic gardens at universities throughout Europe. As new species of plants were brought back by colonial explorers from the New World and botanical knowledge expanded, physic gardens embraced a far wider range of plants and became the botanical gardens we know today.

First published in 1597, one of the most famous herbals is John Gerard's *Herball or General Historie of Plants,* a work based largely on a translation from Latin to English of Rembert Dodoen's herbal, but with the addition of Gerard's own herbal remedies, comments, and rearrangement of the herbs listed in the text. Gerard, like many herbalists of the time, was involved in medicine as well as gardening.

The most popular and undoubtedly most controversial herbalist in England was Nicholas Culpepper, an iconoclastic apothecary who was determined to take medical knowledge away from the exclusive control of physicians and give them to apothecaries and the general public. In 1649 he translated the *London Pharmacopeia* from Latin to English and renamed it the *Physicall Directory.* Culpepper believed deeply in the so-called "doctrine of signatures," a belief that clues to a plant's intended therapeutic purpose were hidden in its shape and color. If a plant looked like a heart, it was good for the heart;

if it looked like a liver, it was good for the liver, etc. In 1651 Culpepper published his most famous work, *The English Physician* (AKA *The Complete Herbal*), a lavishly illustrated combination of astrology, the doctrine of signatures, and botany. This herbal was immensely popular among laymen.

Culpepper's *Complete Herbal* is seen as the culmination of the Age of Herbals. Scientific reason gained ground as authorities such as Sir Thomas Brown began to question many of the superstitious "truths" propagated for centuries, and apothecaries began to rely more on strict empirical studies of plants.

> The dubious "doctrine of signatures" may not be completely false after all. Recent studies have shown that some of the plants named for body parts they resemble may actually be beneficial in treating diseases for those organs. Lungwort, for example, has been found to actually contain substances that are useful in treating some lung ailments!

Herbs in the New World

In addition to their Western beliefs, clothes, furniture, and culture, the colonists moving to the New World brought with them their treasured herbs as well as their gardening traditions. In Elizabethan England, herbs, flowers, and vegetables were all intermingled in kitchen gardens; likewise, the colonists surrounded their homes in the New World with a hodgepodge of useful plants conveniently located near the kitchen, which was in operation from dawn to dusk as part of the daily routine. This "intensive companion planting," as we would call it today, has shown many benefits in pest and weed control.

> Here's a partial list of herbs grown in the colonies, compiled by John Josselyn in 1672. I've left out his recommendations for which ones thrive here and which don't, but I've retained the charming original spellings. You'll no doubt recognize them all.
>
> - annis
> - baye
> - comferie
> - featherfew
> - ground ivey
> - lavender-cotten
> - penny royal
> - purslain
> - rew
> - tansie

The colonists were perhaps as self-sufficient as their monastic counterparts in the Middle Ages, growing an impressive array of culinary, medicinal, and dye herbs among their vegetables and fruits.

Colonists in the New World also discovered a vast wealth of indigenous plants and herb lore of the Native American population. Although some dismissed the Indian medicine as primitive, many others gained an intense interest in the newfound herbal knowledge after the publication of Dr. Benjamin Barton's study of Indian healing techniques and materials in his *Collections for an Essay Towards a* Materia Medica *of the United States.*

> Anise, angelica, caraway Many of America's roadside "weeds" are actually escapees from colonial gardens native to Europe and Asia. Some examples: Queen Anne's lace, Saint-John's-wort, motherwort, yarrow, soapwort, dame's rocket, celandine, catnip, teasel, tansy, rose campion, and the much-hated plantain. , dandelion, hops, hyssop, marshmallow, thyme, and nettles are all listed in ancient herbal texts as both medicinal and culinary herbs.

Perhaps the most well known herb lover and gardener of the colonial period is Thomas Jefferson, though George Washington's herb garden at Mount Vernon is also well known. Jefferson, in addition to his love of Italian wine grapes, was also an avid herb gardener, interplanting herbs and vegetables in the kitchen garden like his Elizabethan ancestors. Jefferson was particularly fond of French tarragon and nasturtiums, which he planted in an enormous bed at his Virginia home, Monticello.

The Decline and Renewal of Herbal Medicine

With all the native plants and European imports, coupled with the healing traditions of European and Native American cultures as well as the growing scientific knowledge of the Enlightenment, the herbal healing world was in full bloom.

As the eighteenth century drew to a close and the Industrial Revolution emerged, chemists began to isolate more and more of the alkaloids that gave herbs their healing powers and subsequently began to develop synthetic substitutes as the medical establishment moved further away from folk medicine.

In the twentieth century, particularly during the 1930s and 1940s, pharmaceutical science exploded and twentieth century medicine, relying on powerful synthetic drugs, began to dominate. Herbal medicine and herbal healing knowledge quickly waned. Nevertheless, many prescription drugs contain active plant ingredients, and the vast majority are synthetic derivatives of herbs.

However, partly as the result of the counterculture movement of the 1960s, and more recently as a backlash against large, impersonal healthcare, herbal and folk medicine have seen a tremendous renaissance in the past twenty years.

Despite the prevalence of orthodox Western medicine in the United States, more than seventy-five percent of the world's population relies primarily on herbal medicine.

CHAPTER 3

A Little Botany. *Very* Little.

You don't need to be a botanist to garden, but it's not a bad idea to have a basic familiarity with this stuff. This chapter is going to explain (painlessly, I hope) some of the differences between annuals and perennials, why it's a good idea to know both the common names and the Latin tongue-twisters, and a little about the actual structure of the plants in your herb-garden-to-be.

Scientific Names

When you see plant names in a book, you'll frequently see two different names; the common name, followed by the Latin, or scientific name: Sweet Basil (*Ocimum basilicum*).

It may not seem important to you yet, but it's a good idea to familiarize yourself with both names. The use of Latin is the basic language of all scientific nomenclature, not just botany. That's because at the time of the development of this classification system, Latin was nearly universally understood by the better-educated classes.

The system in use today was first introduced by Carl von Linné, a Swedish botanist and biologist who lived in the 1700s, who even Latinized his own name—to Carolus Linnaeus. He coined the term *Homo sapiens*, which means wise man, to classify humans.

Botanists all over the world use the same Latin names to describe plants, and have been doing so for centuries. They've established a uniform system for naming plants; the system uses a binomial (two name) system to identify plants, much like our own names for people. The generic name (genus) corresponds to a person's last name (like Smith) and the specific name (species) is like the first name (John). But the generic name is always first and the species second, similar to how names appear on bureaucratic lists, e.g. Smith, John.

FAMILY NAMES

Families are groupings of similar plants, all given a generic name. Knowing which family a plant belongs to goes a long way in helping you know how to care for it.

Some of the larger and more familiar families in the herb world are below.

Mint, *Labiatae* (sometimes called *Lamiaceae*)

This family includes mint (imagine that!), basil, lavender, rosemary, and thyme.

Things these plants have in common: flower shape and growth by runners—or in the case of the woody-stemmed lavender and rosemary, stems that readily take root when they have contact with the ground.

Daisy, *Compositae* (sometimes called *Asteracae*)

This family includes chamomile, feverfew, dandelion, and calendula.

Again, flower shape is a very good clue; almost all *compositae* family members have round, daisy-like flowers. Their primary method of reproducing is by prolific seeding.

Carrot, *Umbelliferae* (sometimes called *Apiaceae*)

This family includes parsley, chervil, angelica, and cilantro.

See, you're getting it . . . it's the flower shape again! In this case the flowers are umbrella shaped and are called umbells. These guys also reproduce primarily by seeding themselves rather than by spreading or sending runners.

Other well-known families include:

- rose, *Roseaceae*: contains roses (duh!), meadowsweet, salad burnet, lady's mantle, and strawberries
- lily, *Liliaceae*: contains chives, garlic, and many other bulb producing plants, as well as aloe
- cruciferae, *Brassica*: Their vegetable cousins are well known, but did you know that horseradish, mustard, sweet rocket, and arugula are in this family too?
- *Caryophyllaceae*: contains *Dianthus* (pinks), carnations, and soapwort
- *Boragaceae*: contains borage, comfrey, vipers bugloss, lungwort, and forget-me-not. Distinguished by very hairy leaves and stems, and by flowers that turn from blue to pink as they age on the plant.
- *Malvaceae*: contains marshmallow and hollyhock
- *Myrtaceae*: contains myrtle and eucalpytus
- *Violaceae*: contains pansy, heartsease, and violets

You can think of plant families as the largest groupings of people, and the genus names as a smaller division, followed by even smaller divisions for the species. For instance, in the family Labiatae there is the genus *Mentha* (its "last name") and the species epithet *spicata* (its "first name"). *Mentha spicata*, therefore, refers to the particular type of mint called spearmint. *Mentha aquatica* is water mint, and *Mentha x piperita* is peppermint. Did you notice the second name is sort of descriptive? That's because they were designed to describe the plant. In theory, it's a good system, but sometimes it doesn't work out that way.

Examples of commonly used species epithets:

USES

- *officinale (officinalis)*: medicinal, of apothecaries
- *sativum (sativa, sativum)*: cultivated, planted, sown, not wild
- *satureja*: culinary
- *vulgare (vulgaris)*: common
- *tinctoria (tinctorius)*: for dye

COLOR

- *alba*: white
- *nigra*: black
- *purpurea*: purple
- *cinerea*: light gray
- *rubrum*: red
- *variegate*: variegated

GROWTH HABITS

- *angustifolia*: narrow-leafed
- *millefolium*: having many leaves
- *perforatum (perfoliatum)*: having perforated leaves
- *digitalis*: thimble-shaped (from the German "fingerhut")
- *quinquefolium*: having five leaves

- *grandiflora*: large-flowered
- *spicata*: spiked
- *dentate*: toothed
- *graveolens*: strong-smelling, heavily scented
- *tormentosa*: woolly, hairy
- *tomentosa*: trailing
- *serpyllum*: mat-forming
- *procumbens*: trailing
- *odorata*: fragrant
- *citriodorus*: lemon-scented

With the above list, you can look at a plant catalog, see the name *Thymus serpyllum*, and realize that the thyme plant offered is a creeping one rather than

Sometimes plant names come from Greek mythology. For instance, the genus *Achillea* was named for the Greek war hero Achilles, because he used these plants in battle to stop bleeding wounds.

an upright variety. And if you're ever in a field full of yellow flowers that you can't identify, you can look at the leaves. If they look "perforated," you'll know you have Saint-John's-wort (*Hypericum perforatum*). Pretty cool, huh?

Sometimes after the species epithets in the name, there are further subdivisions, called subspecies, varieties, and forms. These terms refer to natural variations. In these cases, you'll see the word stuck on the end of the binomial name, like *Mentha suaveolens* var. *variegata*. This one means that *Mentha suaveolens* (applemint) has a variegated variety: pineapple mint.

Cultivars, however, are distinct horticultural types that have been developed by cultivation. You'll recognize them by their single quotation marks, e.g. *lavandula angustifolia* 'Munstead.'

Finally, if you see an *x* in the name, it indicates a hybrid, which is a crossing of two genera, species, or cultivars. This is usually done by breeders, but— especially in the case of mints—can happen naturally. Peppermint, mentioned above, is an example.

Occasionally you'll see the genus name abbreviated to the first letter, as in *A. schoenoprasum*. This only occurs in lists when it is clear what the genus is. The complete name is used for the first item in the list, and the rest are abbreviated, as follows: *Allium schoenoprasum* (chives), *A. tuberosum* (garlic chives), *A. sativum* (garlic), *A. cepa viviparum* (Egyptian Onion).

Some rules seem to have been invented just to confuse lay people like us, like the fact that family names are never italicized but always capitalized, but genus names are always capitalized and always italicized. Species epithets are always italicized, but never capitalized, except in a few cases where they have been changed from genus names or are named after people. Another odd rule is that sometimes with epithets you'll see *officinalis* and *officinale,* or *vulgare* and *vulgaris*. This is because they need to agree in gender, just like in French. But don't worry, just recognizing the basic root of the word is all that's needed.

Common Names vs. Latin Names

Don't get me wrong—common names are easier for everyday use. But we still need to use Latin names when referring to plants because sometimes the common names are so darn confusing. Here are a few examples.

You go to buy a scented purple heliotrope from a nursery, but you come home with valerian. Why? Because when you asked for heliotrope, the clerk thought you meant garden heliotrope (*Valerian officinalis*) when you really meant *Heliotropium arborescens*.

Or you have a friend who offers to give you some bergamot out of her garden, but you'd really prefer to get some plain old beebalm. You're in luck, because the two are different common names for the same plant: *Monarda didyma*.

Or worse yet, you try to identify a plant your neighbor calls "all-heal" and discover there are twenty different plants with that name! Balm of Gilead is another example; nobody really knows which was the original plant mentioned in the Bible, but today dozens of plants claim the title.

See why it's a good idea to use the Latin? I promise you won't sound pretentious when you're trying to pronounce these tongue-twisting names!

A NOTE ABOUT PRONUNCIATION

Since Latin is pretty much a dead tongue, there are no hard and fast rules about pronouncing these words. There are a few guidelines, though.

- Most vowels are long, not short. So *linum*=LYE num, not lih num; *spica*=SPY cuh.
- When there is an *e* on the end, pronounce it. So, *perenne*=per REN ee; *umbelifferae*=um bel LIF fer ee; *liliaceae*=lil ee AY see ee.
- Pronounce the *es* at the end, too: *tagetes*=ta JEE teez; *onites*=oh NYE teez.

Life Cycles: Annuals, Biennials, and Perennials

OK, now the Latin lesson is over and the science lesson begins. This part is a little easier, because we're going to be using plain old English. We briefly covered some of this ground in Chapter 1, but here's a little more detail.

ANNUALS

An *annual* is a plant whose complete life cycle, from germination through flowering, setting seed, and dying, all occurs in one growing season. Because of their short lifespan, annuals grow and bloom very quickly. Their flowers usually last the whole season, blooming until frost. For the most part, they are very low maintenance plants, and very easy to care for. Some annuals require no care at all, like nasturtiums, which don't even need deadheading! Others require minimal care, like regular watering and feeding. Basil is in this category. All it really needs is water, compost, and a little trimming to get rid of the flowers—so you'll keep getting those delicious leaves!

Annuals are further broken down into *tender* and *half-hardy* classifications; tender plants will croak at the first hint of frost (like basil), but half-hardy ones will continue to grow and bloom after cold weather arrives (like calendula). Eventually, though, half-hardy annuals will succumb to winter in all but the warmest climates.

Some annuals, like Johnny-Jump-Ups (*Viola tricolor*), self-sow, meaning they produce seed that sows itself. Plant these guys once and you'll never have to plant them again. Some people love this attribute; others are annoyed by all the "volunteers" popping up in unexpected places.

Most annuals need lots of sun and plenty of water. They can often be sown directly into the garden, so purchasing seedlings is unnecessary.

BIENNIALS

A *biennial* is a plant that lives for two years, growing its leaves in the first season, then flowering, setting seed, and dying during its second year. Biennials frequently form a rosette of leaves close to the ground their first year, and send up a tall flower spike the second. The bloom time is usually not as long as with annuals, but it lasts longer than in a lot of perennials. This relatively small group of plants consists mostly of good self-sowers, and these plants will establish themselves in your garden if the conditions are right.

Many biennials are classified in the plant family *Umbelliferae*, the carrot family. This means they have long taproots and don't appreciate being transplanted—have you ever tried to transplant a full grown carrot?—so it's best to try to sow them directly in the garden. If that's not possible, start them inside, in peat pots, so there will be less transplant shock. Don't let this scare you, though; every year garden centers (including mine) sell thousands of parsley seedlings that are transplanted into their new owners' gardens with no problem at all. Transplant concerns are just something to be aware of.

How you grow a biennial herb depends on what you want out of your plants. For instance, the biennial parsley (*Petroselenium crispum*) is usually grown for its first-year leaf growth, and goes to flower early in its second year, pretty much ending leaf production. While you can hope for lots of volunteers the *following* year, if you use a lot of parsley you'll be better off getting new plants each year. On the other hand, most people grow caraway (*Carum carvi*) for the seed, so you'll have to wait a year before you harvest it.

Occasionally, you can cut the flowers off ornamental biennial herbs and prevent the plant from going to seed. You *may* be able to get another year out of it, but make no mistake: These plants know they can't keep going forever, and they'll do whatever it takes to complete their life cycle.

PERENNIALS

A *perennial*, as I noted in Chapter 1, is a plant that lives for more than two years. There are long-lived perennials, like mint, tansy, and wormwood, and there are short-lived perennials like foxglove. These short-lived plants usually set lots of seed, and sometimes you won't even notice that the following year's plant is really just the offspring of the original.

Depending on the specific plant, perennials can bloom for very short times or they can keep going most of the summer. For instance, lungwort and bloodroot are among the earliest herbs to bloom in the garden, but they wither away when the weather warms. But purple coneflower and yarrow are just getting going when warm weather comes, and they'll keep blooming for the rest of the summer.

Deadheading is the secret to a long bloom time for most perennials. These plants think if they can just get to the ripe seed stage, their work is done and they can go back to sleep. But if you're vigilant about getting the dying blossoms out of there before the seeds inside ripen, they'll keep sending out more new flowers, trying to get some seed out of it. Frequently the flowers will grow smaller and smaller, but at least they're still coming. Even some flowers people don't usually consider re-bloomers will do just that if the seed heads are removed early enough. Foxgloves are an example of a "comeback special" in my garden; last summer I had a brand new crop of foxgloves blooming in early September!

Perennials are further broken into groups of *herbaceous* and *woody*. Herbaceous plants die in winter but grow back every spring, usually in larger and larger clumps. Tarragon and mint are herbaceous perennials—feel free to cut them to the ground at the end of the season because they always grow back from their roots.

With woody perennials, the stem gets woody with age, like on a tree, and new growth each year comes from those stems. Examples are sage and lavender. It's important *not* to trim woody perennials too much at the end of a growing season, especially in cold climates, because they need their woody growth to get through the long winter ahead. It's also a good idea to protect these guys with mulch

in the coldest climates, but we'll cover that in more detail later.

Tender Herbs

Some herbs of each group are *tender*, meaning that in most parts of the United States they must be taken inside for the winter. The plants we grow in our gardens today have been collected from natural species growing all over the world, and can therefore tolerate wildly different temperature extremes, either naturally or by adaptation. Tropical plants growing wild in the rainforest would certainly die if exposed to frost there, but that's not of too much concern—until they're brought to Vermont. At the same time, plants that can take full sun in Vermont need shade in the South. Tarragon needs a dormant period of

In 1672 a colonist named John Josselyn put together a list of familiar herbs and flowers that were brought over from the mild climate of Old England and grown in the earliest gardens of New England. He described how many of the plants were simply not suited to this climate. Many of the plants struggled to get through their first few winters, but later adapted themselves to their new climate and became staples of the American herb garden. Rue, southernwood, mint, and lavender are among the notable survivors.

cold or it won't thrive, so it typically has trouble in the desert Southwest.

The point is, just because some varieties of lavender are hardy in the Mediterranean doesn't mean they'll survive where temperatures fall below zero, and the lovely rosemary shrub in your North Carolina cousin's yard must be kept in a pot and brought inside anywhere north of New Jersey. Oh, and that beautiful thirty-foot-tall bay tree you admired in your California friend's garden? That, too, must be put in a tub for indoor protection anywhere the ground freezes in winter. It'll only get to maybe five or six feet high in a tub, but at least you'll still have it!

Leaf and Flower Forms

I bet you think you know this part already. Flowers are flowers, right? What's to know, besides what color they are? Well, there's a little more to it than that. Almost every herb produces a flower, which you probably know is the reproductive organ of the plant. The leaves are the food producer, and the roots are the storage cellar.

Flowers

Whether showy or insignificant, a plant's flowers are usually the key to its identification. If a plant has daisy-like flowers in England, it's going to have daisy-like flowers in the tropics, the desert, or the tundra. Whether the plant can live in those conditions is a whole other story.

Very quickly, then, here's a crash course in flower structure.

Petals are the showiest and most colorful part of most flowers, and they're what attract pollinating insects and birds. All the petals together make up the *corolla*. Within the corolla are the male parts (*stamens, filament,* and *anther*) and female parts (*pistil, ovary, ovules,* and *stigma*) needed for pollination. Pollen produced by the anther is received by the stigma, where it travels down to fertilize the ovules in the ovary. The ovules eventually become the seeds, and the ovary becomes the fruit.

The forms that flower clusters make are widely varied. Flowers that are arranged along a tall stem are called *spikes*, while flowers that are arranged in the shape of an upside down umbrella are called *umbels* (not "umbrells"!)

Leaves

Most herb lovers admit that the reason they grow herbs in the first place is for the flavor and fragrance of the leaves. Coming in a close second is the incredible array of herb shapes, colors, and textures.

Roots

In addition to the storage functions they perform, roots form the foundation that holds the plant firmly in the ground, and they allow the plant to absorb water and nutrients from the soil. Most herbs have a *fibrous root system* that can be (relatively) easily divided and transplanted to make new plants. This root system is shallower in the soil, too, which makes these plants more susceptible to drought.

Herbs in the carrot family, as mentioned earlier, have a long, fleshy *taproot* that makes them impossible to divide and much more difficult to transplant. On the other hand, this type of root is better able to withstand severe conditions.

Getting Started

2

Here are the basic facts you need to know before you rush out and start planting. First we'll cover how to choose the site for your garden; then we'll talk about your climate, soil, sun, and hardiness zones. And then we'll move on to the fun stuff: picking out the plants!

CHAPTER 4

First Things First

If you're a beginning gardener, hopefully you're reading this section in the dead of winter—that time after Christmas when things seem hopelessly gray outside. That's the perfect time to gather your thoughts on garden design, what plants to try, and so forth. But first, you have to know a little about the particulars of your proposed garden site.

Know Your Place

Before you start planning your new garden, there are some initial things you need to consider, such as garden size, utility obstacles, budget, time, workload, etc. Here's how to figure it all out.

WHERE TO BEGIN?

You've already decided you want an herb garden, or you wouldn't have this book in your hands right now. But what kind? How big? Where in your yard? For beginning herb gardeners, the best place to start is by thinking small. You'll thank me in the end, I

promise. I know, you've seen pictures in magazines of two-acre herbal paradises, and you want that *now!* Well, take it from me, it ain't that easy. The most economical and sensible approach is to start with a small dooryard-type garden. That way, you'll get a sense of how much you can handle, how things grow, and how much time it takes to take care of an herb garden. It's also a good idea to start with the easier plants. That's no problem, though, because most herbs *are* easy-care plants!

I've devoted a whole chapter to the easiest herbs. Check out Chapter 10!

But before you decide on that dooryard garden, you need to think about a few other things, like where the electrical and gas lines are buried on your property. I discovered that the hard way: While digging around the porch foundation, I hit a copper tube and cut it right in half! Fortunately, it was an abandoned gas line that had never been completely removed when the lines were changed by the previous owners, and it wasn't hooked up to anything. But if that had been the working gas line leading to my house, it would've meant an expensive service call to repair it—not to mention dangerous!

Water lines are also easily damaged. If you have a septic tank, you'll need to know where the tank and the leach field are. It's best not to plant anything but grass on top of a leach field, for several reasons:

1. You don't want taproots going down into the leach field and clogging it.

2. You don't want to eat herbs that are grown over sewage.

3. If you ever have to do work on the septic system, you'll destroy your garden!

You should also keep in mind the needs and priorities of your family. Do you spend a lot of time outside during the summer? Put the garden around your terrace or porch. Do your kids play football every day on that patch of lawn you have your heart set on for an herb garden? Playing fields are difficult places to garden in. Of course, the kids will smell great!

Try to put the garden where you'll most enjoy it, not where you can't see it from your house or where you have to hike a long way to it—unless you want the solitude the walk would provide. Siting it in just the right place makes the garden enjoyable all the time, not just while you're working in it.

GOOD FENCES MAKE GOOD NEIGHBORS

Keep in mind your property lines and boundaries, too. Just because you share a chain-link fence does not mean your neighbor will appreciate the morning glories you plant at the base of it to cover it up. This is, again, the voice of experience talking. I had a neighbor who ripped out my almost-ready-to-bloom morning glories because she thought they made the fence look "messy." This happened every single year for three years! The same neighbor used to unplant the annuals in my three-square-foot front lawn because she thought they were weeds.

Don't plant trees that will shade your neighbor's house, and don't put up obstructions that will block their view of the mountain without first talking to them. You wouldn't want them to do that to you, would you? At the same time, if your neighbor's tree is creating too much shade for your garden, please don't cut it down. Finally, think twice about planting invasive creepers too close to your property line. While these hints are directed at gardeners with small town lots, it's something for anyone in close proximity to other houses to think about.

Finally, if you rent, please ask your landlord before putting in a garden. While most landlords would appreciate the improvements you want to make, that's not always the case. Also, you can ask them about the electrical and gas lines, and they should be able to provide you with all the info you need.

Budgeting Time

If you can only schedule ten minutes a week for gardening duties, you can't expect to take care of a fifty-foot garden. You need to be realistic about the time you can spare for gardening.

Keeping things small and choosing low-care plants will make a big difference in the amount of time you spend doing your "chores." Don't be surprised though, if you're like most of us gardeners and get addicted—spending more and more time in the garden, puttering, deadheading, pulling a weed here, a flower there. It's a wonderful life! Also don't assume you'll be able to recruit your spouse or kids into helping you with the gardening—they may or may not take to it.

Budgeting Money

Gardens take some financial investment, ranging from the initial packets of seeds and a tool or two, to doing the whole shooting match with fences, ornaments, full-grown plants, and a garden tractor. Herb gardening doesn't need to be expensive, but beware: There are a lot of very tempting toys out there. Just know in advance if you have tight budgetary constraints. If you do, work with them by starting your own seeds rather than buying all your plants, or making fences from materials you have on hand rather than buying those convenient but costly premade sections from the home center.

Also, keep in mind that if you're renting or planning to move in the near future, investing in a lot of perennials may make the move more painful when the time comes. There's no need to plant an herb garden with nothing but annuals, but unless you'll be able to dig them up and take them with you, leaving behind a garden full of expensive perennials you've doted on will not be easy.

Garden Size

Now's the time to measure the dimensions of your proposed garden. If you want a small dooryard garden to start with, go out and look at how much room you have for it. You can cram a lot of herbs into a small area, so don't be discouraged if it doesn't look like a big enough space to begin with. It's also surprising how much larger a garden becomes when you're taking care of it!

HOW I DID IT

In my own dooryard garden, I started on one side of the brick sidewalk leading to the driveway. Since the driveway crept right up to the house, it was more like a sidewalk stuck *in* the driveway. No matter, I was putting a garden there. The sidewalk was about five feet long, so that became one dimension. Then, standing in the driveway looking at the house, I saw a window beside a beam in the wall. That looked like a good place to take the garden out to, so I measured and came up with ten feet. Great! Now I had my dimensions to work with.

I knew I could put quite a little collection of plants in an area that size, but had to come up with a better idea of what I wanted there. Since it was right by the kitchen door, it was the perfect spot for things we use a lot in the kitchen, such as basil, chives, and sage, but I also wanted a lot of flowers to dress up this back entrance to the house. I also knew that it was a south-facing, sunny—*really* sunny—gravelly spot, so I couldn't put certain plants there, like shade-loving lungwort (*Pulmonaria officinalis)*. What this means to you will be covered in detail in the next chapter. The point is that I knew at this point basically what I wanted to do in that spot, and I knew how much space I had to work with. I was then able to map it out on paper, making changes and revisions as I went. Revising on paper is a lot easier than after you've got the plants in the ground!

> Houses retain heat, so plant your tender or heat-loving plants near your foundation.

Planning Your Garden

You'll need to take a look at the specifics in Chapter 5 on sun, soil, and climate before you actually do this part, but for now, I want to cover some more details on the planning stages.

While you're still in these early stages of planning your garden, you might want to start playing with an initial garden plan. It can be anything from doodles on cocktail napkins to watercolors on graph paper, but making a plan is really going to help in the later stages. And it's fun, too!

If you're leaning toward putting the garden right by your house, begin by sketching a rough outline of the dimensions of the house, driveway, and any other existing buildings, fences, trees, or other large landscape plantings. Then fill in where the garden will go, visualizing the basic shape—square, round, undulating curves, whatever. Remember that this is the first draft, and you can change anything you don't like. Then, using the information you'll get from reading Chapter 5, fill in your plan with a few of the herbs you really want to use. Start with your favorites, and if there's room, add a few more.

YOUR GARDEN NOTEBOOK

Now is also a good time to start a gardening notebook or journal. This is a place to record everything from ideas for color combinations to the actual last frost dates. You can keep notes about which plants work well together and which ones don't, which ones take over in the garden and which simply die for no apparent reason. Most gardeners find they can't possibly remember all the little details from year to year, and a journal helps keep track of these things.

Using your journal to help plan your garden is a great way to help remember the point of certain decisions down the road, and actually mapping out the locations of the plants will help you remember what you put where next spring when all those little green shoots start to appear.

You can include a calendar, where you will mark important dates for ordering catalogs or seeds, when to harvest, reminders to replant, or phases of the moon, if you garden that way. A farmer's almanac is particularly helpful in figuring out those dates.

> Use a notebook with a plastic cover so it will be weatherproof. Also, using a waterproof pen will keep your notes from getting washed away in the event of a sudden shower.

Making a List

Finally, while you're making out that first draft garden plan, start a list of plants that you'd like to put in it. Begin with your favorites, of course, but let yourself go nuts at this point. You can (and should) pare it down later. But for now, go crazy and put in everything that strikes your fancy. Be sure to leave space to put growth habits, size, and color for each plant, so you'll be able to pick and choose the final cut.

CHAPTER 5

Getting to Know Your Site

Before you can really choose the style of your garden, you'll need to understand the importance of climate, sun, and soil, and what your herbs are going to need from you.

Climate: What It Is and What to Do About It

Climate is the way temperature, wind, and precipitation work together to influence the weather of a certain area. It's really important for gardeners to take climate into account when choosing the plants for their gardens.

Is your area very hot, very wet, or very dry? Gardeners in New Mexico have very different requirements than those in Virginia. And those lucky devils in Southern California rarely have a frost and can garden nearly year-round—when do they rest? Those of us in Northern New England, however, spend much more time thinking about gardening than actually doing it!

If you live in an area where the temperatures fall below freezing, what are the dates of the average first frost in fall and last frost in spring? While vegetable gardeners have to worry more about days to maturity than herb gardeners, it still makes a difference regarding what can go in the ground and when.

A great source to find out these statistics is your local extension agent. They keep track of all these numbers so you don't have to. You can find them in the phone book or online.

How low do temperatures go in winter? The hardiness of plants hinges on these numbers. Most plants have an upper and lower limit to what they can take, and every plant has a different range. It's just like people—some love heat and humidity but hate the cold, and others love snow but can't take temps over 80°.

And what about rainfall? Does your area usually get a good amount each summer, or do frequent droughts occur? We'll talk more about water later.

Never thought about any of this before? If you become passionate about gardening, don't be surprised if you find yourself addicted to The Weather Channel!

Hardiness Zones and Microclimates

The map that follows was designed by the USDA to show the different hardiness zones in North America. It breaks up the United States and Canada into ten different zones, based on a ten degree difference in average annual minimum temperatures. Zone 1 is the coldest (below -50° F) and zone 10 is the warmest (only as low as 40°–30° in winter).

There are certain "island" zones within other zones that indicate warmer or colder minimum temperatures. For example, most of Virginia is zone 7, but the high peaks of the Blue Ridge Mountains form a little pocket of zone 6 because of their elevation. On the other hand, large urban cities or areas next to water tend to be a little warmer than their inland neighbors. Burlington, Vermont, on the shores of Lake Champlain, is frequently considered zone 5, while the surrounding area is zone 3 or 4. And New York City and its boroughs are much warmer than their neighbors across the river in suburban New Jersey.

WHERE AM I?

Find where you are on the map. For instance, if you live in southeast Nebraska, you're in zone 5. So, if you're reading an herb catalog and see that a plant you want to grow is listed as hardy to zone 3, you should have no problem because the plant is considered hardy in a colder zone than you're in. By the way, just because the map lists the *average* minimum temperature does not mean that the temperature *always* goes that low every year. In an El Niño year, for example, even though we are zone 4, our temps may not go lower than zone 6! (Boy, was that a great spring!)

SO WHAT DOES THIS MEAN?

Plants grow best within an optimum range of temperatures. Sometimes it's a wide range, and sometimes it's pretty narrow. These zone ratings indicate where a plant will thrive, not just survive. Many will survive in zones other than their recommended range, but you really have to pamper them. In our case, lavender is an example. It's not supposed to be hardy in my zone, but if you plant it in front of big rocks and mulch the heck out of it, you can coax it through a winter with temperatures between -20° and -30°.

Sometimes you'll see a range listed for a plant, like "hardy in zones 3–7." This means that it should survive the cold of a zone 3 winter and the heat of a zone 7 summer. Some plants, like tarragon (*Artemsisia dracunculous*), require a dormant period of cold or simply can't live in very warm areas.

Microclimates

These zones are pretty accurate, but only generally. That's where microclimates come in. In my yard, the line between zones 4 and 5 runs right between my house and the colonial garden. The south-facing, house-protected dooryard garden stays considerably warmer than the more exposed garden in the yard. But even that garden is protected on the north side by several barns, so it's warmer than the garden we put on an exposed, unprotected hill in the middle of the back field. All of these areas are considered *microclimates*.

> ### MICROCLIMATE
>
> The topography, or lay of the land, will influence the climate of that particular area. Other influences that affect microclimate include water, wind, and reflected light.

THE LAY OF THE LAND

Even though higher elevations cause cooler temperatures, valleys tend to be a little cooler than hillsides because cold air sinks and drains into them. This causes them to be prone to later frosts in the spring and earlier frosts in the fall.

Gardens on hilltops have their own set of issues, though. They are usually exposed to much more wind, which dries out both plants and soil. Even though you may escape some of the extremes of early or late frosts, you'll still find your temperatures lower than on flat land. And the soil may not be as good as in a valley because of *erosion*.

> ### EROSION
>
> The action of water going downhill that carries topsoil with it. It's the reason soil in valleys tends to be richer than on hilltops.

SLOPES

Gardens on gentle slopes have the best of both worlds. They are often cooled by afternoon breezes, while warm air rising over them helps keep away frost. A slope with a southern exposure warms earlier in the spring and stays warm later in the fall, providing a longer growing season. And slopes provide essential drainage. However, too much of a good thing can mean too much drainage, leaving you with dry soil, and too steep a slope may make the act of gardening itself difficult, unless it's terraced.

Another slope issue is how it affects water. If a great deal of water collects at the bottom of a hill and drainage is poor, the ground will be spongy and wet, especially if air circulation is also poor. This makes for a great setup for fungal disease on your plants.

WATER AND MICROCLIMATES

Large bodies of water such as oceans and lakes have a dramatic influence on the microclimates of their shores because their temperatures rise and fall more slowly than the surrounding land. For this reason, they frequently don't have the temperature extremes of inland areas. Depending on its size, the body of water may be enough to keep early frosts away, and it will probably mitigate summer heat as well.

So even if all you have is a little spring-fed pond, it will affect the climate of your garden.

HEAT AND LIGHT IN MICROCLIMATES

Light and heat also play a role in microclimates. Remember my dooryard garden? It's in its own zone not just because it's on the south side of my house, but also because of the light and heat reflected off the walls. It seems to get much more sun than the unwalled garden in the yard, even though both have full sun all day long. That's why the lavender plants I put there are much larger and healthier than the ones in the exposed garden. But it also means that I have to water this garden more in the summer, because it gets baked on summer afternoons.

DIFFERENT TYPES OF MICROCLIMATES
- hills
- valleys
- banks or slopes
- exposed flat areas
- windy areas
- stone or rock walls
- ponds or streams
- marshy or wet areas
- dry, sandy spots
- cold spots (note where snow lingers after all the rest has melted)

Special Problems

Some areas have their own little sets of problems. The seashore is one of those. Wind and salt spray create conditions that not every plant can tolerate, so keep that in mind when planning your garden. Some plants that are particularly suited for seaside gardens are rugosa roses and potentillas. Many plants that have grayish foliage work well at the shore, as they have tiny hairs that help resist the drying effect of winds. And since coastal areas tend to be a tad warmer, you may be able to grow plants that your inland neighbors can't!

And just as you would not plant a cactus in the rainforest, you shouldn't put a tropical plant that needs constant rain in a high desert area. Of course that doesn't mean you can't garden there at all, it just means you need to take a little time to learn the needs of certain plants before you attempt to grow them. If you're willing to do some pampering, you might be able to pull it off. Or maybe not, but at least you learned something from it, right?

The Sun

In addition to climate, the next consideration in planning your new garden is exposure to the sun, a critical part of *photosynthesis*. All plants need some sun to survive; the amount varies from plant to plant, and even from site to site!

> ## PHOTOSYNTHESIS
>
> *Photosynthesis* is the process that enables plants to make their food. Leaves contain the pigment *chlorophyll*, which absorbs the radiant energy of sunlight in order to convert carbon dioxide to carbohydrates, otherwise known as dinner!

ALL SUN IS NOT CREATED EQUAL

The sun has different characteristics at different times of the day, and also during the different seasons. You probably know that the sun's intensity is greatly diminished during the winter months, but it also follows that, in the summer, morning sun is not as brutal as afternoon sun. So, when looking at your potential garden, if you see an area that would be scorched by August afternoon sun, you probably won't want to put plants that need a little shade in that spot. Here then, is a quick rundown of sunlight amounts:

Full Sun: At least six hours of direct sun, ideally between 9 a.m. to 5 p.m. Many plants benefit greatly from morning sun (9–3) and afternoon shade (3 p.m. on), even if they are described as full-sun lovers. This is especially true in southern gardens, or spots that have southern exposure and sandy soil.

Partial Shade (Partial Sun, Light Shade): These interchangeable terms simply mean approximately four hours each of shade and sun. They can also mean dappled or filtered light, like the shade created by trees whose branches let in little "holes" of light. Bright shade refers to an area that doesn't receive any direct sun, but is still filled with reflective light, like beside the sunlit wall of a house. Partial shade can also be created out of lath, arbors, or trellises in an area that has no trees.

Full Shade: Also known as "deep shade," these areas get neither direct nor reflected sun, and can sustain only a very few shade-loving plants. The ground directly beneath large branches of evergreens is the deepest of deep shade, where only mulch will grow, and the degrees of full shade go up from there. The shady north side of a house may be bright enough to grow shade lovers like sweet woodruff (*Galium odoratum*), but under a large deciduous tree you may be able to grow springtime sun-lovers like bloodroot (*Sanguinaria canadensis*) that go dormant by the time the tree leafs out and creates denser shade. If there are trees shading too much of your garden, you may want to consider pruning the lower branches to let more sun in. Or you can plant a shade garden there.

One great thing about herbs is they can take a little less sun than vegetables because they're gen-

Too little light and you'll have either long, leggy shoots that lean toward the sun, or tiny leaves, or few leaves at all. Having an idea in the first place about their individual needs will help you choose the best spot for them. And then, be ready to experiment!

It's a good idea before you etch your garden in stone to go take a look at where the sun falls at different times of the day; where it is in the morning, at high noon, and afternoon; where the shade of the existing trees in your yard is cast, as well as the shade cast by your house, outbuildings, walls, and fences. And don't forget, if you're doing this exercise in the middle of winter, the sun will be considerably farther south in the sky than it will be in midsummer, and will cast a whole different set of shadows.

Water

Plants need water. That's a basic fact of life. The process of photosynthesis can't happen without it. But different plants have different needs, and it's important to know how to choose which plants have water requirements that match what you have, as well as how to water them properly.

LOCATION

It stands to reason that if you have a marshy area next to a pond, a garden there will have more moisture available than a garden on a hot, dry, sandy slope, right? That's why a water lily grows in a pond, and a cactus grows in the desert—they have differ-

Here's a partial list of herbs that can tolerate some shade: angelica, bay, beebalm, catnip, chamomile, chervil, cilantro, costmary, feverfew, germander, hyssop, lemon balm, lovage, pennyroyal, tarragon, thyme, valerian, wormwood.

erally being grown for leaf production rather than for their flowers. There are quite a few herbs that can tolerate light to moderate shade (even though they really prefer full sun).

Your plants will let you know if you haven't chosen the best spot for them. If they are getting too much sun, they'll respond with wilted or scorched-looking leaves, or they may look stunted.

ent needs. In the section that describes individual herbs, you'll see the water requirements for each plant. In the meantime, while you're planning your new garden, keep in mind the natural water availability at the proposed site. So, for your pond garden, you'll want plants that can stand "wet feet." Likewise, for your desert rock garden you should choose drought-tolerant plants that require good drainage.

WATER FROM ABOVE

Rain is generally the best watering option for your herb garden. The rule of thumb is one inch of rain per week. If you're getting that much, you're in good shape, and probably won't need to supplement. Rain gauges are cheap and easy to find at hardware stores; invest in one. (Just don't leave it out in freezing temps or you'll be reinvesting every spring!)

But what if it isn't raining that much? Even in Vermont's legendary cool summers, we don't always get our weekly inch, and if the temps start climbing, the plants start to look wilted. That's the time to jump into action.

> Sandy soil dries out quicker than loamy or clay soils, so it may need watering more frequently.

HOW TO WATER

You'll want to make sure that when you water, you're getting the precious liquid deep enough into the soil to reach the plant's roots, not just at the soil surface. The reasoning behind this is that you want to encourage the plant to reach very deep into the soil (and maybe find some of its own water in the process) rather than just keeping its roots at the surface, where the hotter temps evaporate the water before it does any good. Deeper roots enable the plant to withstand heat and drought better, too.

By the way, young plants need more water than their grown-up counterparts. So keep that in mind during the early part of the season; the youngsters must be well-watered to get them off to a good start.

> Instead of overhead sprinkling, try to water with a slightly heavier stream right at the base of the plant, even sticking the hose end slightly into the soil or into the mulch—you did mulch, didn't you?

HOW NOT TO WATER

That said, I try not to do the overhead sprinkler thing because I feel it's wasteful. Handy, but wasteful. All that water just flying through the air evaporates before the roots can get it. An exception is in cases where dust is a problem; plants like a good shower every once in a while to keep their foliage clean.

It's also a good idea to try to water in the morning, before the heat of the day gets the evaporation machine going. Some people say never to water at midday, or in the heat of the afternoon. I agree in principle, but if your garden is frying out there, and high noon is the only time you can get out to do it, it's better than letting things get totally crispy.

Some garden gurus say never to water in the evening, either, because of the increased risk of fungal diseases coming from the foliage not drying out overnight. In all the places I've gardened, I've never had a problem with this. Your beebalm is going to get powdery mildew in August whether you water at night or not, so if the only time you can water is after work, you have my permission.

WATER, DROUGHTS, AND . . . SPONGES?

Sometimes, if there hasn't been a good soaking rain in a long time and the soil is very parched, the initial rain will roll right off without soaking in. That's because soil is much like a sponge—it needs a little moisture in it to be able to absorb more. So if it's been really dry and I hear there's rain in the forecast, I like to go out and water a little just to get the soil ready for the rain. The same principle goes for container plants; if the soil is very dry and contracted away from the edge of the container, water a little at a time until the water has been reabsorbed into the roots. Otherwise the water will just drain out the sides of the container.

You can conserve the water that you do get in your garden with a good soil-covering mulch. Shredded bark or leaves, cocoa hulls, or even compost all make great choices for a "summer mulch." Mulch not only keeps the moisture in, it also keeps

the soil temps down and slows evaporation. We'll talk more about mulch in Part 6.

HOSES

Concerning water, another thing to consider is the location of the proposed garden in relation to your watering method. If you're going to stick with above-ground hoses, keep in mind the rather unpleasant task of dragging them all over creation. Hoses tend to knock things over, get kinked up, and generally be a great big hassle. There are some better hoses out there that are advertised as non-kinking lifetime hoses, and they work great. They're just a little more expensive than regular hoses.

UNDERGROUND WATERING

One of the best methods for supplemental watering is a drip irrigation system. There are all different types on the market, from soaker hoses made from recycled tires to complicated emitter systems with lots of little connectors and t-joints and things like that. If you're a gardener without a lot of spare time, the soaker hose is the way to go. Just thread it around your garden beds, cover it with a little mulch, turn it on and go. The water is "sweated" out of the whole length of the hose and seeps into the soil. And since it's covered with mulch it goes to the soil, where it's needed, and doesn't evaporate into the air, where it's not.

On the other hand, if you love little projects like putting puzzles together, emitter systems are the toy for you. They're very effective at conserving the water they put into your garden, and they can be hooked up to timers and gauges. It's a little more time consuming, but probably worth it. I myself am still at the soaker hose stage, waiting for the time to put together a good permanent drip irrigation system. Any volunteers?

TOO MUCH OF A GOOD THING

Too much water can be as bad, if not worse, than too little. Drowning a plant can flood the root system and keep the plant from absorbing oxygen and other nutrients it needs to grow. This can lead to root rot, or insect and fungal problems.

KILLED BY KINDNESS

Houseplants are especially susceptible to overwatering by loving owners. It's the main cause of death of container plants! Don't water without checking to see if the soil surface is dry. Wilting and leaf drop are signs of overwatering. Check the saucer; if the water is still standing in it after a couple of hours, be sure to drain it out.

> Did you know that plants need to breathe? They absorb oxygen through their roots and carbon dioxide from the air. The leftover oxygen they can't use is released through their leaves for *us* to use.

Wind

It's important to know if you have windy sites on your property, or if you live in a generally windy area. Since wind dries things out, plants in windy areas need to withstand a little dryness. A windy site also demands strong-stemmed plants that won't get knocked down. Or you could try shorter plants in those spots.

Soil

We'll cover more in detail later, but here's the basic info you need to start.

Soil has many faces. It's composed of various percentages of minerals, water, air, and organic matter, and it can vary greatly according to where you live. Soil is classified by the size of the particles that

TYPES OF SOIL TEXTURE

- fine gravel
- coarse sand
- fine sand
- sandy loam
- loam
- silt loam
- silt
- clay

make it up. This classification of *texture* goes from one extreme, coarse gravel, to the other extreme, microscopic clay particles. In between is a gradation of particle sizes in the soil.

So gravelly and sandy soil, which has a lot of air space between the particles, is very well-drained (sometimes too much so) and warms early in the spring. Sandy soil is often called "light."

As you move down the chart from sand to loam, there is more *organic matter* in the mix, so the soil contains more nutrients and holds water better. Loam has the consistency of fluffy chocolate cake, and is generally considered to be the ideal soil mix.

Clay, the other extreme, often has microscopic particles that are too close together to allow oxygen in or to allow water to drain out. It's difficult for plant roots to move around, and they frequently get water-logged. On the other hand, clay soils usually have a lot of nutrients, but if the plant roots can't get at them, it doesn't do a lot of good. Clay or silt soils are often referred to as "heavy."

DETERMINING SOIL TYPE

It's easy to tell what kind of soil you have in your own garden. (Except in the middle of winter when there's a foot of snow on the ground.)

Go out and dig a hole. That right there will be a clue; if the hole is pretty easy to dig, you may have sandy soil, but if it's really hard, you may be starting out with clay. Anyway, it's best to do this test when the soil is slightly damp. Take a handful of soil and squeeze it into a ball. If it runs through your fingers

without clumping at all, your soil is very sandy. If, on the other hand, it clumps so tightly that it's a sticky lump, you've got clay. The happy medium, loam, will clump together just enough so that if you tap it slightly, it will fall apart.

There are a million different combinations that your soil may take, and you may even have different soil textures in different parts of your yard. Don't worry. If your soil is on either extreme, it's really easy to fix it. We'll cover that in Chapter 15.

TOPSOIL VS. SUBSOIL

If you go out and dig that hole deep enough to see the layers as you go down, you can see the *topsoil* on top (imagine that!); it's a dark layer rich in organic matter. Underneath you'll find the *subsoil*, which is usually denser. The topsoil layer can be anywhere from a couple of inches to a foot deep, and can have a different texture from the subsoil below it. It can be a rich dark brown, or sandy white, or brick red; it can be light and fluffy or full of rocks and pebbles. Subsoil is usually much more difficult to dig through, and it's of lighter color than topsoil.

Sometimes, if you live in a newly built house, the contractors will have scraped away all the topsoil, leaving you with nothing but subsoil. But sometimes they'll fix the damage by bringing all new topsoil. You just have to go out and look at it to know for sure.

MATTER MATTERS

Organic matter, or *humus,* is the remains of plants and animals in varying stages of decomposition.

Decaying organic matter adds vital nutrients to the soil in the form of nitrogen and potassium, and improves the structure of the soil. Most plants thrive in soils rich in organic matter, which have that chocolate cake texture we spoke of before. It's the stuff that makes soil "fertile" (rich in nutrients) and "friable" (easy to work) and encourages everything from good root growth (because the roots have the room to move freely) to high earthworm populations (which means your soil is good) to ease of weedpulling when that time inevitably comes.

You can add organic matter to your problem soils in the form of compost, mulch, or manure, and solve all kinds of problems. Adding it to sandy soils helps improve water retention so you have to water less often, and adding it to clay soil helps with drainage problems.

COULD YOU "HUMUS" A FEW BARS?

Actually, it's pronounced *hyew-mus*, and has nothing to do with music. Humus is decayed animal and plant material that contains sticky substances that bind soil particles together.

THE BIG THREE: NPK
The three most important elements in soil fertility are nitrogen, phosphorus, and potassium, known in the scientific community as NPK. Each contributes to the overall health of the plants in your garden.

NITROGEN (N)
The most important of the three is nitrogen. It's the nutrient that contributes to leaf and stem growth and maintains the plant's green color. In nature, nitrogen in the soil is "fixed" by bacteria that convert it to a form the plants can use.

Certain plants, like clover and pea-family members, are nitrogen-fixers. They collect nodules of nitrogen in their roots and share it with other nearby plants.

Nitrogen can be used up very quickly by plants, and can get drained out of the soil; this makes keeping a good supply of it a challenge. It's also water soluble, and it leaches out of the soil and into the groundwater. That's one of the problems with commercial agriculture—when heavy doses of nitrogen are applied to large areas, it can leach out and drain right into rivers or other sources of drinking water, polluting them.

Although you could conceivably feed nitrogen to a plant anytime, spring is the best time because that's when you want new growth to start. Nitrogen can be like a candy bar; it's a quick jolt of energy that really shows up dramatically when you feed it directly to a plant. So if you feed a plant nitrogen right before cold weather hits in the fall, you may spur tender new growth that could be harmed or even killed by frosty temperatures. There are other reasons, too, but we'll get into that in the care and feeding chapter.

PHOSPHORUS (P)

Phosphorus is crucial for development of flowers, seeds, and fruit, as well as healthy root development of plants. It also aids in disease resistance. It's especially important for root-vegetable crops and flower bulbs to have plenty of phosphorus. Since it's not water soluble, it can be applied in the fall.

POTASSIUM (K)

Potassium is essential for overall healthy plant growth and resistance to disease. It, too, is highly soluble and leaches out quickly, so you'll probably have to add more of it from time to time.

There are several other elements in soil that contribute to its fertility, including magnesium, calcium, iron, sulfur, boron, and zinc. We'll cover them more in detail in Chapter 20.

SO WHAT DO THOSE NUMBERS MEAN?

If you've ever looked at a bag of fertilizer in the garden center, you've seen those three numbers: 5–10–5. These numbers refer to the percentage of nitrogen, phosphorus, and potassium, always in that order. These don't add up to 100 percent because of the inert ingredients the elements are mixed with. The numbers on organic fertilizers tend to be lower than the numbers on chemical fertilizers, but that doesn't necessarily translate to less effective action. It just means organics do their work a lot more gently.

ACIDITY AND ALKALINITY

The last piece of the "good soil" puzzle is pH, which is the measure of acidity or alkalinity. The scale ranges from 1.0 (acid) to 14.0 (alkaline), with 7.0 being "neutral." Most soil falls between 4.5 and 8.0, with acid soils referred to as "sour" and alkaline as "sweet." The pH level of the soil has a direct impact on how the plants are able to absorb the nutrients within it, and most plants have a range they prefer. For instance, blueberries, rhododendrons, and heather love acid soil, while lavender and lemon balm prefer their pH a little on the alkaline side. Most plants tolerate a fairly wide range, though, and thrive best around neutral, or between 6.0 and 7.0.

It's only when your soil is to one extreme or the other that it becomes necessary to modify your soil with lime, wood ashes, or sulfur.

TESTING YOUR SOIL

If you're new to gardening or in a new place, it's a good idea to have your soil tested for pH, fertility, and other factors, depending on the sophistication of the test. Most garden centers and hardware stores sell inexpensive test kits that consist of a plastic container in which you put a soil sample, the testing powder, and water, then shake it up and wait a few seconds. Then you compare the colors to the supplied chart. It's pretty simple to do.

Another home method is to use one of the profusion of meters that are appearing on the market: pH meters, NPK meters, etc. You just stick the meter in the soil and read the gauge. Or you can do the old-fashioned farmer's trick of tasting the soil. If it tastes sweet or sour, well, you figure it out. This is not the most recommended method, though!

The most sophisticated way to find out about your soil is to have it tested by your local extension service. For a small fee, they'll send you all the stuff you'll need, including the mailer. When they're done with it, you'll have all kinds of information about what elements are in your soil, what the pH is, clay and humus contents, and what you need to add to bring your soil up to snuff. Private labs can also provide this service, but they're usually more expensive than the extension service.

Now that you know what you have to work with, you'll be better able to choose the plants that are best suited to what you have.

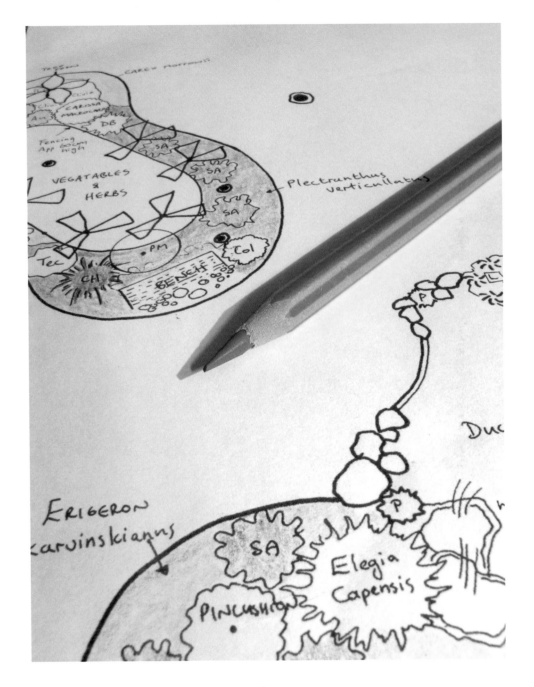

CHAPTER 6

Winter Fantasizing, Spring Frenzy

OK, here we are at the fun part—the part where we talk about designing your new herb garden! I know it got a little boring there, talking about climate and dirt and Latin names, but it had to be done. With all your newfound knowledge, you can now start to think about the specifics of garden design.

Garden Style

The next consideration is planning your new herb garden's style. There are as many garden designs as there are gardeners—the only limit is your imagination. The style of your garden is a reflection of your tastes. An herb garden is by definition really just a garden planted primarily with herbs. There is no set-in-stone style, though there are some styles that are extremely popular.

To begin planning your style, look in books and magazines to get ideas of your preferences. This goes a long way toward helping you narrow down your choices.

Next, think about your lifestyle, your home's architecture and furnishings, and what you want out of the garden—whether it will ultimately be a place to entertain or just a place to run out to while you're cooking in order to grab a few snips of thyme. Do you envision it enhancing your house, or will it be located a distance from it? Do you want a lot of flowers or interesting groupings of foliage? Will it be historically accurate or freestyle? Rustic or urban?

Formal vs. Informal

Do you absolutely adore the untamed look of an English cottage garden? Then an informal design is for you. Do you crave neatness and geometric order? Think more toward formality. Or perhaps you could combine the two into a combination that pleases you.

When talking about gardens, *formal* structure tends to mean neatly clipped hedges that act as boundaries, geometric lines and patterns designed to give a sense of balance, and sparse plantings that emphasize individual plants. Because of all this, well, formality, these gardens tend to look and feel more rigid. Gardens of the Italian Renaissance were very formal.

Informal means romantic, jumbled, massed together in a profusion of color and texture. It's still well thought-out, though, so that colors blend together rather than clash, and beds are still accessible by pathways for maintenance. Informal gardens often have flowing, curvy pathways, and the plants spill over into them. The English cottage garden is the very definition of informal.

THE WILD SIDE

The extreme of informal is a wildflower meadow, where a fairly large area is sown with wildflower seeds and let go. There's no weeding or mowing, except at the end of the season, and there's usually a lot of grass in the mix, too. I mention it here only because wildflower mixes frequently contain a lot of herbs like echinacea and Saint-John's-wort, and these can be very beautiful at their peak. These gardens tend to look weedier than the wildest cottage garden, though, and they're not for everyone.

COMPLEMENTING YOUR HOUSE

Your home's architecture makes a difference here, too. Formal houses (like colonials and Georgians) tend to call for more formal plantings, but cottages, bungalows, and ranches lend themselves to infor-mal groupings. Contemporary homes are a whole other matter; many are informal, but with an artistic flair.

Again, though, this is not etched in stone. You can do anything you want, really. If you have a colonial home, you can put a cottage garden in the front yard, surrounded by a white picket fence, and it will look great! And you can "formalize" a ranch home with ordered, symmetrical plantings, too. It's all a matter of your personal taste.

SPACE AND TIME

One last point in this formal vs. informal debate: Smaller spaces lend themselves better to formal design, not only because a formal garden is easier to care for (all that trimming and snipping takes time!) but also because of the sense of scale. On the other hand, informality needs room to breathe (and flop over, in many cases). Curves and flowing paths need more space to develop so they can look graceful rather than constrained. The same is true for borders; they need to be given room and depth to really show off the way the textures and colors play against one another.

Small Gardens

Do you have space restrictions and hard boundaries, like adjacent buildings and walls? Use them, rather than considering them a liability. If you live right in the middle of town, chances are you'll have the little "postage-stamp" lot like we had in metropolitan New York. It's boxed in on all sides by other people's walls, and usually shaded by them, too. That's OK, though, because you can use it to your advantage.

Do you have a concrete or brick wall? Plant some ivy to climb it. A chain-link fence? Mask it with flowering vines like morning glories or clematis. An ugly concrete terrace? Fill it with containers planted with all kinds of colorful herbs and flowers. Nearly any herb can be grown in a pot, as long as it's kept watered in the heat of summer. And if you actually have some yard space in which to plant, remember that you can cram a whole lot of plants into a very tiny space. It's possible to transform an ugly urban eyesore into an herbal oasis—and the smaller the space, the easier it is to do!

Here are some of the endless possibilities of garden styles:

- border along house
- tiny plot next to kitchen door
- containers on a patio
- elaborate knot garden
- winding path along a hillside
- rock garden
- garden for scent
- secret garden

Many of these will be laid out for you in the next chapter, Foolproof Herb Garden Styles.

Your Garden's "Bones"

While you're thinking about your own personal style, also start thinking about some of the other structures, otherwise known as the "bones" of the garden.

GARDEN PATHS

Along with the actual boundaries like walls, pathways form the skeleton of the garden (unless you are gardening in the tiniest space). In larger gardens, pathways should be wide enough that two people can walk side by side; even in smaller ones they should be wide enough to bring in a wheelbarrow for compost or mulch, and just for ease of weeding. Your paths can be formed with anything from grass (high maintenance) to gravel, paving stones, or brick (high dollar) to sawdust or mulch (must be replaced yearly). Each has its own look and charm.

Also, if you find you have a wide border, and it's difficult to reach the back of it, you can put in a nearly invisible "maintenance" path, perhaps consisting of stepping stones, that only you use during gardening chores.

FENCES

Most people like to enclose gardens that are out in the middle of a yard. To this end, there are many different choices available. You can enclose your herb garden with everything from pickets to boxwood

In large gardens, the rule of thumb for pathways is five feet wide, while in smaller gardens, four feet is a good width.

hedges to rustic saplings to elaborate brick or stone walls. Again, this goes along with the style you've chosen, the architecture of your home, and how much time and money you want to put into it. A rustic twig fence may look great out in the country, but may not work as well in an urban environment.

EDGING

This is not a decision you have to make right now, but you can start thinking about it: to edge or not to edge? By this I simply mean you should decide whether or not you want to outline your beds with some durable material that shows the, well, edges of it. The edge can be made of bricks, paving stones, rocks you find around your property, or old boards stood up on their sides and pushed partway into the ground. You can also buy plastic strips at the garden center.

Or you don't have to edge at all. The advantage to edging is that mowing around the outside of the garden is made easier, as is string trimming. Edging helps slow the progress of grass creeping into your garden, and it helps keep mulches in and pathway material out of beds. And it looks really nice, too. One way to avoid edging—but this actually takes quite a bit more work—is to buy a tool called an "edger," which looks like a metal half-circle stuck on a shovel handle. You force it into the ground all along the outside perimeter between your bed and the grass, and it severs the grass roots, keeping them outside the bed (at least temporarily).

The Next Step: Graphing It Out

So now you have an idea of the style of your new garden. No, you can't just run out and start throwing stuff in the ground. I know you want to, but it's not time yet. The next thing to do is get your hands on some graph paper and sketch out a rough outline of the new garden. You don't have to be an artist!

Start by drawing in any buildings, existing trees or shrubs, and other features like driveways that are already there. If you're having a really hard time deciding what kind of garden you want, get some tracing paper and use that over the main drawing of the buildings; now you can make as many different plans as you like. This exercise doesn't need to take a long time or be excruciatingly perfect, but it's really going to help you have a good-looking garden when the time comes to plant.

BORDERS

For a border garden (one that's right up next to a building, fence, or other hard boundary), get approximate measurements of the wall and make sure you draw it to scale. Also note any windows, doors, or staircases. A good width for a border is approximately two to four feet. Any less, and it will look tiny and out of proportion. Any wider, and you'll need a pathway or stepping stones in it so you don't walk on the planting bed. Of course, if the spot you're looking at is bounded on one side by the house and on the other side, only three feet away, by a driveway—then that's what you'll have to work with.

Your border garden can have a straight or curvy front, depending on the style you're going with, so draw that in, too. Make sure you include the dimensions, and whether the garden is in sun or shade.

Some people use stakes and string to lay out new gardens, but I don't think it's necessary when you're doing a border with predefined limits, like one that's right up against a house. It does, however, help to take a tape measure out and make sure you're not going outside your four-foot limit. You can mark the corners with a stake or stones.

Also, keep in mind that it's best not to put your plants right up next to the house. Give the back of the border a little breathing room—no less than one foot from the foundation—or you'll have problems with both the house and the plants. Another thing to consider is the drip line of the house. If your house has gutters, it's less of an issue, but for older buildings without gutters, heavy rainstorms can dump unbelievable amounts of water directly below the eaves, knocking over and sometimes drowning plants. If this is the case with your house, take the time to see where the water hits the ground and try to plant outside that line.

ISLANDS

Island beds are a whole different matter. Of course, you'll still want to do your measurements, and include existing buildings and trees, but this time using the stakes and strings will be a big help. Island beds can be round, curvy, or straight-sided boxes. Their dimensions can be in relation to a row of trees close by, or near a fence or outbuilding. The difference is that they're not smack up against the structure like a border garden is.

STAKING OUT YOUR GARDEN

You'll want to have some idea of the dimensions of your garden-to-be so you can graph it out on the paper. But once that's done, you can take your little map outside and begin staking out the actual lines. Some people use flour or limestone for this step, and others skip it entirely, which is OK, too, if you have those predefined limits.

WHAT YOU'LL NEED:

- tape measure
- string
- stakes
- hammer or mallet
- garden hose (optional)

If there's tall grass where you're going to be working, you should mow it very short before you begin. You can either start where you know the corners are going to be, or start where you know the center will be, and pound stakes in the ground at those points.

> Be careful when you pound those stakes in the ground—know where your underground utility lines and pipes are!

For a circular garden, use the center stake as a compass point, tying the string to the stake and marking the outside edges with new stakes, as in the figure below. Then take long string or rope, tie it around the stakes, and pull it around the edges of the garden. This is the part where some people use flour or limestone, but I've found that, during the time of year when I'm laying out a new garden, it's usually too windy for the lines to fall neatly.

You should also lay out your pathways at this point, and then you'll be able to visualize the beds. If your garden has curves or wavy lines, it may be easier for you to use a garden hose or thick rope to lay them out. It holds shape better than the strings.

Now that you've got a bunch of stakes and strings in the ground, a word to the wise: Don't get distracted and put off the next stages of preparation, or you'll end up with a weedy mess that you can't mow!

The Facts of Herbal Life

Before you plant your garden, you should be aware of the different forms that plants take. You wouldn't want to put a creeping thyme in the back of the border where it can't be seen, or a tall valerian right in the front so that it blocks the view of all your other plants, right?

So, here's a short course on planning your planting, size-wise and otherwise.

SIZE

Generally, you'll want to place taller plants at the back of a border or along the fence, medium-tall plants in the middle, and short plants in front. That's a common sense rule, but it's one that beginning gardeners don't always remember when they're faced with a greenhouse full of four-inch-high plants at the garden center! As you read through the index of plants later in the book, you'll get an idea of which ones grow tall, medium, or short, and which ones hug the ground. This is also why, on your graph, you should draw in the windows of your house; you probably don't want to put a six-foot sunflower in front of the window and block the view.

MEDIUM HERBS: 1.5 TO FOUR FEET

- basil (*Ocimum basilicum*)
- borage (*Borago officinalis*)
- catnip (*Nepeta cataria*)
- calendula (*Calendula officinalis*)
- chives (*Allium schoenoprasum*)
- dill (*Anethum graveolens*)
- feverfew (*Tanacetum parthenium*)
- German chamomile (*Matricaria recutita*)
- horehound (*Marrubium vulgare*)
- lemon balm (*Melissa officinalis*)
- mint (*Mentha* spp.)

TALL HERBS: FOUR FEET AND OVER

- angelica (*Angelica archangelica*)
- comfrey (*Symphytum officinale*)
- elecampane (*Inula helenium*)
- hop (climber) (*Humulus lupulus*)
- lovage (*Levisticum officinale*)
- foxgloves (*Digitalis purpurea*)
- tansy (*Tanacetum vulgare*)
- valerian (*Valeriana officinalis*)

SHORT OR GROUND-HUGGING HERBS: UP TO ONE FOOT

- Johnny-jump-up (*Viola tricolor*)
- nasturtium (*Tropaeolum majus*)
- pennyroyal (*Mentha pulegium*)
- Roman chamomile (*Chamaemelum nobile*)
- sweet marjoram (*Origanum majorana*)
- sweet woodruff (*Galium odoratum*)
- thyme (*Thymus* spp.)
- violet (*Viola odorata*)

COLOR

Most people think of color as the realm of flower gardens, but if you've been paying attention you'll know that many, if not most, herbs also flower. A plot of cheery yellow and orange calendulas will brighten up a dark corner, and drifts of vibrant red beebalm will bring loads of hummingbirds.

The color wheel below shows how colors that are next to each other complement each other, and those opposite on the wheel contrast. These opposites can make a beautiful statement in the garden, though. Picture a border of all yellows and purples—gorgeous!

Most herbal flowers fall into the cool category on the color wheel—that is, pinks, purples, blues, and whites. As cool colors, they have a calming, peaceful effect. Fortunately, they all harmonize with each other, as well. On the other side of the wheel are the hot colors: reds, oranges, and yellows. These colors tend to create energy and passion, and they, too, harmonize with each other. But don't put pink and orange next to each other; they'll clash and destroy the peaceful effect. So, keep in mind the plants you're putting next to each other, or you may get a less-than-perfect combination.

WHITE: THE GREAT EQUALIZER

White flowers tend to soften the vivid hues of the hot colors, and they can work as a buffer in a garden filled with all different colors on the wheel. If you put a white flower in between those pink and orange flowers we mentioned before, everything has a better chance of working together.

White by itself can be gorgeous, too. White flowers glow in the moonlight, and entire gardens have been planted just for the purpose of night viewing.

Gray herbs, like lamb's ears (*Stachys byzantina*) and artemisia "Silver King" (*Artemisia ludoviciana*), serve much the same purpose—they can bring elements together when planted as a backdrop, and they have the added advantage of being drought tolerant.

TEXTURE

Herbs are especially suited to groupings by texture. For instance, common, purple, and golden sage planted next to each other make a great combination, as do different kinds of thyme or mint planted together. Contrasting types of foliage also work well together. Picture the ferny bronze fennel behind a row of blooming chives, or stately foxgloves blooming behind delicate sweet cicely.

GROWTH HABITS

Finally, you'll want to take into account the growth habits of the plants you're considering putting together. It's usually best to put perennials where they won't be disturbed by the replanting of annuals, for one thing. But also be aware of how quickly some plants can grow to a huge size. You can put small things next to slow growing large things, but the small things will be swamped if you put them near a fast grower. By the same token, invasive herbs like mint and yarrow can quickly overtake their meeker neighbors, who won't have a chance.

My Method

Here's a quick description of how my husband and I got started putting together our colonial garden beside the greenhouse. We began by choosing a large rectangle that had actually been the sandy floor of a previous greenhouse, which had been removed. The dimensions were laid right out for us, but we had to bring in load after load of manure to help the sand that was left behind. Anyway, the front two corners lined right up with the remaining greenhouse, and the back was constrained by another outbuilding. Since we knew we needed to walk between that building and the garden, we left a good chunk of space there.

We measured the area, which turned out to be about twenty feet by fifty feet. Then I went inside and started working on the plan. On graph paper, I came up with the scale (for example, one square=one foot) and drew out my large rectangle, showing its proximity to the greenhouse (seven feet) and the other outbuildings and trees.

For a larger-scale garden like ours, I knew I needed pathways. This is the next step in the design. For my twenty-by-fifty-foot garden, I had already planned on having a traditional four-quadrant layout, so I put one path running right down the middle, crossed by a shorter one midway down. There would be openings in the fence on the front and both long sides. I made the pathways each four feet wide, giving me four beds that were each twenty-three feet by eight feet. And just to add an interesting touch, I put a little four-foot-diameter circle right in the middle of the path in the front half, in which to plant lavender. The figure below is what my sketch looked like at this point.

We went back out and marked the three fence openings. Steve could now start building the fence since he knew where the boundaries were and where

the openings in the fence needed to be. In the meantime, I started working on a plant list, starting with the herbs I knew had to go in and adding more as I learned what the colonists actually planted in their herb gardens.

The style I was going for had different types of herbs in each quadrant: one for culinary herbs, one for medicinal herbs, one for tea herbs, and the last for useful household herbs—and of course, the lavender circle by itself.

I divided up the plants that would go in each section, then marked each one as tall, medium, or short. The tallest plants would go in the corners, anchoring them, and shrubby perennials had a place of honor by the gates. Around the beds opposite the circle would go smaller edging plants like thyme and parsley, and accenting midway down each long side would be other tall plants. I decided to sprinkle calendulas throughout to unify the color and brighten the whole garden, and dedicated the front half of the culinary side to ornamental basils, which would flower profusely by midsummer. I had to find a place for the potted rosemary and lemon verbena, so I left room on the chart for them, too.

At this point I still hadn't decided on pathway materials or other ornaments, but there was plenty of time for that later on. At least I had the basic sketch for my new garden.

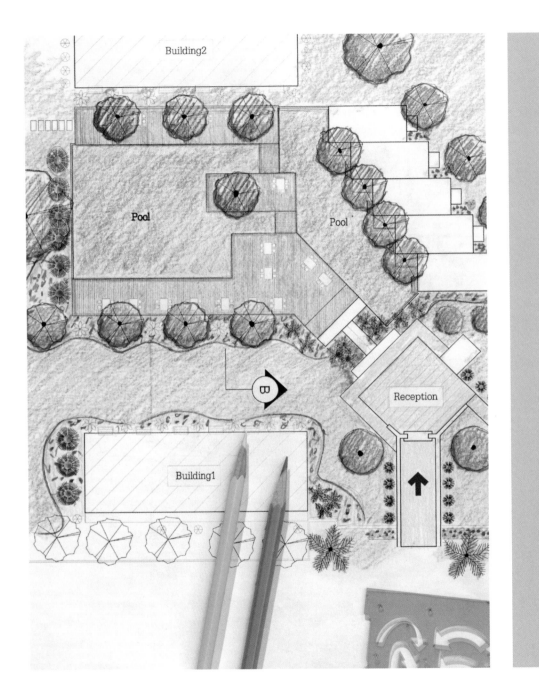

Designing the Herb Garden: Actual Plans for Your New Herb Garden

3

In this section, I'll provide descriptions of popular herb garden themes, easy-to-use plans for different styles of herb gardens, lists of the easiest herbs to grow, and tips on landscaping and how to use furniture and other ornaments to complete the picture.

CHAPTER 7

Foolproof Herb Garden Styles

Herb gardens are especially suited to themes, and half the enjoyment is deciding which one to go with. Tons of flowers? Neat little green mounds? Just enough for the kitchen, or big enough to supply a craft store?

In the next chapter I'll give you actual plans to use for your own garden, but in this chapter I wanted to talk about the endless variety of themes that could be used for designing herb gardens, just to give you some inspiration. We've already talked about how to decide what style suits your needs and tastes, and the difference between formal and informal. Now you can take it all one step further and put that information to more creative use.

Classic Formal Herb Garden

The most familiar herb garden has wide, brick-paved paths that intersect in the center, creating precise squares and rectangles as the planting beds. In the beds are neatly clipped mounds of all the basic herbs: thyme, rosemary, sage, lavender, chives, oregano, etc. In the center is either a birdbath or a sundial, and the entire garden is surrounded by a picket fence, preferably white. The beds are edged with bricks, or in more formal examples, with a very short hedge of box, germander, hyssop, or thyme. To soften the edges, a few ground cover thymes are allowed to spill over into the pathway.

Even in this seemingly rigid style, there are millions of possibilities. You can still put whatever combination of plants pleases you into the beds. You can alter the formality by planting everything closer together and letting things blend, or you can leave out the edging.

Themes

Here are some more ideas for themed gardens. The lists of plants I've included are by no means all-inclusive; I've tried to give the more familiar and easier to acquire herbs, rather than impossible-to-find (or grow) rarities.

Gardens Based on the Usefulness of the Herbs

CULINARY/EDIBLE FLOWERS GARDEN

This plan can be formal or informal, and placed nearly anywhere. Just fill your beds with all your favorite culinary herbs—and perhaps a few you've been wanting to experiment with—and edible flowers (use the list in Chapter 12). Just remember not to spray pesticides on anything you plan to eat! Other spins on this could be a pizza garden (tomatoes, basil, and oregano planted in a circle), or Asian herbs like garlic chives (aka Chinese chives), lemongrass, shiso (perilla), Thai basil, and cilantro (Chinese parsley).

TEA GARDEN

A small garden entirely devoted to herbs you can use for teas can be very charming. Include different flavors of mints, chamomile, anise hyssop, beebalm, lemon verbena, lemon balm, thyme, sage, and roses. This garden could be formal or informal.

DYE (TINCTORIA) GARDEN

Another very colorful formal or informal garden can contain plants used for dyeing fabric. This garden should have woad, madder, poke, lady's bedstraw, dyer's chamomile, marigolds, safflower, dyer's broom, calliopsis, coreopsis, false indigo, anchusa, tansy, heather, and calendula.

MEDICINAL GARDEN

Call this garden your herbal medicine chest: chamomile, calendula, horehound, feverfew, yarrow, valerian, peppermint, comfrey, lavender, catnip, echinacea, marshmallow, sage, rosemary, and thyme. Please do a little reading on the uses of the herbs before treating yourself, though!

COSMETIC/HOUSEHOLD GARDEN

There are so many useful household herbs that you can give them a garden all to themselves. They include tansy, pennyroyal, rosemary, lavender, horsetail, lemon balm, orris root (Florentine iris), balsam, southernwood, and costmary—all for the house. For cosmetic uses, plant calendula, chamomile, rosemary, borage, comfrey, elderflower, lady's mantle, lavender, roses, sage, thyme, and violets.

HERB AND VEGETABLE GARDEN

Although this could easily be informal, this garden is suited to a more formal layout, for ease of maintenance and harvest. You can include many of the "salad" herbs like salad burnet, sorrel, borage, nasturtium, garden cress, chervil, and arugula; nutritious weeds like dandelion, chickweed, and purslane; and, of course, vegetables like lettuce, endive, mustard greens, Egyptian onions, beans, tomatoes, and whatever else strikes your fancy. Mix and match, and include combinations of both herbs and veggies in each bed.

FRAGRANCE/POTPOURRI GARDEN

This can be a wonderful area to relax in at the end of a stressful day, enjoying the fragrances as you meander the pathways. Formal or informal, this garden is also useful, as you can pick the herbs and dry them for sachets and potpourri. Plant lavender (of course!), scented geraniums, lemon verbena, cheddar pinks, roses, heliotrope, orris root (Florentine iris), mint, calendula, mignonette, mock orange, stocks, violet, beebalm, patchouli, sweet woodruff, and sweet alyssum—which is now considered a bedding plant, but was once used as protection from witchcraft!

CUTTING GARDEN

A garden dedicated to plants that can be used for bouquets, wreaths, or other crafts is beautiful, in addition to being useful. Again, for ease of maintenance and harvest, a neatly laid out formal design works best. You could also lay out long narrow beds or rows. Plants to include are:

Herbs: lamb's ears, artemisias (Silver King and Queen), southernwood, wormwood, dwarf Roman wormwood, santolina, sweet Annie, catnip, mints, tansy, yellow yarrow, and pot marjoram

Everlasting flowers: baby's breath, German statice, annual statice, globe amaranth, crested cockscomb, strawflowers, and pearly everlasting

Fresh flowers: aster, delphinium, campanula, cosmos, bachelor's button, sweet William, dame's rocket, mignonette, daisy, salvias, stocks, and zinnia

Theme Gardens Based on Different Time Periods

ANCIENT ROMAN COOK'S GARDEN

How's this for very specific, huh? And you don't need to be an expert in ancient Roman cooking for this style to appeal to you! This classic-style formal garden would have raised beds, statues, and perhaps a vine-covered pergola. Pots stuffed with herbs might line the patio or courtyard pathways. Plants once (and still!) used in Roman cooking are anise, arugula, basil, bay laurel, caper bush, caraway, coriander, cumin, dill, garlic, hyssop, lovage, mint, mustard, myrtle, oregano, parsley, safflower, saffron, savory, and thyme.

BIBLE/SAINTS GARDEN

This style is more suited to informal meandering with curvy paths leading to secluded bowers for meditation. Bible-themed gardens, containing plants mentioned in the Bible, are quite popular. Some of these herbs have been confirmed to be the same plants, while there is controversy surrounding others. Here's a list of some common plants used in Bible gardens: anise, coriander, costmary, cumin, hyssop, lady's bedstraw, mandrake, mint, mustard, nigella, pasqueflower, rose, rosemary, rue, saffron, and wormwood.

A variation on the Bible theme, the saint's garden idea came from the late Adelma Simmons, the *grande dame* of the herb world, who owned Caprilands Herb Farm in Connecticut. When I asked her for advice on starting my own herb business, she said the first thing I should do is plant a saint's garden, and that all the others that followed would prosper. A saint's garden contains herbs having some symbolism or relation to specific saints, like Saint-John's-wort, angelica, rosemary, calendula (once called Mary's gold), lady's mantle (virgin's cloake), teasel (virgin's basin) and Jacob's ladder. Appropriate statues to include in this garden would be St. Francis, the familiar patron saint of the birds; St. Fiacre, the patron saint of gardeners; and the Virgin Mary.

MEDIEVAL/MONASTERY/PHYSIC GARDEN

If you've ever read the Brother Cadfael mysteries, you know about the importance of the herb garden in monastic life. Cadfael is constantly running out to his garden to get a pinch of this or that to make into a potion, in between solving all the mysteries that seem to beset his tranquil village of Shrewsbury.

Life in medieval monasteries had to be completely self-contained, and everything they needed was available within their walls. So, to define the different types of gardens in this topic: *physic gardens* contain only medicinal herbs; *monastery gardens* contain a little of everything that would be needed on a daily basis, from food, to medicine, to the occa-sional flower for pleasure; and a *castle* or *pleasure garden* was a flowery paradise used for sheer enjoyment, usually reserved for royalty.

All of these gardens are usually enclosed and have formal, geometric designs. The pathways are generally bricked or paved, but could be gravel or grass. In the monastery garden, the beds are rectangles, lined up side by side, and edged with wide boards or a wattle fence, which is made from thin saplings woven together to form a short barrier.

Plants for the kitchen were not divided up into vegetable and herb groups, but were all planted together. The healing herbs were planted close to the infirmary, in beds of their own. The monks would also have planted brewing herbs like hops, alecost, and alehoof. Pleasure gardens usually consisted of wide, flower-filled borders around a "mead" or meadow. Today this can be grass, but you might also use creeping thymes or chamomile as a lawn if you won't have too much foot traffic. Other features to include would be an arbor with a seat under it and living benches—soil-filled benches covered with turf, thyme, or chamomile. There are hundreds of appropriate plants that you can put in a medieval garden.

Plants for a medieval garden: dill, fennel, cilantro, chervil, parsley, sorrel, lovage, burnet, sage, thyme, rosemary, lemon balm, bay, lady's bedstraw, pennyroyal, woad, lady's mantle, feverfew, calendula, clary sage, hyssop, chamomile, rue, costmary, chives, comfrey, teasel, mugwort, angelica, wormwood, milk thistle, southernwood, and roses.

SHAKESPEARE/ELIZABETHAN/ TUDOR GARDEN

This is a very formal patterned style, filled with the plants mentioned by the Bard himself. His verses are full of references to herbs and flowers, and gardeners have been designing gardens around his work for years. In fact, this style is one of the most popular of all the theme gardens. A Shakespeare garden is ideally completely enclosed by a tall brick or stone wall, but that's sometimes a tough order. If you're able, at least enclose it with a wooden fence. If you can't enclose it at all, that's OK too. Just say you're taking artistic license. The paths should be brick or crushed gravel, and the garden should contain a bench, an arbor for climbing roses, and a small statue, if possible. The beds should be edged with wooden planks. And now, the stars of our show: the herbs!

Plants for a Shakespeare garden: bay, calendula, fennel, sweet (knotted) marjoram, myrtle, parsley, heartsease (Johnny-jump-up), rosemary, wormwood, lemon balm, dianthus (gillyflower), columbine, English daisy, hyssop, lavender, peppermint, rue, creeping thyme, sweet violet, box, broom, and old roses—eglantine (sweetbrier), musk, and apothecary. No longer considered herbs, but still welcome additions in this space, are peony, lily, and anemones.

KNOT GARDEN

A twist, if you will, on the Elizabethan garden, this is the most extra-super-formal garden in our list. An actual plan is included in the next chapter. Knots came into popularity in Tudor gardens around 1525, and they have been evolving ever since. Today, most knots are created with santolinas, hyssop, box, and germander clipped tightly into geometric patterns. Sometimes the patterns loop around each other, forming the "knot." Two different colors of foliage plants (i.e. silver santolina and green box) can provide contrast and interest, and the area inside the loops or patterns can be filled with flowers or other herbs. Knot gardens are especially suited to small spaces, and they're pleasant to look down on from upstairs windows. The pathways should be brick, crushed stone, or closely shorn grass.

COLONIAL GARDEN

Again, I've provided an actual plan for this garden in the next chapter. As you would expect, a perfect setting for a colonial garden would be next to a colonial house, but it would certainly be appropriate for newly built "revivals" of both colonials and cape-style homes. This is a more formal style, but it can be adjusted to your tastes and made more rural or more elegant.

The colonists filled their gardens with the plants they had brought with them from the Old World as seeds, or sometimes cuttings that somehow withstood the long ocean voyage. In very early times, they only planted the most necessary of plants; very few flowers were planted just for ornament. As survival became easier and the settlers prospered, more and more ornamental plants were included in their gardens. Even then, the colonial housewife knew she needed to have a whole apothecary in her yard, ready to use in case of illness or accident. And in an age before refrigeration, pungent herbs were used liberally to mask foods that had gone past their prime.

The style of the colonial herb garden, then, is orderly and neat, surrounded by a white picket fence, with brick pathways and beds edged with wide boards. In a more rural setting, the fence can be made of saplings or other rustic material, and the pathways may be grass, sawdust, or mulch. In nearly every colonial garden you'll find a bee skep—a woven hive that was once used to keep bees near the house—or a flat sundial. Many colonial herb gardens are divided into quadrants, each devoted to herbs with different uses. Refer to the plan in the next chapter for more details on the plants used.

VICTORIAN GARDEN

The opposite of the utilitarian colonial garden, a Victorian herb garden is like everything else in that grand age: bold, bright, and overflowing with flowers and every kind of ornamentation you can think of. Gardening was a passion during the Victorian era, and several garden styles gained popularity, from super formal to super casual—and occasionally horribly gaudy.

Today, what we usually think of as a Victorian garden is a colorful combination of cottage garden borders surrounding trimmed beds, usually containing very large potted tender perennials. Beautifully ornamented urns, birdbaths, gazing balls, stone statues of cherubs, and sundials are everywhere, and occasionally you'll find a gazebo if space allows.

Wrought-iron fences have become popular, but pickets are still in common use. Pathways are frequently assembled with brick or crushed stone. Benches made of formed concrete, carved wood, or wrought iron can be tucked into corners.

Plants to include in large tubs (or whiskey barrels) would be bay, myrtle, scented geraniums, and lemon verbena. The Victorians loved new hybrids and unusual forms of plants, so any herbs with variegated leaves would be perfect to include. Many of our favorite herbs and flowers were favorites then, too.

Plants for a Victorian garden include angelica, sweet basil, butterfly weed, calendula, pinks, catmint, chamomile, chervil, clary sage, fennel, feverfew, flax, heliotrope, hops, horehound, hyssop, lady's mantle, lamb's ears, lavender, sweet marjoram, mints, nasturtiums, oregano, pennyroyal, rosemary, sage, savory, tarragon, thyme, valerian, and wormwood.

Floral favorites would be bleeding heart, candytuft, celosia, cleome, delphinium, forget-me-not, four o'clocks, foxglove, geraniums, hollyhock, larkspur, lily-of-the-valley, love-lies-bleeding, nigella, peony, petunia, poppy, salvia, snapdragons, stocks, sweet pea, Sweet William, pansy, veronica, and, of course, roses.

Informal Garden Styles

GARDEN OF NATIVE PLANTS

This is a growing area of interest, especially in this era of endangered species. Contact your extension agent to determine which plants are native to your area. Some regions even have wildflower farms that sell the seeds of native plants. The good news is that many herbs are actually natives of North America.

Here's a partial list: echinacea, wild beebalm, Joe-pye-weed, boneset, goldenrod, elder, Jerusalem artichoke, witch hazel, evening primrose, butterfly weed, horsetail, meadowsweet, coreopsis, skullcap, and vervain.

DROUGHT TOLERANT/ XERISCAPED GARDEN

This gardening style is in keeping with making your plants happy by giving them conditions close to their own environments. So if you don't get a lot of rain, don't plant herbs that need a lot. It sounds like a simple idea, right? You don't necessarily need to eliminate watering entirely, but in many areas where water is in short supply and lawn watering is banned in the summer, this type of garden is a great alternative.

Pathways should be paved with stones, crushed gravel, or sand, and should avoid the use of grass, which needs a lot of water. The heavy use of mulch is of utmost importance, because it helps conserve water, especially if drip irrigation is being used. Accessories often have a Southwest flavor, usually because these gardens are situated in that region, but the theme could work nearly anywhere. The Mediterranean is another arid area whose decorative touches work well in an American low-water garden.

Plants with gray foliage are usually considered drought-tolerant: lamb's ears, santolina, lavender, the artemisias, the yarrows, sage varieties, curry plant, rosemary, thymes, and savory, as well as coneflower, Joe-pye weed, and goldenrod.

SHADE GARDEN

On the other end of the spectrum is the shade garden, whose plants require less sun; in many cases these plants actually need the shade to survive. For sun-starved yards filled with old trees, a charming alternative is to have meandering paths leading to shady nooks and crannies. And you can still have color, too! See the plant list in Chapter 5 for shade-loving herbs.

WATER/POND GARDEN

There are some herbs that don't mind the wet feet of a pond environment—for example: angelica, chives, lemon balm, lovage, mints, valerian, watercress, and sweet woodruff.

BEE/BUTTERFLY/HUMMINGBIRD GARDEN

Here's a garden that can be styled any way you like. I've seen bee gardens shaped like bee skeps, and I've included a butterfly garden shaped like a butterfly in the next chapter. What's important here is the selection of plants that goes inside. By choosing the right plants, you can lure all kinds of butterflies and hummingbirds to your garden. These guys prefer less housekeeping in the garden, and they would probably appreciate a shallow water source.

As far as what flowers have the right kind of nectar for them to feed on, butterflies and hummingbirds have similar needs. But guess what? Butterflies come from caterpillars, and you need to share some of your foliage to allow them to reach their more colorful life phase. Not all caterpillars become beautiful butterflies, so get to know which are which. One of the most common caterpillars, with the yellow, lime green, and black stripes, becomes the black swallowtail butterfly. They *love* to munch on members of the carrot family during their pillar phase, so you'll need to plant some parsley, dill, or Queen Anne's lace to lure them. Share your bounty. They won't take too much; you may not even notice!

Here are some herbs to help lure all three of these creatures into your bee/butterfly/hummingbird garden: borage, heliotrope, marigold, nasturtium, stock, beebalm, purple coneflower, coreopsis, hollyhock, nicotiana, and snapdragon.

Especially for the bees: thyme, lavender, basil, chamomile, comfrey, sweet marjoram, hyssop, lemon balm, and oregano. Bees love all flowers, which means they appreciate the tiny flowers of dill and fennel, and those of the mint family.

And for the butterflies: parsley, chives, butterfly weed, butterfly bush (*Buddleia davidii*), and false indigo.

Hummingbirds really like red flowers, especially if they're trumpet shaped, but quite a few other flowers also have the right kind of nectar, globe thistle, pinks, and delphinium among them.

CHILDREN'S GARDEN

Planting a garden just for your kids can be a real joy. I still remember the first little area that my parents let me tend in their large vegetable garden in Virginia. I had mint, nasturtiums, and sunflowers of my very own! It doesn't have to be large—in fact, it really shouldn't be, if they're going to be responsible for the care of it.

Let your kids have a hand in the design and choice of plants. You can also include some fun structures like "sunflower houses" and teepees. This is another free-for-all style, where the plants matter more than the format. Kids love big, colorful, interesting plants, especially if they "do stuff" like snapdragons (they talk!), giant alliums (great big lollipops), lamb's ears (very fuzzy), nigella (cool seed pods to pull apart), bleeding hearts (odd-shaped flowers that can be pulled apart), pansy (cheerful "faces"), lavender (you can make wands with it), catnip (it drives kitty nuts!), chamomile (Peter Rabbit's favorite), hen and chickens (they make "babies"), and hollyhocks (they make great dolls), as well as other good-smelling and pretty herbs like basil, lemon thyme, and Johnny-jump-ups.

You should also be aware of some flowers and herbs that aren't safe in a young kid's garden. Never plant foxglove, delphinium, larkspur, bittersweet, or monkshood, especially if you're encouraging sniffing and tasting right in the garden. It's also a good idea to tell them "Never, *ever*, eat anything without checking with Mom or Dad first!" Then explain why.

URBAN/ELEGANT

Here is a garden that depends on the style, and not the plants. Town gardens are frequently elegant, just because they're so constrained, either by brick walls and stone patios or by some type of fencing. You can turn nearly any urban eyesore into an herbal oasis with a little imagination. Elegant touches include thyme plants tucked between flagstones on a patio, or masses of potted herbs like rosemary, bay, lemon verbena, scented geraniums, and lavender. Trellises and screens can be used to grow vining plants like nasturtiums, climbing roses, and wisteria.

RUSTIC/COUNTRY

On the other end of the spectrum is the rustic country garden, filled with antique watering cans, tools, and wheelbarrows, often with a backdrop of outbuildings with weathered barn boards and peeling paint. The garden can be surrounded by fences made from split rails, peeled logs, pickets (painted or not), or wattle (thin saplings woven together to form a barrier). You choose the layout within the garden, and you choose the plants.

EVEN MORE THEME GARDENS

- all one plant, many varieties (thymes, lavenders, scented geraniums, alliums, or other herbs)
- color gardens: all blue, all silver, all gold, moonlight (all white)
- garden of old roses
- lemon garden (lemon-scented herbs, highlighted by bright yellow flowers)
- secret garden
- wagon wheel
- wild garden

CHAPTER 8

Ten Easy-to-Follow Garden Designs to Use for Your Own Garden

In the last chapter we discussed many different styles of herb gardens, and I tried to give you some inspiration to create your own.

Here I've made it even easier. I've given you ten different predesigned garden plans to follow. Some are super-easy, with only a few plants, while others are a little more complicated and include a larger list of plants. Nothing here is etched in stone, so feel free to change things that may not work for you. You can scale down or swap shapes, sizes, and plants, or you can combine elements you like into your own design. The only rule to follow here is to have fun!

Basic Small Kitchen Garden

You can't get much more basic than this little garden that's just the right size to tuck by your kitchen door. It can be situated right up against the house, or it can be an island bed in a lawn. It contains twelve of the most familiar herbs, in enough quantity to supply a family for a summer. You can edge this little plot with just about anything, from bricks to boards to rocks you find around your yard.

Larger Basic Garden

OK, so maybe this is a little fancier than you originally thought, but it's not really that complicated. It consists of two diagonal paths that cross in the middle, with a circular path around a small bed of seven common cooking herbs. In the center of that arrangement is a sundial on a pedestal. In two of the four outer beds, you'll place more cooking herbs, planted in greater quantity than in the previous plan. The mints should probably be confined to containers, or they'll try to take over the rest of the bed. We've thrown in more ornamental herbs like lavender, purple basil, and woolly thyme, and we've also included some common medicinal herbs like chamomile, feverfew, and comfrey. Along the outer fence are taller plants like beebalm, foxgloves, and valerian.

The paths can consist of anything that strikes your fancy: sawdust, grass, gravel, or bricks. I've put stepping stones in the middle of the outer beds for ease of maintenance. The fence can be formal or rustic—or not there at all. You might also put a bench at the far corner, surrounded by flowering herbs.

Formal Knot Garden

This one's not cheap or easy, but it's a beautiful style for someone who loves the formal look and has a small space. It's very important to keep a knot garden well-trimmed, because it can get messy very quickly. In our example, the space is ten feet by ten feet. You'll only need three kinds of plants for this garden, but you're going to need a lot of them. Unless you can afford to buy them, your best bet would be to start the seeds yourself. Have I talked you out of it yet? Don't let me scare you; it's completely do-able if you have the time.

One quick consideration: If you live in a severe climate, herbs that are not one hundred percent hardy may not live through the winter and thus may not be the best choice. Holes in the design where plants have died can spoil the effect.

One last thought: Some people have tried making small knots from globe basils. This is a good alternative to avoid the upkeep of a knot year after year if you decide you don't like it. This method also provides lots of clippings for pesto!

Salad Garden

The French really like to keep their gardens well-kept and trimmed. Here's an example of a French *potager*, or salad garden. It looks similar to our knot garden but has a greater variety of plants, and all of them are delicious in a salad. The central star consists of (relatively) taller herbs like basil, sorrel, and salad burnet, while the corner beds contain four types of lettuce (both green and red leaf) and salad greens, surrounded by edgings of parsley and edible flowers.

This colorful little garden would look terrific with crushed gravel pathways, and it can be contained with a short wattle or Victorian wire edging.

A Flower-Filled English Cottage Garden

By definition, a cottage garden is not plotted out but instead evolves naturally over the years, mixing annuals, biennials, and perennials in a "happy jumble." This garden has more flowering herbs and stretches the definition of "herb" to its broadest; it includes many plants that are no longer considered herbs but were once held in high esteem. Because of this, it's possible to include so many flowering herbs in this garden that it will look more like a flower garden than your standard herb garden.

I've provided a basic shape and layout for a cottage garden in a fifty-by-thirty-foot front yard, along with diagrams on how to arrange the plants by height. You pick and arrange the plants according to the list provided. It's not necessary to try to incorporate every plant on the list; just pick your favorites. The color scheme runs toward English cool colors, like pinks, blues, and purples, with a few bright colors thrown in for emphasis. The plan shows all the romantic features you'd expect in a cottage garden, like an arbor, birdbath, white picket fence, and roses climbing around the front door. The main sidewalk can be grass or gravel, and the stepping stones around the birdbath should be interplanted with creeping thymes.

- Place short plants beside the walkway and stepping stones.
- Place medium plants in the middle.
- Place tall plants along the fence and house.
- Put creeping plants between the stepping stones.

SHORT HERBS FOR A COTTAGE GARDEN

- artemisia "Silver Mound"
- bachelor's button
- candytuft
- catmint (*Nepeta mussini*)

- chives
- clove pinks
- creeping soapwort
- forget-me-not
- garlic chives
- germander
- heliotrope
- hen and chickens
- lamb's ears (remove flower stalks)
- lily-of-the-valley
- lungwort
- marigold
- nasturtium
- pansy
- parsley
- Roman chamomile
- santolina
- snapdragon
- spicy bush basil
- strawberry
- sweet alyssum
- upright thymes
- violets
- winter savory

MEDIUM HERBS FOR A COTTAGE GARDEN

- aster
- baptisia
- basils, decorative purple types (cinnamon, red rubin, purple ruffles, "African Blue")
- bleeding heart
- borage

- calendula
- carnation
- clary sage
- columbine
- feverfew
- flax
- German chamomile
- honesty
- hyssop
- lady's mantle
- larkspur
- lavender
- lemon balm
- lupine
- marguerite daisy
- mignonette
- nicotiana
- nigella
- orange mint
- ornamental sages (purple, golden, tri-color)
- painted daisy
- peony
- pineapple mint
- Roman wormwood
- rudbeckia
- rue
- silver tansy
- southernwood
- stock
- sweet pea
- yarrow

TALL HERBS FOR A COTTAGE GARDEN

- artemisia "Silver King"
- artemisia "Silver Queen"
- beebalm
- delphinium
- echinacea
- Elecampane
- fennel
- foxglove
- hollyhock
- iris
- mock orange
- roses (climbing)
- sunflower
- tansy
- teasel
- valerian
- wormwood

CREEPING HERBS FOR A COTTAGE GARDEN

- creeping yarrow
- creeping thymes: red, white, pink, miniature
- English ivy
- pennyroyal
- sweet woodruff (shade)
- woolly thyme
- Butterfly Garden

This charming design was inspired by Adelma Simmons's butterfly garden, but I've included plants specially selected to lure real butterflies. The body of the butterfly is the central pathway, and it can be made of gravel, bricks or sawdust. Grass would be too difficult to mow and keep out of the beds. The butterfly's head is a shallow birdbath, essential for the "winged flowers" that you're trying to attract. The two wings are the planting beds, filled with both flowers and foliage that should bring in several different species of butterflies. The beds are edged with two different types of thyme, and when they're in bloom, they are covered with tiny flowers. The plants should all be spaced close together and allowed to grow into each other. Don't keep this area too tidy, because your new friends will need peace and quiet to grow and develop.

Colonial Garden

In the previous chapter I discussed the history of colonial gardens. Here's a classic example of a four-quadrant herb garden. The pathways are sawdust (but could be any of the materials we discussed in Chapter 7), the edging is brick, and the beds are mulched with shredded bark. In the center of the lavender bed is a bee skep perched on a short tree stump. Our garden is fenced with saplings, but could be fenced with pickets, and there's a bench at the far end.

CULINARY BED
- angelica
- basil
- borage
- chervil
- chives
- dill
- English thyme
- fennel
- horseradish
- lovage
- nasturtiums
- oregano
- parsley
- sage
- savory, summer
- savory, wintersorrel
- sweet marjoram

TEA HERBS
- anise hyssop
- applemint
- beebalm
- lemon balm
- peppermint
- pineapple mint
- spearmint

BREWING HERBS
- alecost
- alehoof
- hops (on a teepee in corner)
- meadowsweet
- mugwort

MEDICINAL BED

- beebalm
- comfrey
- echinacea
- evening primrose
- feverfew
- flax
- horehound
- hyssop
- lamb's ears
- mallow
- poppy
- Roman chamomile
- valerian
- white and pink yarrow

HOUSEHOLD BED

- lemon balm
- pennyroyal
- soapwort
- southernwood
- tansy
- teasel
- thyme
- wormwood

DYER'S HERBS

- bedstraw
- calliopsis
- dyer's chamomile
- goldenrod
- hyssop
- madder
- St.-John's-wort
- woad
- Rock Garden

Here's a relatively simple design for a small rock garden, only seven-by-four feet. It includes a stepping stone pathway interplanted with woolly and miniature thymes.

Classical Garden

Inspired by the formal gardens of eighteenth-century Europe, this parklike setting is suitable for an elegant home with a larger yard. In the center is a reflecting pool, with urns filled with sweet myrtle at each corner. Surrounding the pool is a gravel walkway, which in turn is surrounded by a grass lawn. The outside perimeter is bordered on all sides by neat plantings of flowering herbs, mostly blues and purples. There's a large statue along the back wall within the flower border, with apple trees at each corner, climbing roses along the short sides, and a screen of Lombardy poplars behind the rear wall. This garden wouldn't be too difficult to maintain, as it contains only sixteen varieties of herbs, but would be expensive to install because of the pool, statues, and trees. But you can't beat it as an elegant backdrop to an elegant house.

Container Garden

Don't think you can't have a garden just because you don't have any ground to plant in. If you have a sunny windowsill, fire escape, terrace, or porch, you can still catch the herb-gardening bug. Groupings of plants in pots look great together, and some herbs can even be planted together in a single pot. I have a windowbox that has contained the same creeping rosemary, golden sage, and silver thyme plants for at least five years. I've considered separating them, but it would be like tearing apart a family; they all look healthy, so I just add fresh soil to the box every spring.

Strawberry jars are especially well-suited to plantings of herbs, like thymes. But they tend to dry out faster than other planters, so keep that in mind in the hot summer months.

CHAPTER 9

Landscaping with Herbs

Up to this point, we've just been talking about garden design, as if the only option you had was to design a special herb garden from scratch. Well, that's simply not true! If you have an existing garden, or limited space for a new one, you can incorporate herbs into what you have.

Incorporating Herbs into Your Existing Landscape

Herbs don't have to be confined to their own special spot. Remember our earlier definition of herbs? Well, look in any book on perennials, and every other plant listed could be considered an herb! With that in mind, if you already have a lovely perennial border established, you can easily tuck a few of your new friends into it. The same goes for rock or shade gardens, and even vegetable gardens! There are a lot of people out there who consider ornamental gardens a waste of space—I'm definitely *not* one of them!—when you could be growing your own food.

But why not beautify your utilitarian veggie patch with a few fragrant herbs? The fact that they're useful should excuse their beautiful blooms.

For a perennial bed or border, you can add tall accent plants like Joe-pye-weed, meadowsweet, angelica, or valerian. You can fill the middle with colorful additions like calendula, soapwort, foxglove, poppies, and echinacea. Shorter herbs like catmint, lady's mantle, santolina, and lavender add both color and texture to the front. And there's absolutely no reason you can't tuck a few of your favorite culinary herbs in there, too.

See the list of cottage garden plants in the previous chapter for more herbs that are suitable for mixing in with your perennials.

GROUND COVERS AND HERBAL LAWNS

If you have places in your yard that are hard to mow because they're steep or full of obstacles, that's the perfect place for herbal groundcovers. If you have space under trees or on slopes or ditch banks, there are herbs to suit your needs. For shady areas, try sweet woodruff, bugle (ajuga), mints, pennyroyal, wild ginger, and violets. On sunny banks, other spreading herbs like creeping soapwort, ground ivy, lady's bedstraw, lamiums (dead nettles), dwarf comfrey, creeping thymes, wild yarrow, and some sedums will quickly cover difficult spots.

HERB LAWNS

Hate mowing? Why not change from high maintenance grass to practically no-mow herbs in your lawn? OK, you won't be able to play putt-putt in your front yard any more, but herbal lawns can stand up to varying degrees of foot traffic, and some can even handle a little roughhousing with the kids. And boy, do they smell good!

Some people use just one variety of herb for their lawns, but others have suggested that using a combination of varieties gives the best results. Here are a few of the best:

Roman chamomile (*Chamaemelum nobile*), the perennial kind, is the most famous of our grass replacements, perhaps because with its feathery foliage it most resembles a traditional lawn. Depending on the climate, it stays lush green all year and will continue to spread by runners, getting thicker and fuller as years pass. Chamomile needs plenty of sun to spread, and in severe climates some patches may die out. That's OK; just let it flower and go to seed

and the bare spots will fill in no time. The time to mow is during flowering season, but since the flower stalks never get woody, they flop over at the first hard rain. Removal of the flowers will help the plant spread throughout your lawn. And you can always use the clipped flowers for tea!

> One caveat: If you're allergic to ragweed, you should avoid chamomile lawns.

While chamomile is the most familiar choice for herbal lawns, there are other good candidates, too. Creeping thyme, also known as wild thyme, forms a thick, hardy carpet that stands up to walking and playing with the kids. But don't use English thyme (*T. vulgaris*), which forms a small upright shrub and is NOT comfortable to walk on! There are several creeping varieties, and many more cultivars, but the two basic groups are *T. serpyllum* and *T. praecox*. *T. serpyllum* is also called mother of thyme, and it forms a mound. *T. praecox* is a mat-forming creeper with smaller leaves than *T. serpyllum*. Depending on your needs, the dense mat of *T. praecox* may be better for a lawn. Choosing several different cultivars can give a rainbow of flower colors.

Thyme loves a sunny, sandy location, and it will creep between crevices or rocks. This makes it a natural choice for planting in patios and stone or brick walkways. Thyme lawns shouldn't be mowed, but you probably won't want to anyway because the mat-forming varieties never get more than a couple of inches tall, and the woodier *T. serpyllum* only grows to about five inches.

> Watch your step! Bees absolutely love thyme flowers, so you may not want to walk barefoot on your new lawn while it's in flower!

Wild marjoram (*Origanum vulgare*) is another good choice for herbal lawns. You may have heard people talking about how their oregano took over their garden. Well, it was really wild marjoram, which is a rampant grower that forms thick, fast-growing mats. The plant's pink flowers form in late June and come on tall stalks, so you'll need to mow as soon as you see the stalks appear.

> We'll cover the confusion between marjoram and oregano in detail later, but for now, look for seeds or plants of *Origanum vulgare*, which is the hardy wild marjoram we're talking about here.

Wild marjoram thrives best in full sun with lots of water, but it can easily handle less-than-ideal conditions, including little kids playing on it!

Pennyroyal (*Mentha pulegium*) is a smaller, creeping member of the mint family that also forms a dense mat. It has a very pungent aroma, sometimes described as peppermint, that has been used for centuries as a flea repellent. If you've got pets, pennyroyal lawns may be just the ticket!

A pennyroyal lawn should be mowed when it flowers to encourage spreading. Unfortunately, pennyroyal is not reliably hardy in severe climates, so north of zone 6 it may not be the best choice. But even though I'm zone 4 in Vermont, I've grown pennyroyal successfully for years, so it's certainly worth a try.

Corsican mint (*Mentha requienii*) is another great ground cover that's iffy in severe climates. Only hardy to zone 7, this smallest of all the mints is sometimes confused with moss! Where it does grow, it grows fast, as long as it has enough sun and water. It has a wonderful scent, and it's very tolerant of heavy traffic.

In planting an herbal lawn, you might want to start small and increase the area as you get more familiar with the growth habits and requirements of each herb. Renting a power sod remover will make your job a lot easier. Add compost and rake the area until it's weed free. You can then either plant starts (lots of them!) from a nursery at four- to nine-inch intervals, or you can sow seed. If you decide to grow a combination of herbs, you can mix the seed together and broadcast it over the area. Water it well and—just like with a grass lawn—don't walk on it until the plants are well established.

TRELLISES, WALLS, ETC.

Whether you're short on space, you need to screen an ugly area, or you just have a wall to cover, climbing herbs can fill the bill. Hops, climbing nasturtiums, and jasmine can all be trained to climb up trellises, pergolas, arbors, screens, and walls. Climbing roses make a gorgeous cover for trellises, arbors, and pergolas. Choose repeat blooming varieties like "new dawn" or "Cécile Brunner."

When you grow heavier plants that develop woody stems, keep in mind the weight limitations of your plant supports. A flimsy five-foot trellis from the garden center cannot support the weight of heavy plants like roses, but it can handle smaller vines like climbing nasturtiums and hops. On the other hand, a rustic arbor made from sturdy cedar logs can take the added weight of roses, grapes, and wisteria. OK, wisteria isn't really an herb, but it's a good example of a really heavy vine.

Herbal Shrubs

Roses make a repeat appearance here in the shrub section, because of the great variety available for screening. Rugosa and sweetbrier roses can be used as an informal hedge, with the added bonus of thorns to keep out unwanted four-legged guests.

Yew (*Taxus* spp.) is a traditional formal hedging plant, and you can comfortably call it an herb because it is being investigated for use as a cancer drug. Box (*Buxus sempervirens*) and juniper (*Juniperus com-*

munis) are other famous evergreen herbal hedges. Keep in mind, though, that planting a few little two- or three-foot babies will not give you a beautiful full-grown hedge in a single season. It's going to take several years to mature into a nice, lush screen.

More familiar herbs that can be used as low shrubs include rosemary and lavender. Creeping rosemary, with its gracefully curving trunk, can be trained like a bonsai tree; upright rosemaries can reach heights of three to six feet in warm climates. I've seen rosemary shrubs that entirely replaced the usual boxwood foundation plantings around homes in the southern US. Lavender can line sidewalks or pathways, or it can form the border of a garden.

Germander, hyssop, santolina, southernwood, wormwood, rue, winter savory, and shrubby thymes can all be planted close together to form hedges—either formally clipped or left to grow into their natural shapes.

> Remember the climate issues we've already talked about, because nurturing a hedge through its first couple of years only to have a severe winter kill it can be a heartbreaking experience.

Herbal Trees

This was probably the most mind-blowing concept for me when I first started learning about herbs:

This is by no means a complete list, but here are a few herbal trees and their uses:

- elder (*Sambucus nigra*): medicinal, cosmetic, flavoring
- English oak (*Quercus robur*): medicinal, dye, tannin, ink
- eucalyptus (*Eucalyptus globulus*): medicinal, perfumery, crafts, insect repellent
- ginkgo (*Ginkgo biloba*) (maidenhair tree): medicinal, dye
- silver birch (*Betula pendula*): flavoring, beverage, medicinal
- slippery elm (*Ulmus rubra*): medicinal
- sugar maple (*Acer saccharum*): provides sap for maple syrup
- white willow (*Salix alba*): medicinal
- witch hazel (*Hamamelis virginiana*): medicinal, cosmetic

trees, of all things, can also be herbs! It turns out they're not just good for furniture, house building, and fuel, but they also provide sap, bark, leaves, berries, and nuts that can have potent herbal properties. Trees make a dramatic statement in the garden and landscape, and can be a stunning focal point. They can also frame the garden area.

Garden Decoration

So you've got your paths laid out, and you've decided on the type of fence style, and the style of the garden itself. Now you can begin to think about the little stamps of personality you'd like to add when it's all finished. To wrap up our section on garden design, I want to quickly cover garden ornaments and other decorations.

The style of your garden should be reflected in your accessories. For instance, if you've got an extremely formal knot garden, a rustic scarecrow would be, well, inappropriate. But an elegant urn situated in the center of the knot would be perfect. On the other hand, a cottage garden may not be the best place for a seven-foot replica of Michelangelo's *David*. But let me contradict myself here by saying that adding less formal elements to formal gardens may give it a more approachable feeling. So play it by ear, and put what makes you happy in your garden. If that includes brightly painted gnomes and plastic pink flamingoes—hey, it's your garden, go for it!

Mail-order catalogs and some garden centers

carry a huge assortment of ornaments, but also keep your eyes open at flea markets, antique shops, and salvage yards. Sometimes the absolute perfect urn or statue will be hidden away in a corner.

Here are some ideas to get you started:

Wheelbarrows: Antique ones can be hard to find, and they're very expensive in some parts of the country, but they can often add the perfect touch to a country garden. The same goes for old farm carts and wagons.

Birdbaths: These come in every conceivable material and in every possible style, from super formal to super fun. Look around to find what's right for your garden.

Bee skeps: Woven from straw or grapevine, bee skeps are almost considered a requirement for every herb garden. You can perch them on logs or simple pedestals. But you might want to bring them in for the winter so they'll last longer.

Birdhouses: Birdhouses have become incredibly popular in recent years, coming in designs from elegant to country, indoor or outdoor. You can perch them on top of posts or set them right in the garden.

Sundials: Another "requirement" for herb gardens, sundials come in many different designs, from the familiar flat circle to the armillary (globe shaped).

Large urns and pottery: Terra-cotta, concrete, stone, lead, and hypertufa (a lightweight artificial stone) all make statements in the garden.

Manufacturers are recreating old styles to look like antiques, and modern styles are available, too.

Statues, large and small: You can find everything from Greek heroes to bunnies and toads to stone fruit baskets to simple stone orbs or millstones. Whatever your pleasure, there's a concrete form out there for you. If you collect turtles, for instance, combine your two hobbies by adding turtles to your garden.

Garden signs and markers: Whether you mark your plants with the plastic tags from the nursery or you hand-paint your own slate markers, complete with images of the plants, what you use adds your personality to the garden. There is a huge selection out there, from terra-cotta disks on stakes to engraved copper, to hand-painted shutter slats.

Trellises, arbors, pergolas and obelisks: These are larger investments, and make a bigger statement in the garden. Trellises are usually flat latticework panels, and they can be used against a building or as a screen. Arbors are freestanding structures that often form a small enclosure. They can be used over gates or as a garden centerpiece. Pergolas take arbors a step further; almost like a series of connected arbors, pergolas are tunnel-like structures consisting of parallel colonnades with an open roof. Any of these can be bought ready-made or constructed from the materials you have on hand, depending on whether your style is formal or rustic. Obelisks and other teepees are simply elaborate posts for training climbing plants. Again, they can be bought or made from local materials.

Fountains and wishing wells: Another long-term investment in your garden, manufacturers have developed kits for do-it-yourselfers, or you can buy pre-made ones. These, too, come in styles ranging from super-formal concrete fountains with classical themes to rustic whiskey barrels with old well pumps. I've seen wishing wells for sale at the same places that sell gazebos and other wooden yard structures.

Architectural remnants: These can make very interesting focal points in gardens. Look for old porch balustrades, chunks of concrete city building decoration, old Victorian gingerbread, or whatever. Just use your imagination.

Gazing balls: First popularized in Victorian times, these reflective globes have made a huge comeback in recent years. They're available in many colors, and can be perched on pillars or pedestals.

Weathervanes, whirligigs, and wind chimes: Not just ornamental, these old-time weathermen of the garden had real jobs. If properly mounted, weathervanes indicate sudden changes in wind direction that may mean bad weather is on the way. Whirligigs and chimes have a different purpose: Their constant motion or sound can help keep pests away from the garden. Please note that you should not mount whirligigs and chimes too close to birdhouses, feeders, or birdbaths, because you may repel the very creatures you're trying to lure!

Furniture: Every garden needs a place for you to rest and enjoy the fruits of your labor. Benches and seats, whether made of stone, formal wood, cast iron, or twig, make any garden an inviting space, and with all the different styles to choose from, there's no excuse not to!

Stepping stones: Pavers, log slices, or anything flat can be used as stepping stones. There are some new products that allow you to make your own with a little Quikrete and forms, and you can add your own personal touches to them such as hand- or footprints, the names of family members, or even embedded mementos.

MORE IDEAS

- antique garden tools
- buckets
- hose guides: terra-cotta, stone, etc.
- rain barrels
- scarecrows
- wagon wheels
- watering cans
- whiskey barrels

CHAPTER 10

Choosing the Plants for Your New Garden

OK, you've got a basic understanding of what you'll need and how these plants grow. Now comes the best part! In this chapter I'll give you lists of the easiest herbs to grow in your new garden. The first two are culinary, and the third is ornamental. But remember, most herbs cross over into more than one category.

Because of space limitations, not every herb in these lists will be included in the index of plants in the back of the book. So, where the herb *is* listed in the back, I'll abbreviate the description in this chapter. In cases where the herb is *not* listed in the back, I'll give you a better description here.

For each entry, I'll include the common, Latin, and family names; whether it's an annual, perennial, or biennial; and the mature size. Remember, tender means very susceptible to frost; hardy means it can withstand either a few degrees of frost (for annuals) or a severe winter temps (for perennials).

Top Ten Basic Herbs

BASIL, SWEET

Ocimum basilicum
Mint family (Labiatae)
Annual (tender)
1–2 feet tall
Full sun; rich moist soil

Basil is one of the best known and beloved of all herbs. The incredibly fragrant foliage can be used fresh or dried for pasta sauces (including pesto), salad dressings, and many other dishes.

ROSEMARY

Rosmarinus officinalis
Mint family (Labiatae)
Perennial (woody), ever-
  green shrub (in mild
  climates)
Hardy to zone 7/8
2–6 feet tall
Full sun to part shade; light, well-drained soil

Rosemary comes in a very close second in the race for favorite herb. It's used medicinally and in cooking, cosmetics, and crafts. The needlelike leaves are dark green on top and light grayish-green underneath, with a piney aroma. Although easy to grow in the garden, in cold climates it must be brought inside during the winter.

SAGE

Salvia officinalis
Mint family (Labiatae)
Perennial (woody), hardy to
  zone 4
12–30 inches tall
Full sun to part shade; moderately rich,
  well-drained soil

Sage is another very easy herb to grow. Once established, it's covered with beautiful little blue flowers in spring that can be used as garnish on salads. The pebbly bluish-gray leaves of common garden sage are famously used as poultry seasoning.

CHIVES

Allium Schoenoprasum
Lily family (Liliaceae)
Perennial (herbaceous),
  hardy to zone 3
1½ feet tall
Full sun; moderately rich, well-drained soil

I think it should probably be a law in most areas that every herb garden contain chives! This onion-flavored herb, related to garlic and scallions, is incredibly easy to grow and goes with just about everything in cooking.

DILL

Anethum graveolens
Carrot family (Umbelliferae)
Annual (hardy)
3 feet tall
Full sun; moderately rich,
  well-drained soil

Dill is a carefree annual that can be grown in many conditions. You can use both the ferny foliage and the seeds in cooking (dill pickles!).

OREGANO, GREEK

Origanum hirtum (or *O. heracleoticum*)
Mint family (Labiatae)
Perennial (herbaceous),
  hardy to zone 5
Up to 2 feet tall
Full sun; average, well-drained soil

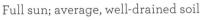

OK, let's get this out of the way right now: The oreganos are a very confusing group of plants. There are many different varieties, all with different growth habits, but the *only* one to grow for cooking is Greek oregano. It grows into a dense, spreading cluster, has inconspicuous white flowers, and smells like pizza! Beware of imitations that have little or no culinary value.

THYME

Thymus vulgaris
Mint family (Labiatae)
Perennial (woody), hardy to
    zone 5
1 foot tall
Full sun to partial shade; light, dry,
    well-drained soil

Another required plant for every herb garden, thyme is a small woody shrub. There are many forms, but probably the best to choose for your first garden would be the upright English thyme, *T. vulgare*.

MINT

Mentha spp.
Mint family (Labiatae)
Perennial (herbaceous),
    hardy to zone 5
Up to 3 feet tall
Full sun to partial shade; rich, moist, well-
    drained soil

Here's another huge family of herbs, but for a first herb garden, the best choices are spearmint and peppermint. These guys are exuberant growers—and that's putting it nicely!—so if you have a large space you can let them run rampant. Otherwise, plant them in bottomless pots to (try) to control their root growth. They spread by runners that quickly creep out into pathways, lawns, and other garden beds.

PARSLEY

Petroselenium crispum
Carrot family (Umbelliferae)
Biennial, hardy to zone 5
1½ feet tall
Full sun to partial shade;
    rich, moist,
    well-drained soil

Today it's thought of as just a garnish, but did you know that parsley became an addition to your plate because of its breath-freshening qualities? It's also high in vitamins, so eat up! Parsley forms neat little clumps of leaves its first year, and then sends up flower stalks early in its second. There are two types to choose from: curly and flat-leaf (Italian). The curly is famous as a garnish, but most cooks consider the flat-leaf type better for cooking.

TARRAGON, FRENCH

Artemisia dracunculus
Daisy family (Compositae)
Perennial (herbaceous),
    hardy to zone 4
2 feet tall

Full sun to partial shade; average,
well-drained soil

Last but certainly not least in our list of top ten herbs, tarragon is another very easy herb to grow in nearly any garden. It grows in clumps that spread each year, and has soft lanceolate leaves that have a distinctive flavor. It is one of the French *fines herbes*, and is the main seasoning in béarnaise sauce.

Another Ten Culinary Herbs

These next herbs are almost—but not quite—as popular as our top ten herbs, but they're all deserving of a spot in your garden.

SWEET MARJORAM

Origanum majorana
Mint family (Labiatae)
Perennial (tender), hardy to
zones 9–10
2 feet tall
Full sun; light, dry, well-drained soil

This is one of the herbs that is frequently confused with oregano. The one we're speaking of here is known commonly as "sweet" or sometimes "knotted" marjoram, a term which comes from the little knotty flowers. The leaves are much smaller and more delicate than any other marjoram/oregano, and have a very distinctive sweet fragrance. Sweet marjoram is very well mannered in the herb garden, growing into a shrubby little bush; it doesn't creep or spread like its cousins.

LEMON BALM

Melissa officinalis
Mint family (Labiatae)
Perennial (herbaceous),
hardy to zone 4–5
2 feet tall
Full sun to partial shade; average,
well-drained soil

It was difficult for me to put my namesake in this "second string" list of favorite herbs, because I personally can't imagine an herb garden of any size without lemon balm. A close cousin of the other mints, but with a much more restrained growth habit, lemon balm self-sows in *great* numbers, so if you need to keep it in bounds, just keep the flower stalks cut back. Your efforts will be rewarded with lots of fresh new lemony growth for teas and salads.

CILANTRO/CORIANDER

Coriandrum sativum
Carrot family (Umbelliferae)
Annual (hardy)
2–3 feet tall
Full sun to partial shade;
moderately rich, light, well-drained soil

A relative newcomer to herbal top ten lists, cilantro and coriander are the same plant. The leaves of the plant are the herb called cilantro, and they are used in Mexican, Middle Eastern, and Chinese cuisines. Coriander is the seed of the same plant, and is a spice used in Indian, Mediterranean, and Eastern cooking. The two have completely different fragrances, too. The aroma of fresh cilantro leaves is very strong and pungent, and has been compared to the rather unpleasant odor of bedbugs. For this reason, many people have a love/hate relationship with this herb. But once it goes to seed, the aroma becomes warm, pleasant, and citrusy.

SUMMER SAVORY

Satureja hortensis
Mint family (Labiatae)
Annual (tender)
1½ feet tall
Full sun; average soil

Once you get a whiff of savory, you'll understand where the word came from. It smells, well, savory! Summer savory is a very easy-to-grow annual that doesn't much care how you treat it. Well, that's not entirely true; it still needs sun and water, but it certainly doesn't need any pampering in the garden.

FENNEL

Foeniculum vulgare
Carrot family (Umbelliferae)
Perennial (herbaceous),
    hardy to zone 6
4 feet tall
Full sun; average, well-drained soil

Fennel is a lovely tall plant, with feathery foliage and pretty flower heads. It has a long history as both a culi-

nary and a medicinal herb. There are several types, from common fennel, *F. vulgare*, to *F. vulgare dulce*, sweet fennel or Florence fennel, whose stem swells so large it's considered a vegetable. There is also a decorative version of *F. vulgare* called bronze fennel that's lovely in the garden. Fennel's flavor is like licorice, and you can use both the foliage and the seeds, if your growing season is long enough to produce them.

CHERVIL

Anthriscus cerefolium
Carrot family (Umbelliferae)
Annual (hardy)
2 feet tall
Partial shade; moist, humus
    soil

Chervil is one of the daintiest, most delicate of all the herbs, at least in the kitchen. In the garden, chervil is one of the few herbs that likes some shade, especially in hot climates. A happy plant will reward you with lush foliage and lots of tiny white flowers, which in turn become lots of seeds. If you've picked the right spot for it, it'll keep seeding itself year after year.

CATNIP

Nepeta cataria
Mint family (Labiatae)
Perennial (herbaceous),
    hardy to zone 3–4
1–3 feet tall
Full sun to partial shade; average, sandy
    well-drained soil

If you set it, the cats will get it, but if you sow it, the cats won't know it. Sowing seeds may be the way to go, but plants are readily available at herb nurseries. Catnip is super easy in the garden—unless you have cats that will get to it before you do! All it needs is well-drained soil. To harvest catnip, gather the leaves and tops when the plant is in full bloom.

SORREL

Rumex spp.

Dock or sorrel family
  (Polygonaceae)

Perennial (herbaceous),
  hardy in zones 5–9

2–3 feet tall

Full sun; rich, moist, well-drained soil

Sorrel comes in two varieties, French sorrel (*R. scutatus*) and garden sorrel (*R. acetosa*). Both are hardy and easy to grow, but I prefer the more lemony flavor of the French variety. It's much less acidic than garden sorrel, and looks prettier in the garden. The leaves are smaller and have silvery patches on them. French sorrel grows in lower mounds than garden sorrel, which can look a bit weedy when in flower.

SALAD BURNET

Poterum sanguisorbia
  (formerly *Sanguisorbia
  minor*)

Rose family (Rosaceae)

Perennial (herbaceous),
  hardy to zone 3

2 feet tall

Full sun to partial shade; average,
  well-drained soil

Cucumbers don't agree with you, but you love the taste in salads? You, my friend, are in luck. Salad burnet tastes just like cucumbers but without the gastric distress. And it's so easy to grow! The clumps are well behaved, don't spread out of control, and even make a nice medium-sized edging.

LOVAGE

Levisticum officinale

Carrot family (Umbelliferae)

Perennial (herbaceous),
  hardy to zone 3

5 feet tall

Full sun to partial shade; rich, moist,
  well-drained soil

Need another veggie substitute? If you like celery but find it difficult to grow, then lovage is for you. It's much easier to grow than celery, is a hardy perennial, and makes a dramatic tall accent in the garden. The leaves, stems, and seeds all taste like celery. It's a famous addition in potato salad and goes with many potato, rice, and stuffing dishes.

Top Ten Ornamentals

Here are some of the best-loved, easiest-to-grow ornamental herbs. Some of them are no longer considered herbs except by the broadest definition, but they're still right at home in an herb garden. Most are perennials, and all would look lovely grouped together, or as part of a flower garden.

LAVENDER

Lavandula angustifolia
Mint family (Labiatae)
Perennial (woody), hardy to
    zones 5–8
Full sun; light, sweet, well-
    drained soil

There are dozens of varieties of lavender, some of which are easier to care for than others. If you're in an area that has frost in the winter, choose the hardy varieties. All of them are beloved the world over, in both flower and herb gardens.

ROSES

Rosa spp.
Rose family (Rosaceae)
Perennial (woody), hardy to
    zones 4–8
Full sun to partial shade;
    well drained,
    loamy soil

Of the many types of roses to choose from, the rugosas, the old varieties, and the wild roses are the easiest to care for and the most appropriate for the herb garden.

PINKS

Dianthus caryophyllus
Pink family
    (Caryophyllaceae)
Perennial (half hardy ever-
    green), hardy to
    zones 5–8
8–20 inches tall
Full sun; sweet, well-drained soil

The predecessors to carnations, pinks have many varieties available commercially. The clove-scented ones are generally considered the best for herb gardens.

FOXGLOVES

Digitalis purpurea
Figwort family
    (Scrophulariaceae)
Biennial or perennial, hardy
    to zones 4–10
3–5 feet tall
Full sun to partial shade; rich, moist,
    well-drained soil

The beautiful tall spires of foxgloves make lovely background accents, and will self-sow profusely if happy in their spot. However, all parts of foxgloves are toxic and should not be eaten.

LADY'S MANTLE

Alchemilla vulgaris (also *A. mollis*)
Rose family (Rosaceae)
Perennial (herbaceous), hardy to zone 3
6–20 inches tall
Full sun to partial shade; rich, well-drained soil

The soft bluish green leaves of this lovely little plant catch dew in the morning, giving it the name "dew-cup." Delicate clusters of chartreuse flowers appear the second year.

ARTEMISIAS

Artemisia spp.
Daisy family (Compositae)
Perennial (deciduous sub-shrubs), hardiness varies with species
2–4 feet tall
Full sun to partial shade; light, dry, well-drained soil

There are several species of artemisias that are particularly attractive in the herb garden, including southernwood (*A. abrotanum*), wormwood (*A. absinthium*), Roman wormwood (*A. pontica*), "Silver King" (*A. ludoviciana* "Silver King"), "Silver Queen" (*A. ludoviciana* "Silver Queen"), and Sweet Annie (*A. annua*). Most have very fragrant silvery foliage and are quite drought tolerant.

HOLLYHOCK

Alcea rosea (syn. *Althaea*)
Mallow family (Malvaceae)
Biennial or short-lived perennial (herbaceous), hardy to zones 2–9
4–8 feet tall
Full sun; average, well-drained soil

Hollyhocks are closely related to marshmallow (*Althaea officinalis*). Both have similar medicinal properties, but hollyhocks seem to be slightly less effective than their cousin. They're still a beautiful addition to the garden!

LUNGWORT

Pulmonaria officinalis
Borage family (Boraginaceae)
Perennial (herbaceous), hardy to zone 3
Up to 12 inches tall
Part sun to shade; average, moist soil

Once used as a treatment for lung ailments, this herb has now retired to the ornamental garden, loved for its striking spotted leaves and flowers that turn from pink to blue—just like its larger cousin, borage. Another plus is the fact that it thrives in shade, a relatively unusual attribute in the herb world.

COLUMBINE

Aquilegia vulgaris
Buttercup family
    (Ranunculaceae)
Perennial (herbaceous),
    hardy to zone 3
2–3 feet tall
Sun to part shade; average to rich,
    well-drained soil

The dainty columbines are another of the herbal retirees that have been favorites in gardens for hundreds of years. Once used in lotions, these plants are now known to be toxic but are still valued for their graceful beauty.

SOAPWORT (BOUNCING BET)

Saponaria officinalis
Pink family
    (Caryophyllaceae)
Perennial (herbaceous),
    hardy to zone 2
1–3 feet tall
Full sun to light shade; fertile, moist soil

A colonial escapee into the countryside, bouncing bet is a lovely, easy-to-grow perennial that was (and still can be) used as a very gentle soap. Another species, *S. ocymoide*—rock soapwort—is a trailing front-of-the-border plant that is covered with bright pink flowers in early spring.

CHAPTER 11

More Top Ten Lists!

In the last chapter, I gave you the top ten and "second-string" culinary and ornamental herbs. Now we'll cover a few more categories of favorite easy-to-grow herbs. As in the previous chapter, we'll include the common, Latin, and family names; whether it's an annual, perennial, or biennial; and the mature size. Remember, *tender* means very susceptible to frost; *hardy* means it can withstand either a few degrees of frost (for annuals) or severe winter temps (for perennials).

A Foray into Medicinals

One of the biggest reasons people decide to start their own herb garden is for the convenience of growing their own medicinal herbs. Here, then, are the easiest medicinal herbs to grow and use. Keep in mind, please, that we aren't here to diagnose problems, and if you're really sick, you need to seek advice from a health care professional.

CHAMOMILE, GERMAN

Matricaria recutita
Daisy family (Compositae)
Annual (hardy)
30 inches tall
Full sun to light shade; sandy, well-drained soil

Perhaps best known from Beatrix Potter's story of Peter Rabbit, chamomile is famous as a soothing tea for tummy aches. There are two types, both easy to grow. German chamomile is a taller annual and flowers more profusely than its perennial cousin, Roman chamomile.

PEPPERMINT (see "Mint" on page 103)
Mentha x piperita
Mint family (Labiatae)
Perennial (herbaceous), hardy to zone 5
2 feet tall
Full sun to partial shade; rich, moist, well-drained soil

Peppermint, with its smooth, purple stems and unmistakable aroma, is a rampant grower in gardens and should be confined if possible. It does, however, deserve a place in your medicinal garden because of its soothing qualities. A tea made from peppermint leaves will help insomnia, upset stomach, indigestion, nausea, and headache, among other things.

HOREHOUND

> *Marrubium vulgare*
> Mint family (Labiatae)
> Perennial (herbaceous),
> > hardy to zone 4
> 2–3 feet tall
> Full sun; sandy, well-drained soil

Ever heard of horehound candy? Well, it's made from the horehound plant, and it really does seem to help coughs and sore throats. Even a gentle tea made from the fresh or dried herb can help. The plant is very pretty in the garden, with its pebbly gray-green foliage, and it's very easy to grow.

CALENDULA

> *Calendula officinalis*
> Daisy family (Compositae)
> Annual (hardy)
> 1½ feet tall
> Full sun; average, well-
> > drained soil

A garden favorite for thousands of years, calendula was once known by the name "pot marigold." Today the herb is valued not just for its cheerful yellow and orange flowers, which blossom from early summer right through hard frosts, but also for its gentle treatment of minor external skin cuts and sores. The flowers are edible, and have also been used as a saffron substitute.

ECHINACEA (PURPLE CONEFLOWER)

> *Echinacea purpurea*
> Daisy family (Compositae)
> Perennial (herbaceous),
> > hardy to zones 3–9
> 2–4 feet tall
> Full sun to light shade; fertile, well-drained soil

A Native American prairie plant that has become a mainstay of perennial gardens, echinacea has enjoyed a resurgence of popularity due to its effectiveness at strengthening the immune system. There are several varieties available for gardeners, but the easiest is *E. purpurea*, both as far as gardening and use after harvest. Only *E. purpurea* has been shown to have medicinal properties; its above-ground parts (leaves and flowers) are effective in immune system boosting.

VALERIAN (GARDEN HELIOTROPE)

> *Valeriana officinalis*
> Valerian family
> > (Valerianaceae)
> Perennial (herbaceous),
> > hardy to zone 4
> 3½–5 feet tall

Full sun to light shade; rich, moist soil
Another favorite of old-time perennial gardens, garden heliotrope is a striking ornamental with incredibly fragrant white flowers. The roots, however, are another story. They stink, but they make a valuable tranquilizer without the unpleasant side effects of their chemical cousins like Valium. Before going out and digging up your valerian plant, though, take the time to do some more reading about how to use it.

HOPS

Humulus lupulus
Cannabis family
    (Cannabaceae)
Perennial (herbaceous) vine,
    hardy to zone 3
20–25 feet tall

Full sun; deep, humusy, well-drained soil
This fast-growing vine is better known for its use as a flavoring in beer, but it also has a long reputation as a sedative. The small, greenish cones are an important ingredient in herbal sleep pillows. Hops grow well on arbors, pergolas, trellises, screens, or simply on tall poles or mature trees.

COMFREY

Symphytum officinale
Borage family
    (Boraginaceae)
Perennial (herbaceous),
    hardy to zone 3
3–5 feet tall

Full sun to partial shade; rich, moist soil
You'd better be sure you want comfrey in a garden before planting it, because if you change your mind you'll never get it out. That said, comfrey is very easy to grow, and will withstand a variety of conditions. Use the large, coarse leaves as a hot compress for bruises, sprains, and strains, as well as for other skin problems like burns, insect bites, and eczema.

YARROW

Achillea millefolium
Daisy family (Compositae)
Perennial (herbaceous),
    hardy to zone 2
3 feet tall

Full sun; rich, well-drained soil
Another ancient herb, yarrow's Latin name comes from the Greek warrior Achilles, who supposedly used this plant to help heal wounds on the battlefield. This traditional use was continued as recently as the Civil War. Applying a poultice of crushed, fresh yarrow directly to a bleeding wound will quickly close it—so quickly, in fact, that you must be sure to clean any dirt out before you apply it. In the garden, yarrow has a tendency to spread. Choose the white or pink flowered varieties, as the yellow types are more ornamental than medicinal.

SAINT-JOHN'S-WORT

Hypericum perforatum
Saint-John's-wort family
(Hypericaceae)
Perennial (herbaceous),
hardy to zone 4
1–2 feet tall

Full sun to partial shade; average to poor soil
Because of its antidepressant qualities, Saint-John's-wort has been in the news lately—and with good reason. People have been using it for centuries; internally, to treat depression and melancholy as well as a host of other complaints, and externally to heal cuts, bruises, burns, and sprains. In the garden, don't give it too much compost or fertilizer, or you may get over-exuberant growth. Saint-John's-wort is a common sight in fields and along roadsides, and this is a good indication that it needs no pampering.

Herbs for Crafts

SWEET ANNIE (AKA SWEET WORMWOOD)

Artemisia annua
Daisy family (Compositae)
Annual (hardy)
3–10 feet tall
Full sun; average soil

A rather large annual needing plenty of garden space, sweet Annie can reach a height of ten feet in a spot it really likes, so give it room. It will self-sow once established if the plants are allowed to go to seed. Its aromatic, feathery branches are great for wreaths and dried arrangements, and they dry very well.

LAVENDER (see page 107)

Lavandula angustifolia
Mint family (Labiatae)
Perennial (woody), hardy to zones 5–8
Full sun; light, sweet, well-drained soil

I know, I've already talked about lavender as an addition to a flower garden, but this time I wanted to mention its usefulness for crafts. The intensely fragrant branches and flowers can be used in everything from sachets and potpourri to laundry fresheners and soap, and it's great for wreaths and dried flower arrangements.

YARROW, FERN-LEAFED

Achillea filipendulum
Daisy family (Compositae)
Perennial (herbaceous),
hardy to zone 3
3–4 feet tall
Full sun to light shade; average,
well-drained soil

A close relative to medicinal yarrow, fernleaf yarrow has flat-topped clusters of flowers in various shades of yellow that dry extremely well for flower arrangements. It is very easy to grow in the garden, but may need to be divided every few years to keep in bounds.

ARTEMISIA "SILVER KING"

Artemisia ludoviciana 'Silver King'
Daisy family (Compositae)
Perennial (herbaceous), hardy to zone 4
2–4 feet tall
Full sun to light shade; average, well-drained soil

Silver King makes a dramatic statement in the perennial border, with its ghostly white-gray foliage. It spreads readily by runners, so must be confined to keep it in bounds. Silver King and its partner Silver Queen both make outstanding wreaths and dried arrangements if harvested in late summer when their seedheads are almost pure white. After that, the rain and wind of autumn will discolor the foliage.

ORRIS ROOT (FLORENTINE IRIS)

Iris x *germanica* var. *florentina*
Iris family (Iridaceae)
Perennial hardy to zone 4/5
2–4 feet tall
Full sun; fertile, well-drained soil

Most people don't think of the stately iris as an herb, but the Florentine iris is an exception. The dried rhizome was once used medicinally, but is now valued as a fixative in potpourri. There are hundreds of iris varieties out there, but for the best results, try to find *Iris* x *germanica* var. *florentina*.

SOUTHERNWOOD (LAD'S LOVE, OLD MAN)

Artemisia abrotanum
Daisy family (Compositae)
Perennial (woody), hardy to zone 4
To 5 feet tall
Full sun; average, well-drained soil

Southernwood is a lovely, gray-green shrubby perennial with very aromatic foliage that has sometimes been described as lemon-scented bathroom cleaner. Because of its strong scent, it is used in sachets to repel moths.

WORMWOOD

Artemisia absinthium
Daisy family (Compositae)
Perennial (woody), hardy to zone 3
3–4 feet tall
Full sun to partial shade; loamy, well-drained soil

One of the best known of all the artemisias, wormwood was once used as liqueur flavoring but is now known to be toxic when used internally. It's still used medicinally in the antiseptic lotion Absorbine, Jr. Today, you can use it as an insect repellent in sachets, or make a tea from it to repel soft-bodied insects like aphids.

TANSY

Tanacetum vulgare
Daisy family (Compositae)
Perennial (herbaceous),
    hardy to zone 4
3–5 feet tall
Full sun to light shade; average soil
Tansy is another old-time insect repellent herb, and you'll find a huge clump of it by the kitchen door of many old New England farmhouses. It was grown because it had a reputation for keeping out the ants and flies. You can make a sachet for your kitchen cabinets that may help repel ants. The pretty little yellow flowers dry golden, and they also make a nice addition to dried flower arrangements and potpourri. Tansy is almost too easy to grow in a garden, and it's difficult to eradicate if you change your mind about it.

CATNIP (see page 105)

Nepeta cataria
Mint family (Labiatae)
Perennial (herbaceous), hardy to zone 3–4
1–3 feet tall
Full sun to partial shade; average, sandy
    well-drained soil
Yes, we covered this one in our "second string" top ten list, but it's worth mentioning again here in the context of crafts. Your kitty will love you for making her some little catnip toys stuffed with her favorite herb. If you don't sew, small muslin bags are available from mail order sources, but they don't hold up to feline ecstasy as well as homemade ones.

PENNYROYAL, ENGLISH

Mentha pulegium
Mint family (Labiatae)
Perennial (herbaceous),
    hardy to zone 5
6 inches tall (flower spikes
    to 1 foot)
Full sun to partial shade; rich, moist soil
There are two types of pennyroyal, American and English. Ironically, English is the type that's more widely available in the States. That's just as well, because English pennyroyal is preferred for herb gardens as a creeping ground cover. Pennyroyal is famed as a flea repellent, a use that goes back to Roman times! You can weave the fresh strands into an herbal collar for your pet or put the leaves in their bedding.

I Thought That Was a *Weed*!

Let me start by saying that I'm *not* suggesting you actively plant these guys in your formal herb garden. The reason I wanted to talk about them is because they've only become "pests" in the age of perfect golf-course style lawns. They were included in the old herbals because they fit the definition of useful plants—either due to their medicinal benefits or some other purpose. There's an old saying that a weed is simply a plant growing where you don't want it. With that in mind, let's talk briefly about these plants that could very well end up being your friends.

DANDELION

Taraxacum officinale

Daisy family (Compositae) Dandelions are so familiar that they probably need no description. They are hardy even in

severe climates, and they self-sow prolifically, as anyone with a lawn knows. But did you know that dandelions are packed with nutrients, and they have been used as a spring tonic for generations? The leaves are bitter, but when picked in early spring before flowering, they can be added to salads for a boost of vitamin A, as well as vitamin C, protein, and fiber. The flowers can be gathered for dandelion wine, and the roots can be dried and roasted as a coffee substitute. Dandelion is a powerful diuretic, as evidenced by its French name, *pissenlit*, or "wet the bed." It's also used for urinary or gallbladder disorders.

SWEET GOLDENROD

Solidago odora

Daisy family (Compositae) Goldenrod has gotten a bad rap. It's not the one responsible for hay fever—that distinction

belongs to ragweed, which blooms at the same time but has inconspicuous flowers. In fact, at one time goldenrod was used as a hay fever treatment! Blue Mountain tea, made from goldenrod, replaced English black tea during the American Revolution, and it was also a source for yellow dye. Goldenrod's sunny yellow flowers dry well for winter arrangements, too.

SAINT-JOHN'S-WORT (see page 114)

Hypericum perforatum

Saint-John's-wort family (Hypericaceae) As mentioned in the entry for medicinal herbs, Saint-John's-wort is a common sight in fields and waste places, and in some areas, eradication programs have been started to get rid of it because it has caused photosensitivity in some light-skinned animals that have foraged it. The Latin name suggests a way to identify this herb—if you hold the leaves up to the light, they appear to be perforated. Gather the flowers when just opened for tinctures, oils, and salves.

JEWELWEED, TOUCH-ME-NOT

Impatiens pallida, Impatiens capensis

Touch-me-not family (Balsaminaceae)

Jewelweed keeps bad company, hanging out with the likes of poison ivy and stinging nettle. But it makes a great first-aid treatment in case of a run-in with one of these bad boys of the great outdoors. Just crush the leaves and apply right on the rash. Jewelweed grows wild in moist, shady areas, and its succulent leaves have been described as "ninety percent water." The pale orange flowers look like little pouches or slippers, and when they develop seed pods the reason for the common name "touch-me-not" becomes apparent—they explode when you touch them!

BURDOCK
Arcticum lappa
Daisy family (Compositae)
OK, you may think I've gone too far—to actually suggest the weed that produces those obnoxious burs could possibly be useful!

Well, yes it is, and it's actually cultivated as a vegetable in Japan. Not only is burdock valued for its culinary uses, it has also been used to treat many illnesses and skin conditions, from rheumatism to gout.

MOTHERWORT
Leonorus cardiaca
Mint family (Labiatae)
Motherwort is an unusual member of the mint family, in that it doesn't have a fresh, pleasant

aroma. *At all.* This escapee from colonial gardens has naturalized in farmland all over North America, and it was adopted by Native Americans for its sedative effects and for the same conditions that both the Europeans and the Chinese used it for: treatment of menstrual problems and heart disease. And it has pretty purple flowers, too.

STINGING NETTLE
Urtica dioica
Nettle family (Urticaceae)
Here's another one you'll think I'm crazy to mention, but it really is a good plant—unless

you walk through a patch of it wearing shorts! The fresh leaves and stems inject an irritating toxin when touched, and boy, does it hurt! So get to know and recognize this plant before harvesting it, and then make sure you're wearing gloves. Stinging nettle makes a great spring tonic, and it has both culinary and medicinal uses. Once dried or cooked, it loses its sting and makes a tasty green vegetable. Medicinally, it has been used to treat rheumatism, gout, skin conditions, and blood disorders.

CHICKWEED
Stellaria media
Pink family (Caryophyllaceae)
Chickweed is a persistent weed that continues to grow even

after fall frosts to produce a thick carpet of green. But this nutritious weed was once sold as a potherb in European markets, and it's delicious in salads. It tastes even better cooked like spinach.

PURSLANE

Portulaca oleracea

Purslane family
(Portulacaceae)

Purslane is a common weed in gardens, driveways, and sidewalks, and while you're busy pulling it up, think about tossing it in your salad rather than your compost heap. Purslane, once known as "pussley," was once a popular garden plant, and it was cultivated as a pot herb for its iron-rich leaves and branch tips. Medicinally, it's considered a cooling herb that lowers fevers and clears toxins.

GROUND IVY

Glechoma hederacea

Mint family (Labiatae)

Ground ivy has been known by many names over the centuries, "gill-over-the-ground" "run-away-robin," and "cat's-foot" among them, but it's probably best known as "ale-hoof" for its use as a bittering agent and clarifier for beer. These days it's better known as a lawn-invading weed, and gardeners have other unprintable names for it. In addition to its uses in beermaking, ground ivy was made into a tea for treatment of jaundice, poisoning, and gout.

CHAPTER 12

Fragrance, Flavors, and Flowers

In this last chapter devoted to lists, we'll talk about two more categories of herbs that you'll want to know about. I must warn you though, once you get started, you won't be able to stop!

The World of Scented Geraniums

Scented geraniums are the ultimate Victorian herb. The name conjures up images of velvet-draped Victorian parlors, their wide bay windows filled with dozens of varieties of these little beauties, from fernleaf to velvety lobed leaves with a purple blotch in the center. And they all have a different fragrance.

Scented geraniums, like common garden geraniums, both belong to the genus *Pelargonium*, and to the large and diverse geranium family (Geraniaceae). The common (non-herbal) garden geraniums you see everywhere are called zonal geraniums, and they are related to our herbal scented geraniums. They are all actually tender perennials in their native South Africa. We call the scented varieties "herbs" simply because of their fragrance, where their showier cousins have the flowers but not the scent. Scenteds made their way to Europe in the 1600s, coming home with sailors as souvenirs from the South African Cape. Interest grew quickly, and by the 1750s, they had reached colonial America. But it was during the Victorian period that scenteds reached their greatest popularity, with hundreds being offered in plant catalogs.

There are at least 250 naturally occurring species of *Pelargonium*, but only a few have been developed into the familiar scented geraniums of our gardens and windowsills. Because of the ease of hybridization, growers have created countless cultivars, and many nurseries offer hundreds of types. Only a few of the varieties out there are the true species, among them rose (*P. graveolens*), lemon (*P. crispum* and *P. citronellum*), mint (*P. tomentosum*), and apple (*P. odoratissimum*). Whenever you see names of cultivars, for example, *Pelargonium graveolens*

"Gray Lady Plymouth," knowing that *graveolens* is the rose group will give you a clue to the fragrance.

THE ROSE GROUP
(P. GRAVEOLENS)

- peacock
- old-fashioned rose
- Rober's lemon rose (lemony-rose)
- mint rose (and variegated)
- Lady Plymouth
- gray Lady Plymouth
- snowflake (lemony-rose)
- *P. capitatum* "attar of rose"
- camphor rose
- little gem
- little leaf rose
- *P.* "Dr. Livingston"

THE LEMON GROUP
(P. CRISPUM)

- lemon
- gooseberry
- fingerbowl lemon
- Prince Rupert
- variegated Prince Rupert
- cinnamon
- peach

There are an infinite variety of leaf shapes, textures, and colors, in addition to the hundreds of fragrances available. Leaves can be nearly circular, oak-leaf shaped, crinkled, or finely cut like a fern leaf; they can be sticky, velvety, hairy, or smooth and leathery; they can consist of all shades of green, some with dark blotches, others splashed with cream or white. And all the flowers are different, too. Though they're not as showy as zonal geraniums, they're still lovely, ranging in colors from white to bright pink and occasionally red.

Geranium Fragrances

The real star of the show here is the fragrance. Really rosy, incredibly lemony, refreshingly minty, fruity, even chocolate; whatever your pleasure, you'll probably find it in a scented geranium. In many cases, the fragrance is unmistakably the same as its name; in others you may have to use your imagination. By the way, remember that "peacock" is not supposed to smell like a peacock—it's a rose! Sometimes, the fragrance will be different, depending on who's doing the sniffing. It's really fascinating!

There are different groups of scented geraniums. The rose group, the lemon group, and the mint group are the main ones. In my greenhouse, to break it down further, I organize my scenteds into groups like fruity (orange, apple, lime, strawberry, and apricot, along with the lemons), spicy (nutmeg, cinnamon, old spice, ginger, filbert), floral (all the various roses including attar of rose, peacock, and Lady Plymouth), and minty (chocolate mint, lemon balm, and peppermint). The rest fall into the miscellaneous category for my purposes: interesting leaf shapes, cool names, nice variegation. I want to stress that this is my own personal method for keeping track of dozens of varieties, and it's not an official "breakdown."

Geranium Growth Habits

Along with the infinite variety of leaves, fragrances, and flowers, there is also an infinite variety of growth habits for scented geraniums. There are some that grow quite tall, some that sprawl all over a garden, and others that remain compact and tidy. In areas that remain frost-free, scenteds planted outdoors can live for several years and can become sizable shrubs and trees. For the rest of us they must be treated like annual bedding plants—plant them right in the garden. By using different types, you can create very interesting contrasts in a bed. Be aware that certain types grow huge in the ground, and may become too large to pot up and bring inside for the winter. In these cases, you can take cuttings in late summer and leave the parent plant in the ground.

Most scented geraniums work great in containers, and can be brought inside for the winter. Scenteds are among the best herbs around for indoor culture. During the summer they can be put in window boxes, where they'll trail over the sides, or in whiskey barrels, where you can plant a mini-garden of several different varieties. Several types also work nicely in hanging baskets. A collection of small pots looks great on a patio or deck, and they can be moved around to suit your needs.

Care and Feeding of Scented Geraniums

You'll be happy to hear that scented geraniums are very easy to care for. Planted right in the ground, they don't need much at all, except for a little occasional grooming. They thrive in full sun but can get along with as little as a few hours a day. They prefer a rich, loamy, well-drained soil. Just remember, they can't stand freezing temperatures—although a few can stand a light frost—so if you're going to take cuttings for the winter, do it in late summer before the frost hits.

In containers, scenteds still need bright light, but they need to be protected from full sun—especially in hot climates. If plants get leggy, move them to a bright spot. As with other container plants, make sure you water well during hot weather. Be careful not to overwater, though, because that promotes fungal diseases and rot. Just let the top of the soil dry out between waterings. Scenteds don't seem to mind being crowded into planters, and they look much better when planted close together.

They do seem to need feeding a little more frequently than some other herbs, but don't feed them too much nitrogen or the fragrance will be diminished. I've heard some people say that organic fertilizers don't work as well on scenteds, but I've never had a problem. Indoors, use liquid seaweed or kelp, and outdoors, use fish emulsion.

Pests are seldom a problem on plants grown outdoors, but once you bring them in for the winter, check them regularly for aphids and spider mites. If properly cared for, even indoor plants are fairly pest resistant. Keep them in a sunny, cool window that gets four to five hours of sun a day. Prune them when they get leggy, and remove any dead leaves. By the way, this is a regular part of scented geranium grooming—leaves die, you take them off. No big deal.

Propagating Scented Geraniums

The easiest way to get scented geraniums is to buy them. Very few varieties can be propagated from seed, and the process is not easy. Once you have a few plants, though, and all your friends are admiring your collection, you may want to share. To propagate scented geraniums, start by taking cuttings from growing shoots of an established plant. Using a sharp knife, cut a two- to four-inch shoot just below a node and stick it in clean sand or soilless potting mix that will allow water to drain off quickly; otherwise the cutting will rot. Some people have had success with letting the cutting heal for a few hours

or overnight before sticking it in the soil. I've tried it both ways, and they both work.

> A *node* is where a leaf grows from the stem. It's usually where new roots will form in a cutting.

Water your cuttings in well, and put them in a bright spot out of direct sunlight. Depending on the variety, it can take anywhere from six weeks to several months before you have enough roots to transplant to a larger container. (Chocolate has been notoriously slow to root for me, while others take off. You'll just have to experiment.) Eventually, they will be large enough to transplant into the containers, and you can keep them there for a couple of years. They'll need repotting every year or two, either to give them more space or just to refresh the soil.

Enjoying Scented Geraniums in Other Ways

Finally, you ask, what the heck can you do with all these plants? Well, scenteds can be used to make desserts, jellies, sugars, and potpourris. While I've recommended certain types of geraniums in these recipes, feel free to experiment with using what strikes your fancy.

Ten Great Scented Geraniums

NAME	SCENT	GROWTH	DESCRIPTION
Apple	apple	compact	small, velvety leaf
Chocolate	pungent	spreading	large leaf, purple blotch
Eucalyptus	pungent	upright	large leaf, bright flower
Fernleaf	pungent	upright	delicate, lacy leaf
Old-fashioned rose	rose	upright	divided leaves
Old spice	spicy	trailing	small, smooth, sweet leaves
Orange	orange	upright	small leaf, showy
Peacock	rose	upright	leaves flecked with white
Rober's lemon rose	rose	upright	leaves like tomatoes
Strawberry	strawberry	upright	small, crinkly leaves

SCENTED GERANIUM SUGAR

One of the easiest things to make is flavored sugar. Take eight to twelve clean rose geranium leaves and layer them with sugar in an airtight canister or mason jar. Leave the jar in a sunny spot for a couple of weeks, to let the leaves scent the sugar. You can then use the sugar for cookies, whether sprinkled on top or mixed in the recipe with regular sugar.

SCENTED GERANIUM JELLY

Here's another easy one. Just put a couple of rose geranium leaves on the bottom of a clean jelly glass or jar, and pour hot apple jelly over them. The heat releases the essence of the geranium, and infuses it into the jelly.

SCENTED GERANIUM HONEY

Along the same lines as the jelly, you can use lemon, orange, or any of the sweet scented geraniums, and pour warmed honey over the leaves in a clean jar.

SCENTED GERANIUM CAKE

This works best with bland cakes like sponge or angel cakes—not chocolate. Just put a few rose (or lemon, orange, etc.) geranium leaves on the bottom of the cake pan, followed by the flour, before you pour the batter in. After baking, you can remove the leaf when you take the cake out of the pan. If you want, you can use fresh leaves to decorate your cake. The flowers make lovely decorations, too!

A Beginner's Guide to Edible Flowers

It's hard to believe now, in our era of plastic and silk flowers, but people have been eating blossoms for centuries! For appetizer, dessert, garnish, or whatever—all cultures have been doing it for ages. The practice fell out of popularity when chemical pesticides came into widespread use; people didn't know whether they couldn't eat the flowers because of the poison on them. Now that we've seen the light, and are using organic fertilizers and pesticides (if any at all), it's safe again to throw some Johnny-jump-ups and nasturtiums in our salads, or make jelly from the unsprayed roses by the kitchen window.

Gourmet restaurants all over the country have launched this revival, and the flames have been fanned by cookbooks, magazines, and cooking shows. You're not limited to garnishes with your edible flowers; you can mince them up and add them to herb butters, cheese spreads, and cake, crepe, or pancake batters.

Some flowers taste better than others, too. The blooms of culinary herbs usually taste like a milder version of the leaves, while other flowers are sweet, bitter, citrusy, or peppery. Each flavor lends itself to a different use in cooking.

Edible=Nontoxic

The main rule of thumb is, if you can eat the leaves, you can eat the flower. So it follows that it's safe to eat the blossoms of any culinary herb. This is not to say, however, that all flowers are safe, so if you are the least bit unsure of what you're about to pop in your mouth, DON'T! If you are in doubt, call your local poison control center. Also, it's a good idea not to eat flowers picked from heavily traveled roadsides, because of the pollution from cars. And eat flowers from greenhouses or nurseries only if you're absolutely sure they were grown organically.

Picking Your Posies

Pick your edible flowers in the early morning, when they're still moist with dew. Choose perfect blooms for garnishes, but if your recipe calls for just the petals, the blossom doesn't need to be picture perfect. Wash them gently in cool water, then wrap them in paper towels and store them in a plastic bag in the fridge until ready to use. Most blooms will last a day or two, but they are best used fresh. Some can be rejuvenated by crisping them in cold water (like with wilted lettuce).

Before long you'll be picking flowers to use in everything from salads to decorating cream cheese to vinegars to teas to candying violets for cakes. Once you start, it's hard to stop!

Here are some of my favorite edible flowers; all can be used as garnishes.

- beebalm: minty, goes well in beverages, teas
- borage: mildly cucumbery; freeze individual blossoms in ice cube trays for summer drinks
- calendula: once used to color cheese and butter; mildly bitter; use as garnish, desserts
- chive blossoms: oniony flavor; use in salads, vinegars
- lavender: unopened flower buds are an essential ingredient in *herbes de Provence;* floral flavor good in cookies, ice cream, desserts
- lemon gem and tangerine gem marigolds: sweetly scented tiny marigolds are great in salads and desserts
- nasturtium: peppery flavor; nice in salads, can be filled with cream cheese for an appetizer
- pansy: slightly minty; gorgeous garnish, good in salads and desserts
- rose: use petals only for sweet floral flavor; can be used for jellies, sugars; can be candied or used fresh as garnish
- squash and zucchini blossoms: mild vegetable flavor; especially nice for stuffing or frying
- violet, Johnny-jump-ups: sweetly minty; good in salads, float in punch, can be candied for garnish

The Potting Shed, Tools, and How to Make Compost

4

Now we'll learn about some of the must-have tools you'll need for your new garden, as well as some more frivolous but useful toys. In addition, we'll learn all about compost and why it's the best thing for your garden.

CHAPTER 13

Gardening Tools

This chapter will cover some of the most essential tools you'll need for herb gardening, as well as others that are handy but not essential. We'll also talk about how to shop for the best quality tools and how to care for your investments.

Quality vs. Economy

Growing up, I was always looking for a bargain; I usually bought the cheapest version of anything I needed. Gardening changed that for me. Now I *really* understand that differences in price are not just because of profit margins for the manufacturer. Going through no less than three cheap trowels in my first gardening season was my first clue.

WHAT TO LOOK FOR

Good quality tools can last for many years if properly cared for. Here are some things to keep in mind while you're shopping.

METAL

Look for tools made from steel labeled as "tempered" or "heat treated," and seek out steel that has been "forged" or "drop-forged." If you can afford the added expense, buy heavy-gauged stainless steel because it won't rust if left out in the rain.

Avoid inexpensive tools stamped out of sheet metal. They'll bend in half or even break, causing you frustration. Plus, you'll spend more money in the end to replace them.

TOOL HANDLES

Some small tools will have plastic handles, but the vast majority of tools have handles made from wood. Look for straight-grained American ash, and avoid knots or splinters. Ash is the best choice for handles because it's light, strong, and resilient. You also want to steer clear of painted handles, because the paint may be hiding flaws like cheap wood.

If you tend to lose tools—and we know how they like to hide under leaves and piles headed for the compost heap!—you can paint them later. Also available is a plastic coating that you can dip the handles in. Red is the usual choice, but any fluorescent color can help you locate your lost tool, no matter how colorful the autumn leaves are.

For a handle that will last even longer, look for fiberglass or solid-core fiberglass, which are both stronger than wood. These add between ten and twenty dollars to the cost of the tool.

> Wrap your tool handles in foam pipe insulation to give your hand more cushion and better grip. You can use it on everything from hand tools like trowels to larger things like rakes, shovels, and rototiller handles.

How the handle is attached to the business end of the tool is crucial to its durability. Look for "solid-shank" or "solid-socket" construction, which means that the socket is one piece of metal rather than two pieces welded together. The socket should completely envelop the handle. If there are rivets or other hardware holding the handle secure, make sure they're heavy-duty.

TOOL WEIGHT

Try to find tools that have a comfortable weight for you to use. A tool that's too heavy for you to lift isn't going to do you any good in the garden, and you'll end up leaving it in your toolshed. On the other hand, sometimes a heavy tool can do more work *for* you if you can use it comfortably.

> If you're on a really tight budget, tend to lose your tools, or are notoriously bad at caring for them, go for midrange items. These will still be better buys than bargain basement cheapos.

Must-Have Tools

Most every gardener I know can get along without anything in his toolshed except his trowel, clippers, and cultivator—either a small, hand-held job or one on a long handle. These are the things you'll need whether you're a container gardener or have a huge herb garden. Of course, there are hundreds of other tools out there that can make your life a lot easier, and we'll get to them in a minute.

Everyone is different, but I find when working in my own garden that no matter how many tools I bring out with me, I always seem to fall back on the same ones—my trowel and clippers. I can't seem to stop using my hands for almost everything else— so gloves are another crucial accoutrement! But I'll never forget how hard it was trying to dig a large hole in hard-packed earth with a cheap trowel, back in the days when I didn't even *own* a shovel!

DIGGING, SOIL MOVING, AND PLANTING TOOLS

My husband and I have a perennial debate: Is the shovel more effective than the digging fork for turning new soil? He swears by the shovel, and I wouldn't trade my fork for the world. This ongoing controversy is a pretty good illustration of how different tools can work for different people. It's probably a good idea to try out tools before investing a lot of money, so if you have a gardening friend, ask if you can borrow theirs. Just be a good friend and return it quickly!

At any rate, the first tool people usually think of for digging is a shovel, and while nothing compares to it for moving earth, it is far easier to loosen the ground first with a digging fork. And then there's the flat-bladed spade, which will cut through sod like nobody's business.

Shovels have curved, scooped-out blades that hold more dirt; they're ideal for digging holes with round sides, filling in holes, scooping compost or mulch into wheelbarrows, and turning soil over. Spades are for more precision digging, and have a flatter blade which makes holes with straighter sides. Kept nice and sharp, a spade will slice through sod and roots and will also lift out established plants with the root ball intact.

Shovels and spades are available with either long or short handles, and it's really subjective on your part which is the best choice for you, depending on your height. The better quality ones often have a little lip on the top where your foot pushes it in the soil, to save wear and tear on your boots. Care for your investment by sharpening the edge of the blade when it doesn't cut well. It will make a huge difference!

Digging forks, also called spading forks, are indispensable for loosening soil, especially when breaking new ground. These forks have heavy square tines that break up clumps more effectively than shovels or spades. Spading forks are useful for working in soil amendments, and they're also essential for lifting clumps of plants and leaving the soil behind, like when you're dividing perennials: Just lift the plant out and gently shake the soil back into the hole. (This is easier said than done in some cases, but that's the basic theory!)

TROWELS

As I mentioned earlier, my trowel is about the only thing I can't live without in the garden. Not only does it dig small holes for transplanting seedlings and other small plants, you can use it to move plants around, too. Trowels are handy for weeding and cultivating, and for mixing small amounts of potting soil or compost. There are many versions out there, but the basic two are wide-blade basic trowels and narrow-blade transplanting trowels, which make smaller holes. Look for one that feels good in your hand and is forged or made from cast aluminum—a cheap one won't last!

All of these tools are important enough to justify spending more money on them; this will ensure more than one season of use. Again, look for ash handles, heat-tempered steel, and solid-shank construction.

On the non-essential tool list are bulb planters, dibbers, sod cutters, transplanting spades, broadforks, and mattocks. Readers may take issue with some of these items being relegated to the "non-essential" list, and granted, I consider the sod cutter pretty indispensable. But that's because of my personal situation; starting brand new gardens every year makes a sod remover impossible to live without.

LIFTING TOOLS

The other kind of forks you'll find at garden centers are for lifting stuff, not for digging. The tines of a *pitchfork* aren't nearly as strong as spading forks, but they're better for moving mulch, fluffing compost, and moving bulky-but-light things like loose hay or straw.

Along the same lines are manure forks, which have ten or twelve tines. These guys will pick up mulches like shredded bark, compost, and (of course) manure without dropping too much between the tines. They're great for loading and unloading these materials from trucks.

Neither of these is really considered a must-have for herb gardening, but both come in very handy. See if you can find second-hand ones at yard or barn sales.

WEEDING AND CULTIVATING

There are dozens of types of weeders out there, all with different design elements and price tags. But in the end, you have to actually use them to get a feel for what works best for you. Here's a quick rundown of what's available:

HOES

Hoes are always included on "must-have" lists for gardens, and there are dozens of types, many with highly specialized uses, like onion hoes. Hoes are used for cutting weeds at or just below the surface of the soil, to make furrows for seeding, and to draw soil up to or away from the base of a plant.

The classic shape of hoe that most people think of is called the American-pattern hoe. It has a wide flat blade on a nice, long handle. Use this hoe by pulling it toward you; it both weeds and cultivates at the same time.

> If you mulch your garden, you won't be able to use your hoe. But then again, if you mulch it well enough, you won't need to!

My personal favorite hoe, the one that actually gets used, is the warren hoe, which has an arrow-shaped head. Using the point, you can make furrows for seeding and chop out stubborn weeds, or you can turn it on its side to use like a standard hoe. It's great for small gardens, and the long handle saves bending and stooping.

Other types of hoes available are the scuffle hoe, which is sharpened on two sides for pushing or pulling; the oscillating hoe, a hinged version of the scuffle; the weeding hoe, which has a narrow blade on one side and a forked weed puller on the other; the swan-neck hoe, with a curved neck that's

All hoes work best when kept sharp and clean.

good for light weeding; and grading hoes, which are really used for breaking ground, chopping, and terracing.

OTHER CULTIVATORS

Just as with hoes, there are many types of cultivators with different designs, uses, and price tags. Long handled versions include three-tined "claw" types, rotating-disk cultivators with teeth, and single-pronged biocultivators.

To *cultivate* means to break up the surface of the soil to let in air and moisture. This is also called *aeration.*

There are even smaller versions, some with three-hooked tines, some with springs, and hand forks with three straight tines, which are better for heavy-duty weed digging. There are dandelion weeders with long, notched blades for digging out weeds with long taproots, and all kinds of other little specialty weeders for sidewalks, hotbeds, and the like. There are also Asian hand cultivators and Cape Cod weeders . . . you get the idea.

RAKES

There are two basic kinds of rakes to choose from: metal garden rakes and leaf rakes. Metal garden rakes—the kind with short tines—are an essential part of your tool collection, even if you only use them a few times a year. Use them for clearing debris like rocks and sticks from garden beds, and as the last step in preparing a bed for planting. You can *grade* the soil, changing the contours of it (on a small scale, of course—this is no bulldozer!), break up compacted soil, mix in fertilizer or lime, or spread manure, compost, and mulches. Turn it upside down (tines up) and you can smooth the soil even more.

Leaf rakes are for raking up leaves in the fall. You can also use them for clearing off perennial beds in the fall, but generally a leaf rake is not considered an herb garden essential like its shorter-tined cousin.

CUTTING/PRUNING

OK, here's my other essential—and this is not a paid advertisement. I *love* my Felcos! For years I used cheap little clippers from the discount stores, and I thought they were OK. But then my husband gave me the best gift I've received in years—a pair of Felcos with a rotating grip. Clipping and pruning has never been the same! I even take care of them—they were expensive—by oiling and sharpening them at least once a season and keeping them in their little holster when I'm not using them. Of course, there are other high-quality pruners out there, and just because I haven't mentioned them doesn't mean I don't like them.

Hand pruners, also called *secateurs*, come in two styles. First, there are *bypass* pruners, which work like scissors, with one blade moving past the other. Kept sharp, bypass pruners make a cleaner cut. *Anvil* pruners, which have a sharp, narrow blade that presses down on a wider plate (or anvil), require less hand pressure to make the cut. Some models have a ratcheting mechanism, which really helps when trying to cut a thicker branch. They're especially useful for those with less hand strength.

When your trusty hand pruner just won't do, go for the loppers. They have longer handles and are used for larger branches on shrubs, or for larger perennials. You'll see them with both wood and metal handles, and some even have nifty telescoping handles. Some people can keep their loppers in good shape for decades, but around here, we've gone through several in a season—broken handles, lost hardware, whatever—so look for the best you can afford.

Depending on the amount of gardening you do and the space you have (and your love of gadgets), you also may want a pair of inexpensive snipping scissors for small jobs around the greenhouse or for your windowsill garden. These are for tidying up, not for major harvesting.

INTRO TO HOSES AND WATERING/ FEEDING TOOLS

Never considered a hose a tool? Well, it's an implement that (supposedly) makes your life in the garden easier, right? If you have only the tiniest of gardens, you might be able to get along without a hose as your water source, but just remember that water is heavy, and carrying around watering cans is no picnic. (More about cans in a minute.)

I know all about life in "hose hell"; the plumbing system in my greenhouse fails every single year (usually on the hottest day of the year) and I have to haul several hundred feet of hose across the lawn to keep the greenhouse from completely drying up. So I've learned a couple of things that I'd like to share.

First, again, go for quality. Those so-called "lifetime hoses" that don't kink and can be driven over are worth the extra couple of bucks. They really work!

Second, invest in a hose reel if you have a lot of hose to cart around. You'll develop a love-hate relationship with it, too, but it's better than not having one.

Third, if you're forced to leave your hose in the yard so long you have to mow over it, please set your mower blades *very* high. There's nothing more annoying than shaving just enough of your hose off to allow a leak in the middle. (This is probably something that only happens to me because of the greenhouse, but I include it just in case it may help you, too.)

Fourth, if you use your hose in the garden and find that you constantly knock over plants with it, consider using hose fenders at the corners of the beds. They range in price and style from free (big sticks stuck in the ground) to mid-range (old concrete architectural elements you can find at flea markets) to high-end (mail order catalogs offer terracotta figures designed for this purpose).

Lastly, at the end of summer, drain your hose and coil it up to store indoors for the winter. It will last much longer.

A NOTE ABOUT NOZZLES

Just like everything else for the garden, there are many different types of nozzles available. The old standby, the metal-trigger type, is usually adjustable from spray to stream and will get you by. They've started making them out of cheap plastic now, and guess what? They're cheap plastic. You'll buy three of them before the season is over. Don't be tempted by all the combinations—flat spray, gentle, hard stream, etc.—in these plastic ones. If you want all that, go for the metal kinds for an extra couple of dollars.

For general garden use, I use an old-fashioned brass nozzle that twists on and off. The farther you open it, the more the stream changes. I've found that it's actually more versatile than the new ones with all the spray choices. Another option is a simple on/off switch, which is especially helpful if you connect a lot of hoses—you can install this in the middle and take the hoses apart without turning off the water at the faucet. I use several of these, especially where the hose reel hooks up to the feeder hose from the house.

Also, watering wands are now available to home gardeners. Once only sold to greenhouses, this long wand with a water breaker at the end saves you from stooping in the garden or straining to water hanging baskets. And the breaker turns an otherwise gushing stream of water into a gentle rain.

SOAKER HOSES

You'll notice I haven't mentioned sprinklers yet. And I won't here either, because I don't like them. I think they waste water, and even in a part of the country where water shortage is not a crisis, I don't like wasting. That's why I'll talk about soaker hoses and other drip irrigation methods instead.

Any kind of drip irrigation system is a good investment if you live in a part of the country where watering is a problem—and even if you don't.

Soaker hoses are made from porous material like canvas or recycled tire foam, or they can have holes punched down the length of them. Water "weeps" out along the hose, soaking the ground below.

SOAKER HOSES

If you use the type that has holes poked in it, make sure you position the holes down toward the ground rather than up in the air, or you'll end up with just another sprinkler!

You can bury the soaker hose under a thick layer of mulch right in the garden, and not only will you conserve water that would've evaporated before it reached the roots, you'll also protect the hose once it's there with the mulch. It's a great system, and it's *easy!* Just lay the hose out, cover it and you're done!

If, however, you love gadgets and puzzles, drip irrigation may be the thing for you. These systems are made of a system of tubing, valves, emitters, pressure regulators, backflow preventers, line filters, and timers, and they can cost considerably more than their soaker counterparts. The companies that sell the equipment for drip irrigation can help you design a system that's right for you. Even with their increased cost and complexity, these systems can more than make up for their drawbacks in areas of the country where water is at a premium. Well-designed systems can use between thirty and fifty percent less water than sprinkling!

The bottom line: These types of watering systems are head and shoulders above standard sprinklers or hand watering. Here's why.

First, you don't have to stand there with a hose, wasting your life, every night when you should be playing with your kids.

Second, watering from below ensures the water actually gets to the plants, rather than evaporating into the air or running off to where it's not needed.

Third, watering from below keeps foliage dry, reducing the chance of inviting fungal diseases like powdery mildew.

Fourth, plants watered with drip systems grow more quickly and are more productive because they are not stressed out by lack of water.

And last, sprinklers, while fun for the kids in the summertime, often end up spraying you or your guests.

WATERING CANS

I couldn't get along without my watering can. In fact, I own two sizes—a large one with two roses, normal size and extra-gentle seedling size, for watering the many houseplants and herbs that I overwinter indoors.

Watering can *roses* are the attachments at the end of the spout that have tiny holes to let the water pass through gently.

I use the smaller can for small watering jobs, like just one windowsill full of plants. I use the larger-size can for larger plants—often without the rose attachment to let the water flow faster. I also use the large can with the rose for starting seeds indoors, and for when I'm transplanting just a few seedlings into the garden and don't want to drag the hose all the way out there. For major transplanting jobs I'll still use the hose to water everything when I'm done.

I also use the watering can for feeding fish emulsion or liquid seaweed to my indoor plants. For feeding the entire greenhouse I use a pump sprayer, but that's not a must-have for the average gardener.

SPRAY BOTTLES

Another useful toy for feeding plants is a one-quart spray bottle from the hardware or discount store. I *would* say quality counts here, but I think they're all cheap, no matter how much you pay. So in this case, go for the bargain, because you'll have to replace it regularly anyway. These little guys, cheap or not, are great for applying all kinds of organic stuff to your plants—liquid seaweed and fish emulsion, insecticidal soaps, baking soda and hot pepper sprays, you name it.

> You can screw the spray handle from the main bottle onto quart soda bottles, and have different combinations of premixed sprays ready to go— just switch the bottles.

HAULING

Most herb gardeners don't absolutely *have* to have wheelbarrows and garden carts, but they certainly are handy for hauling around manure, mulch, and hay. They also make great transportation for bringing your plants or equipment out to the garden. Wheelbarrows are much easier to maneuver, but two-wheel carts can carry more material.

Little red wagons are also handy, but you may have to share them with your kids. Try to find used ones at yard sales.

GET THE POWER!

For every clean, quiet, non-polluting hand tool, there seems to be a motorized, noisy, gas-guzzling equivalent. Most herb gardeners will not have a use for many of the power equipment sold in garden centers, but there are exceptions, most notably the string trimmer. As a matter of fact, it's really the only power tool I need for my herb gardens. It's really handy for trimming weeds and grass along fences, at the base of buildings, or along walls. Available in electric, gas, or battery-powered models, you really need to try them out before buying to get a feel of what's right for you. My first one was a tiny electric one, which would've been great if I had forty acres worth of extension cord. If you have a very small yard and not a lot of arm strength, this is the way to go, even though the power cord is a hassle. The trimmer we use now is battery-powered, and while I can go anywhere with it, it's heavy and cumbersome. I don't enjoy using it nearly as much as I hoped I would. The battery also runs down after about half an hour— which is all I can handle anyway! But it really does a job on the grassy weeds around the main gardens.

The other option is gas-powered, which is even louder and more stinky than the previous two types. But if you have the arm strength and are troubled with really heavy-duty weeds, you can't beat it. Some models use a steel blade that is powerful enough to cut small trees. Please use this type carefully.

DON'T BOTHER

These are the big boys of the power gardening tools—and I only say don't bother with them if all you have is a simple, small herb garden or perennial borders. But if you also have a large vegetable garden, and/or lots of lawn, you might want to have these.

- Rototiller: completely unnecessary for a normal-size herb garden because even the small ones are just too big. Most herb gardens are a mixture of annuals and perennials, and you can't use the tiller once the area is planted.
- Lawn mower: Obviously, if you have a lawn, you'll need a mower. But it's not a tool for the herb gardener—unless you've planted an herbal lawn . . .
- Chipper/shredder: These are very loud—and I mean LOUD—machines that are great for larger scale gardeners who make a lot of their own compost and mulch. I love ours, as long as I'm inside when it's running.

NICE-TO-HAVES

There are dozens—no, probably hundreds—of items that garden centers and mail-order catalogs will try to entice you with. Feel free to spend your money the way you like, and if something strikes your fancy, there's no harm in splurging every once in a while. In the meantime, here are a few more basics you may or may not need, and are usually forgotten until you're out in the garden and actually need them.

- Tape measure: for measuring garden beds
- Twine, along with sticks: helpful for laying out beds
- Scissors: to cut twine
- Baskets/buckets: for hauling hand tools and above items, as well as carrying out weeds
- Notebook: to keep track of what you and the garden are doing
- Waterproof markers: for plant labels and for notebook entries

The Care and Feeding of Your Trowel

Now that you've invested in a few tools, you'll want to keep them in good shape. That means *not* leaving them out in the rain, and cleaning off the dirt when you're finished with them. Even good quality tools will deteriorate and rust if you treat them badly, making them just as unpleasant to use as the cheapos. Here are a few tips to help you keep your tools in tip-top shape:

- Clean off dirt after each use (even if you're really tired!) with a wooden scraper, brush, or rag. Dirt is easier to remove when it's fresh rather than dried and caked-on.
- Store your tools indoors—they'll last longer.
- Periodic sharpening of hoes, spades, and hand pruners will keep them doing their job efficiently. Learn to sharpen your own tools with a file or whetstone, or just take them to a professional.
- Sand and varnish the wooden handles of your tools occasionally. Some people use tung oil to seal the wood.
- Sometimes handles break. I know we live in an era of disposable everything, but don't throw the tool away! Hardware stores sell replacement handles.
- At the end of the season, take a few minutes to thoroughly clean and oil all your tools (to prevent rust) and store them all together in a dry place. You'll be glad you did in the spring!

> Keep a five-gallon bucket filled with sharp builder's sand in your toolshed to dip the metal blade of your tools in. This scrapes off dirt and sharpens at the same time. Adding a quart of oil will accomplish oiling your tool, too!

Spring Fashion: What to Wear in the Garden

Garden fashion is all the rage these days—catalogs offer all kinds of pretty little pants and T-shirts with pictures of flowers or antique tools on them. But the real stuff you need is more utilitarian and less fashion-conscious. It's all a matter of personal taste, but there are still some universal rules of thumb.

You may prefer working in the garden in a long flowing dress so that the whole image looks right out of "Enchanted April," but most of us prefer sturdy jeans or pants and loose-fitting shirts. There are some catalogs that offer pants with removable knee-pads. Ordinarily I'd say this is a frivolity, but I own a pair and absolutely love them. I wear them every time I weed or transplant, or when I know I'll be working on my knees.

Gloves and hats are no longer the stuff of tea parties—for working in the garden you need protection from both sun and thorns. For your hat, choose a wide-brim style. In areas with lots of bugs, you can get a bug net that fits right over the hat. It makes you less of a target for mosquitoes and blackflies. Gloves come in dozens of styles and colors, but plain cowhide gives the best protection from thorns. Plain cotton gardening gloves are good for light weeding, but they tend to wear out quickly. Gauntlet gloves, sturdy long gloves that go up to the elbow, are available for working with roses and other prickly shrubs.

Sneakers are fine for everyday gardening, but in rainy weather you may find that a pair of rubber garden clogs keeps your feet nice and dry. If you're going to be doing a lot of spading or forking new ground, sturdy work boots are a better choice to protect your feet. Boots are also a very good idea if you're using heavy equipment like tillers or string trimmers.

Some gardeners also like to use aprons or vests with lots of pockets to keep their pruners and markers in. You can also get strap-on knee pads, full bug-proof suits, and all kinds of other accoutrements. Some are worth the money, others aren't. Use your best judgment.

Yard Sale Finds and Grandma's Garage

As a footnote, I want to share something. A couple of years ago I inherited my grandmother's gardening tools, especially valuable to me because I spent many childhood summers with her in her beautiful garden. Anyway, at first I didn't want to actually use any of these antiques because I didn't want to break them, but I gave one of them a try last summer, and realized it was still as sturdy as the day it was made. These tools were well designed and well made, and they're a delight to use, not just because they are a direct link to my grandmother, but because they are great tools. My point is, if you happen to find old garden tools at a yard sale, flea market, or junk shop, grab them. They may need a little cleaning to get the rust off, or even a replacement handle, but the work they'll give you in return for a little elbow grease will be well worth it.

CHAPTER 14

How to Make Dirt

You may think that all dirt is created equal, but that couldn't be further from the truth. And you may also think that only nature knows how to make dirt. But guess what? People have been doing it since the beginning of time—or at least since the beginning of agriculture! This chapter will talk about why and how to create compost, the best food for your garden.

What Is *Compost*, Anyway?

When living things die, they decompose. That's a natural part of nature. And when this stuff decomposes, whether it's fallen leaves, dead weeds at the end of the season, animal waste, or an animal that has died in the woods, it all breaks down with the help of microorganisms to become new dirt. (OK, it's called humus at this point.) Everything in its own way is returned to the earth.

So if you ever go for a walk in the woods and notice the thick layer of leaves on the forest floor, or pine needles in an evergreen forest, that's nature's way of replenishing the nutrients for the trees that are living there now. The fallen leaves of the previous years decompose to nourish the trees for next year. It's a never-ending cycle.

This is the absolute easiest explanation of a rather complex subject, but it's really all you need to know. The combination of many different decayed things determines the richness of the soil. The more varied the ingredients, the richer the soil.

Experienced gardeners call compost "black gold" because it's such a valuable addition to the garden.

Remember Chapters 4 and 5, when we talked about soil fertility, and how the best soils were dark and humusy? That's because of the level of organic matter in it. Organic matter (humus) improves both

sandy soils and clay soils by aerating them, and by making the soil better able to conduct water so that plants can use it.

> *Humus* is decomposed plant and animal matter. The term organic matter is pretty much interchangeable with humus. Whatever you call it, it all contains important nutrients that plants need.

Do you see how this makes it possible for you to make your own soil to use in your garden? You can pile up old leaves, grass clippings, kitchen scraps, fireplace ashes, and livestock manure (more about this later). It will all break down together and make beautiful soil for your garden. Composting speeds up the natural processes by adding heat to the equation: When all these ingredients are piled up and begin decomposition, the microorganisms heat up, speeding up the whole shebang.

OK, at this point I know some purists are going to argue that you're not really making soil, but adding to your soil. I think that's quibbling. You're taking raw ingredients, waiting for them to decompose, then when they're dark, crumbly, and unrecognizable from their original form, you're putting them back in the ground. In my mind, that's making dirt. (Yeah, I know, the purists don't like to call it dirt, either!)

THE BOTTOM LINE

Although the best reason for composting is the benefit for your garden, there are a couple of other reasons you might want to think about. One of them is your pocketbook. Using compost on your garden decreases your need to go out and buy fertilizers, organic or otherwise—and it might even end this need altogether! Many herb gardeners use nothing but compost on their gardens, with wonderful results. Also, you won't have to pay to have your bags of leaves and grass clippings hauled away to the landfill (where they don't belong anyway!). You can recycle all your garden debris, so nothing goes to waste. This makes the whole idea good not just for your garden, but also good for your pocketbook *and* the environment!

Last but not least, compost is the best food for herb gardens in particular because you shouldn't use nonorganic fertilizers on your herbs anyway. And most herbs are so tolerant that they'll only need a good meal of compost once in a while.

Compost Happens

Besides the raw ingredients like leaves, grass clippings and kitchen scraps, compost needs a couple of other things to happen: plenty of moisture, some heat, and air. If any of these three are missing, your compost isn't going to "cook" properly, and may smell bad. But a well-made compost pile shouldn't smell at all. We'll cover what to do in case it does a little later.

There are several methods for making great compost, from super-fast "hot" to lazy (my favorite!). We'll start with the easiest and go from there.

Compost Made Easy

Just put everything in a pile and walk away. OK, that may be oversimplifying it, but that's the basic idea. This is a good method if you have lots of room, and can put the pile out of sight, like in a back corner of your yard. This approach is called "cold composting," because just letting it sit there doesn't really generate the heat that other methods create. The downside to this easy method is that it takes patience—like, a year. It'll take that long for everything to break down to a form that you can use in your garden. For this reason, many gardeners that have plenty of room make a new pile (or two) every year, and eventually there will be enough finished compost to always have plenty on hand.

Your pile should not be too large—four cubic yards is ideal—or it will take too long to "cook."

The process goes like this: start with raw materials that have a variety of consistencies, like grass clippings and manure (high in nitrogen), twigs and sticks (to provide bulk), leaves and straw (high in carbon), wood ashes or lime (to offset the acidity of the leaves). To encourage the fastest decomposition, try to use equal parts of high carbon and high nitrogen materials—you don't want all dry materials, for instance, because the pile won't break down properly. Intersperse a layer of regular soil in the pile every once in a while to add the soil microorganisms to get the process started.

Finely chopped materials will break down more quickly. If you have access to a chipper/shredder, use it! You can also use a chipper to shred your finished compost and make it fine enough to use as potting soil.

COMPOST INGREDIENTS
- High carbon materials: usually brown, dry
  — For example: sawdust, straw, dry leaves, pine needles, shredded newspaper
- High nitrogen materials: usually green, moist
  — For example: green weeds, grass clippings, livestock manure, kitchen scraps (everything from fruit and vegetable peelings to eggshells and coffee grounds—filter included!)

OTHER MISCELLANEOUS BUT NUTRITIOUS INGREDIENTS
- to raise pH (use in moderation): lime (also adds calcium), wood ashes (also adds potassium)

- rock phosphate, bone meal (or hoof and horn meal): adds phosphorus
- ground granite, greensand: adds trace elements

> If you decide to go with the "cold compost" method, don't just keep piling new stuff on top forever. After a few months, start a new pile to let the first one have a chance to finish.

Speeding Things Up

Don't want to wait a whole year? There are a couple of things you can do to speed up the composting process. One of them is to make sure your pile is moist enough, which means watering it with a hose when it dries out.

> A compost pile should be about as moist as a damp sponge.

Another thing you can do is turn your pile occasionally with a pitchfork or manure fork. The definition of occasionally depends on how industrious—or how lazy—you are. You can do it once every six months, or you can do it once a week—now that's industrious! The more you turn it, the sooner it will

be finished. The point of this exercise is that even cold piles have a "hot spot" in the middle, where the action is happening. Turning the pile redistributes the material and lets the stuff on the outside have a better chance of breaking down.

Contain Yourself!

The next level of composting is to put the pile in a bin. You can make your own bin out of anything from used warehouse pallets to cinderblocks to poles stacked up "log cabin" style. The attractiveness of the container doesn't really affect the process going on inside—just make sure you build the structure at least three feet long, wide, and high. Bins are usually open on top, and can also have a front door to make removal easier. You can also design bins that have multiple sections, so you can turn the compost in one compartment and start a new pile in the other.

> Another advantage to containers is they can repel scavenging animals that like to forage in compost.

OTHER HOMEMADE BIN IDEAS
- snow fence and metal stakes
- fifty-five gallon drums or trashcans with holes punched in the bottom and sides

- chicken wire wrapped around tomato stakes at the corners
- hay bales

Wrap a length of chicken wire into a three-foot diameter circle, and tie the ends together—not pretty, but cheap and easy!

Of course, if you're into gadgets, you can always go out and buy one of the many different compost bins on the market these days. They're usually made of black plastic, and range from freestanding bins to "tumble-style," which can roll around on the ground or on a rod, eliminating the step of turning with a pitchfork. The combination of black plastic and easy turning makes the compost ready in as little as two weeks! The main drawbacks to these bins are their expense and the fact that they're usually too small to produce the quantities of compost that many gardeners need in the beginning of the season. But, if you have a small garden and not much space for composting, they can be a real help.

Other Ways to Make Dirt

OK, we've gone from a simple pile in the corner of the yard to turning the pile occasionally to putting the whole thing in bins. But there's an even faster way to do this thing called composting.

Using Heat

"Hot" composting is the fastest way to get to black gold. It's the method that the expensive bins use, but you can recreate it yourself without the black plastic. The secret is frequent turning. Remember earlier when I said that if you turn your pile more often it'll be ready sooner? Well, in hot composting, you need to turn that pile every week or so! It's a serious investment in time, but if you need quantities of compost more quickly, it's the only way to go. Even gardeners in northern climates can get several batches of finished compost in a season. It can be usable in as soon as two weeks, and completely finished in about eight weeks.

> The interior of a hot compost pile can reach 160 degrees, and will feel warm to the touch. In cold weather, steam will rise from it.

The biggest advantages to hot composting are the speed of the process, and the fact that the heat kills many weed seeds, roots, and diseases. Make sure your pile is getting hot enough before adding weed seeds or diseased plants, though!

One of the biggest drawbacks to hot composting is that the whole pile needs to be built at once, and you can't keep adding to it. The other major problem is the labor involved in turning that huge pile every week, as well as the time commitment.

Other Things the Industrious Composter Can Do

OK, say you're really into this composting thing, and want to know even more tricks of the trade. Here are a few simple things you can try.

- Protect your pile in wet weather with a tarp or other covering. Too much rain can leach out the very nutrients you want for your garden. A tarp can also protect the pile from drying out in hot, windy weather.
- If the pile is too wet, insert perforated drainpipe to improve drainage.
- Add large sticks or sunflower stalks as you build the pile. You can remove them later to allow air in.
- Don't make layers of leaves or newspaper too thick—they tend to mat down rather than decompose.
- You can buy bags of rock phosphate, greensand, and other organic soil amendments that you can add to the compost pile rather than putting them directly in the garden.
- Adding comfrey and nettles to your compost is a good nutrition boost for it.

Whether you use the cold or hot method, your pile has a better chance of decomposing properly if you build it by alternating layers of green material with layers of brown, and a sprinkling of "other stuff" thrown in between, like kitchen scraps and wood ashes.

COOL TOOLS FOR COMPOSTING
- Riddle: a sieve-like device to screen out large pieces from finished compost. You can buy them or make them yourself.
- Compost turner: a long metal rod with a double arrowhead at the end to jab into the pile and turn it, aiding aeration
- Compost thermometer: tells you if your pile is getting hot enough

THE PERFECT HOT COMPOST RECIPE

INGREDIENTS (PER LAYER):

1 wheelbarrow full grass clippings

½ bale straw or hay

large shovel-full manure (horse or otherwise)

1 armload hollow stalks

1 bucket kitchen scraps

1 fireplace shovel-full rock phosphate

1 fireplace shovel-full wood ashes

INSTRUCTIONS

1. Make sure you locate your pile on a well-drained site. Start with one armload of grass clippings to form the bottom layer. Spread out the half bale of straw; add to grass clippings. Add the manure and the armload of hollow stalks, then spread out kitchen scraps. Sprinkle on rock phosphate and wood ashes with a fireplace shovel. Moisten with hose. This is layer one—repeat four or five more times.

2. After about two weeks, the pile will begin to get hot. Wait another three or four weeks to turn it, then turn it back again two weeks later. Your compost is ready when the original ingredients are unrecognizable and have become black and crumbly.

What Not to Put in Your Compost Pile

Even though pretty much anything that comes from a living source can be composted, there are a few things you want to avoid putting in your pile.

- Don't use pet feces (cat or dog), because it may carry diseases.
- Meat, bones, dairy, or fatty, oily kitchen scraps. Not only do they decompose slowly; they could also attract vermin to your pile.
- Avoid adding weeds with seeds and perennial weeds with spreading roots (unless you dry them out thoroughly before adding) until you have perfected your hot composting skills. Otherwise, the seeds can survive and end up right back in your garden!
- Colored newspapers, magazines, and books, because the colored ink may be toxic.
- Coal and charcoal ashes, which contain toxic residues.
- Very thick, woody stems, which won't break down for a really long time. Put them through a shredder first, if at all possible.

The Scoop on Poop

There are endless debates about what kind of manure is best to add to gardens. I won't try to end this debate here, but I will offer some basic, commonsense advice: If you have only one type of manure available to you, that's the best type to use. Don't lament that all you have is horse poop when you've heard the praises of Parisian Spotted Duck manure. While it's true that different types of manure have different qualities, don't worry if you don't have what you've heard is the best. Of course, the kind of animal waste that most suburban and urban dwellers have the most of is from their pet dogs and cats, which, as I've said before, you shouldn't use because of the risk of transmitting diseases.

In the days when most families had a few chickens and a milk cow or two, all this was no big deal. They cleaned out the stalls, left the stuff in a big pile for a year, and then used it on their gardens. It's not quite so easy anymore. But it can be done if you really want to. The easiest way for home gardeners to get manure is to buy bags of it at the garden center, but that's also the most expensive way to go. The best places to get manure are local farms. You may have to transport it yourself, but these are great sources.

I'll be covering the whole manure subject in greater detail in the chapters on soil amendments and fertilizers, but for now, just know that pretty much any kind of manure you get needs to be composted before you can add it to your garden. Most fresh manure is so high in nitrogen that it can burn your plants—plus it stinks!

Also, manure is a very important ingredient in hot composting. It's an excellent source of nitrogen, potassium, and phosphorus, and is rich in bacteria that help create heat for the composting process.

> Although manure is a prime organic substance, some farms may spray their manure with pesticides to kill flies, and sometimes manure can contain residues from antibiotics or other livestock medications.

When Compost Goes Bad— Compost Troubleshooting

Composting is a really easy way to make a wonderful soil amendment for your garden. But occasionally, you may run into a problem. Here are a few solutions:

The pile smells bad: Add more high-carbon material, like dry leaves or straw. Turning the pile can also help, especially if it's too wet. Finished compost should be sweet smelling, black, and crumbly.

The pile doesn't heat up: Add more high-nitrogen material, like manure or grass clippings. If the pile is too dry, add water. Turning the pile may also help.

Stuff is growing out of your pile: This is a byproduct of the pile not heating up enough to kill weed seeds. Try turning the pile to make sure these seedlings get to the hot spot in the center, or just avoid putting seedy materials on your pile. (On the other hand, some people get a real kick out of growing a prize pumpkin or tomato in their compost pile!)

The material isn't breaking down: You may have too much large, dry material like woody twigs. Try shredding them or chopping them up before adding them to the pile. Adding more high-nitrogen material can also help balance out your ratio of wet/dry.

Ways to Use Your New Dirt

OK, you've built your pile, turned it, watered it, and loved it. It's either a couple of months later, or the following year, and now it's ready to use. So what do you do with the stuff? I thought you'd never ask!

Your finished pile of black gold is a versatile substance that you can use any time of year without fear of burning your plants, as long as it's completely finished.

IN THE GARDEN
You can add compost directly to the garden, top dressing established plants, adding a trowel-full in the holes you dig for transplants, and as a mulch for the whole garden—if you have a *lot* of compost! One caveat: Don't add compost right at the end of the growing season, because you may stimulate growth that will be killed by the frosts that are soon to come.

COMPOST TEA
Here's an especially good treatment for herbs in particular. It's a great liquid fertilizer for a quick boost, or for whenever your plants could use a little extra kick: Put some compost into a cheesecloth or burlap

bag and soak it in a watering can or barrel for a couple of days. The water should turn pretty dark, and it can be used to water the soil around the base of plants. Or, you can dilute the solution to the color of weak tea, and spray it directly on the leaves. Reuse your "tea-bag" a couple of times, then add the leftover solids to the garden.

POTTING SOIL

Compost makes an excellent growing medium for potted plants and even for starting seeds. You don't need to pasteurize your compost, but it is a good idea to use hot compost for this purpose, because any weed seeds will hopefully have been destroyed.

To use compost in this way, just screen out the large pieces with a riddle and mix with sand, vermiculite, or peat moss to create your own custom blend.

It's Planting Time!

5

In this section we'll learn all about what's involved in the actual planting process. This is the hard part, but you'll be richly rewarded by your efforts in a very short time.

CHAPTER 15

Preparing the Site

OK, you're finished fantasizing by the fire—it's time to get out there and work! The good news is that unlike vegetable gardens, with many herb gardens, particularly with perennial herbs, you may only have to do this hard prep work once. In future years the ground will only need to be loosened to add new annuals, gently turned to incorporate compost, or lightly cultivated to remove weed seedlings.

Step One: Remove the Grass

By fork, sod remover, or plastic: Just get it out of there! Since our farm is organic, these are the methods we have used and know best. Although some may recommend clearing the area with a systemic weed killer prior to planting, our own personal view is that it's best not to get into the habit of relying on chemicals. Many of the benefits gardening bring to the mind, body, and soul come from exercise!

FORKING

If the grass in your garden-to-be is in large, tight clumps, forking may be the best way to go. This is hard work and especially wearing on the back, so take frequent breaks, stretch and straighten your back, and try to practice good posture. If you're removing grass and weeds with a fork, you will actually be performing another important task at the same time. By lifting and turning the soil, you're loosening and aerating it; this will vastly improve the health and fertility of the soil. Simply lift out one forkful at a time. Raise it a foot or two above the ground, then drop it back into the hole you created, breaking up the clods and loosening the soil around the grass roots. Now remove the grass, either by hand or with the fork, shaking off as much of the dirt as you can before consigning it to your compost pile.

SOD REMOVAL

When facing a large plot of weed-infested soil, it's all too easy to turn to the rotary tiller to sweep the problem under the topsoil. Out of sight, out of mind, right? Well, not for long. I've done it myself, and I began to regret it almost immediately. The quack grass I proudly conquered soon came back tenfold as the roots I chopped into little bits spread and multiplied; each bit of grass became a full-fledged plant of its own. Ouch!

I'm not going to kid you: Removing sod is one of the hardest gardening jobs you can imagine, especially if you have a well-established lawn of spreading intertwined roots. To make the turf come out in nice compact sections it needs to be moist, and we know what moisture means: weight. Fortunately, there are gas-powered machines that remove sod; they're available at some equipment rental stores.

For the more labor-intensive method, a square-edged garden spade with a very sharp edge is a good tool. You can push down with your foot—wear boots or shoes with a good, solid shank—or raise the spade up high with both hands and chop straight downward, letting gravity do some of the work. This method takes some practice to get your aim right.

A far better choice is a sod-cutting tool that's specifically designed for the job. But you don't see them often in your neighborhood hardware store—they're usually easier to find via mail-order catalogs or the Internet. Costing about 75 dollars, these wonderful implements typically have a spade-type handle with a long curved shaft ending in a sharp half-moon blade. When properly sharpened they cut through the toughest sod like butter. The curved shaft helps to cut under and lift the sod up and away.

To remove the sod, mark off your bed with wooden stakes and twine or thin lines of lime to indicate the limit of your cutting. From there you can either make long thin cuts in the sod and roll it up, or you can cut off square sections of one or two feet. I've tried both and found that the smaller square sections are much easier to move and transport by yourself than the large rolls, but as always, do what works best for you. You may have to cut under the sod a little to get those pesky roots to let go.

You'll notice immediately that sod has never heard the old adage: "You can't take it with you." A lot of good topsoil is pulled away with the turf. It's hard to do, particularly if the sod is removed in a roll, but try to shake loose as much of the topsoil from the roots of the grass. When the topsoil is all gone, I borrow from the "double digging" method by loosening the soil in the bed with a broadfork, then replacing the hole left by the removed turf with compost and well-rotted manure. The turf you now have in a pile can be composted or moved to a spot that needs patching or re-sodding. I've even used it to build a turf bench for one of our display gardens. It makes a very comfortable garden seat that won't rot or break.

USING PLASTIC SHEETS

A highly effective, though sometimes slow and not as visually appealing, method of removing weeds from a potential garden bed, is to lay down sheets of plastic. There are two basic methods of accomplishing this: either with black or clear plastic. With the clear plastic method, you're tricking the weeds' seedlings into thinking they've got a nice warm environment in early spring. They sprout and are sheltered at first, but as the season progresses they quickly cook in the trapped and magnified heat of their little "greenhouse."

With black plastic, you're relying on lack of sunlight and the absorbed heat of the black plastic to kill the weeds' seeds and perennial roots before they have a chance to sprout new shoots. This method works like a charm, but it can take a full year to kill everything you want out of there. And it can often leave the soil horribly dried out and devoid of vital microorganisms needed for good soil vitality. All of these problems will need to be amended (see below) before starting your new bed.

WEEDING BY HAND

Last but not least, you can do none of the above and simply pull the weeds out by hand. This may sound crazy at first, but if the herbs are thickly planted they'll eventually crowd out the recurring weeds once they've established themselves. Some people actually enjoy weeding!

One final note: On the bright side, though the above methods are labor intensive and work for any type of gardening, with herb gardens and borders you're generally covering a much smaller area than in a large vegetable garden.

Step Two: Tilling the Soil

DOUBLE DIGGING

This is a very effective method of improving fertility and soil structure with minimal disruption of the topsoil. Unlike with most heavy duty plowing and rotary tilling, this method keeps the subsoil and the topsoil largely separated. The downside is that double digging is very, *very* hard work! On a scale of one to ten it's an eleven. I wouldn't recommend this method unless you're in very good physical condition and have a very strong back.

The method itself is very simple: You're just moving the topsoil from one spot to the next in succession and aerating the subsoil beneath.

First prepare the garden beds as you normally would, marking off the area to be worked with string or lime, removing sod and weeds, and loosening the top twelve inches or so of topsoil with a broadfork or garden fork. Thoroughly wetting the soil a day or so before makes this task easier.

Next, divide the bed into twelve-inch-wide strips. Remove the top twelve inches of soil—or less if you have thinner topsoil—down one side of the bed, creating a long trench. Throw this topsoil into your garden cart or wheelbarrow, or onto a large tarp.

Third, gently break the subsoil with a garden or broadfork.

Now evenly cover the subsoil with a thin layer of compost, rotted manure or other organic material.

Move a twelve-inch strip of topsoil from the next row onto the loosened subsoil you just worked. Now work the subsoil in the second trench as you did the first, and repeat until the topsoil in the entire bed has been moved.

Finally, when you reach the end, take the topsoil in your garden cart, wheelbarrow, or on your tarp and put it onto the last row of subsoil, covering the top of the whole bed with a layer of organic material. Work it in to a depth of three to six inches.

ROTARY TILLERS

For an increasing number of gardeners, preparing the soil these days means firing up the rotary tiller. These machines work with a series of blades turned at right angles that chop and mix the soil. The convenience, ease, and relative low cost of these handy machines compared to large garden tractors have made them an almost indispensable part of the modern gardener's tool shed. Now available in sizes ranging from those that could almost fit into the palm of your hand to the gigantic commercial models, the rotary tiller, as a time and lower-back saver, is the undisputed champion.

There are two basic types of rotary tillers: "front-tine" and "rear-tine." The rear-tine tillers are generally easier to handle (and more expensive) than the front-tine tillers. Both are likely to feel like you've got a tiger by the tail if you try to turn under established turf or tall weeds with them. You're better off removing the sod and weeds (and stones) first, or at least mowing them close to the ground. Even the strongest tiller is best suited for turning under clean soil.

Unfortunately, as with anything that makes life easier for us, there are drawbacks. The negatives of heavy tilling are reflected primarily in the long-term health of the soil. Under optimal conditions, rotary tilling helps break up compacted subsoil, introduce oxygen to soil microbes, and evenly mix in organic matter such as compost, rotted manure, grass clippings, and cover crops.

If you use the rotary tiller when the soil is too moist, you run the risk of creating large, compact clods that will not hold water and oxygen. But till when it's too dry, and you'll get your own miniature version of the dust bowl, reducing your soil to a fine powder that can easily blow away or run off in those sudden, heavy downpours of summer. Ultimately you'll reduce the amount of organic material in your soil.

Rotary tillers are recommended for those whose health or physical condition precludes work with hand tools, when gently working organic material into the topsoil, or when preparing a garden site for the first time, where the soil is likely to be compacted. Resist the urge to go deep when tilling. It may provide a sense of satisfaction to see all of those layers churning and mixing, but you're not baking a cake. The dark, humus-rich topsoil needs to stay separated from the sand or clay of the subsoil layer.

Heavy-duty tilling works best when you're preparing a garden site for the first time. We used a rotary tiller only when converting a portion of our two-hundred-year-old pasture to a garden site for the first time. For subsequent tilling, we used the good old-fashioned garden fork, broadfork, and spade.

When you do use a tiller on an established bed, set the guide bar so that the tines only work the top three to six inches of soil.

> Avoid soil compaction by not walking on your garden beds. Laying boards across where you absolutely must tread will distribute your weight and reduce compaction. These boards are also a handy place to catch slugs napping in the daytime!

Ideally every time you till you should work some compost or other organic material into the soil. This will ensure that your soil stays healthy and nutritious. Avoid rotary tilling as a weed-control method. Mulch to control weeds, and avoid walking on your beds to minimize compaction. In some cases, as with quack grass for example, rotary tilling makes the weed problem worse since the chopped-up roots simply spawn their own new shoots and rootlets that quickly spread.

OTHER METHODS

There are endless variations and alternatives to the above methods, varying from the simple and traditional to the complex and modern. So-called "no-till" agriculture, in which there is minimal disruption of the topsoil, is gaining popularity even among some large commercial farmers. There is purportedly less stress on the plant and the environment, and less erosion, loss of water, and organic matter. Along

these lines, the garden fork or broadfork (see tools descriptions) can be used to gently loosen the soil to a depth of about a foot before planting—with no real tilling or turning of the topsoil. The surface is just gently "scratched" prior to planting. This works best in a garden with loose, well-balanced soil that has plenty of rich organic material.

> A good way to keep weeds that spread by their roots out of your herb beds is to use edging around the outside edge. Just make sure the edging you use, whether it's brick, plastic, or wood, goes down four to six inches below the surface.

Step Three: Amend the Soil

COMPOST, MANURE, BONE MEAL, AND OTHER SOIL ADDITIVES

Now that you've prepared the topsoil and subsoil in your garden bed, you're almost ready to plant. But wait—there's one more crucial step. You'll need to add some additional organic material, and perhaps some fertilizers and soil amendments, as part of your yearly cycle of building the soil.

Below are many of the most popular and helpful amendments to mix into your soil, either right after you've prepared the bed or when the new plants are in. This is all after you've tested your soil, of course— or else you won't know if you even need it!

Rocks

TYPE	NPK RATIO	BENEFITS AND COMMENTS
Limestone (Calcitic Or Dolomitic)	n/a	Use lime if you know your soil is acid; it slowly raises the pH. Lime also adds calcium and magnesium. DO NOT USE: quicklime, slaked, hydrated, or builder's lime, all of which are caustic and will damage plants.
Sulfur	n/a	Lowers soil pH.
Rock Phosphate	0–3–0	Slowly adds phosphorus, calcium, iron, and other trace elements to the soil. Also gradually raises the soil pH. One application can last 3–5 years.
Greensand	6–7% potash (potassium)	Very slow-release source of potash and other micronutrients. One application can last up to 10 years! Also, its silica content is great for loosening up clay soil, and as an addition to compost.
Granite Meal	3–5% potash (potassium)	Another very slow release source of potash and micronutrients. Does not raise soil pH. One application can last up to 10 years.
Gypsum	22% calcium; 17% sulfur	Use when you have a calcium deficiency in alkaline soil. Doesn't affect soil pH.
Sul-Po-Mag	0–0–22	Very high in potash; also supplies magnesium. Don't use with lime.

ROCKS

Ground rock powders mined from quarries are available for gardens. Because soil microorganisms must first get to the minerals in rock powders in order for the plants to be able to use them, the nutrients become available to the plants very slowly—in other words, *naturally*! Many of them also make fine soil conditioners.

OTHER ORGANIC GOODIES

Besides adding them to garden soil, you can also use most of these products as additions to your compost. As I've said before, unless your garden soil has very low fertility and next to no organic matter, your herbs aren't too picky. I've included this information for the sake of being complete, not necessarily because your garden will actually need it. If you can see that your plants are suffering for reasons other than too much or too little water or sun, watch them

Other Organic Goodies

TYPE	NPK RATIO	BENEFITS AND COMMENTS
Compost	Ranges from 0.5–0.5–0.5 to 4–4–4	Adds nutrients and organic matter to soil. Best all-around food for herbs.
Mushroom Compost	n/a	Ask supplier if material contains pesticide residue.
Cottonseed Meal	6–2–1	Good source of nitrogen; may contain pesticide residue.
Eggshells	1.2–0.4–0.1	Adds calcium plus trace minerals to soil.
Epsom Salts	n/a	Adds magnesium to soil.
Grass Clippings (fresh)	0.5–0.2–0.5	Ideal lawn fertilizer; let the clippings sit after mowing. Otherwise, good source of organic matter for compost.
Peat Moss	n/a	Adds organic matter; increases soil acidity. Good for use in potting soil because of its excellent water retention.
Sawdust	0.2–0–0.2	Adds organic matter to soil; make sure it's well-rotted before adding because it can "tie up" the nitrogen in decomposition rather than releasing it.
Soybean Meal	7.0–0.5–2.3	
Wood Ashes	0–1.2–2	Very good source of potash and calcium; compost or let sit out in rain to leach before using. Don't overuse—one application can last 2 years or more. Raises pH of soil.

closely, then check with your local extension agent to see if they can figure out which nutrients may be lacking and which amendments you should add. Make sure you tell them you're organic!

For a more detailed discussion of fertilizers and soil amendments, see the Fertilizers section in Part 6. And don't forget to mulch!

CHAPTER 16

Seeds vs. Plants

In this chapter I'll help you figure out the best way to obtain the plants you'll be putting in your garden. Should you start all your own seeds? Should you start them inside the house or directly in the garden? Wouldn't it be easier to buy all the plants already started? But how do you choose the right ones? I'll try to make these decisions a little easier.

What to Buy: Seeds or Plants?

There are several schools of thought on this subject. The most thrifty gardeners—and those who seem to have the most time on their hands—would never consider buying a plant at the nursery because it is so much more economical to start the hundreds of seeds they'll be putting in their gardens this year. On the other hand, there are gardeners for whom money is no object, and not only will they buy all their plants at the nursery, they'll buy three or four of each one, just in case. Most people fall somewhere in the middle.

One thing that makes the decision a bit easier is the fact that some plants don't set seed and are available only as transplants. These include tarragon, as well as many named varieties of plants. We'll cover this in more detail in a minute.

DECIDING ACCORDING TO SEASON

In deciding whether to start your own seeds or buy plants, consider the time of year. Is it February? Then you have plenty of time to buy the seed, flats, lights, and other paraphernalia you'll need. But if it's May, and you're planning to actually plant your garden tomorrow, you obviously have less time. In that case, you'd do better to start with plants. Or you can put the seeds directly in the ground, but again, you have to consider the length of your growing season and what kind of harvest you're hoping for from these seeds.

KNOWING WHEN TO SOW

Some seeds can be planted in the ground much earlier than others. For example, compare basil with peas. Peas can be planted well before the last frost, and they don't need warm soil to germinate. Basil, on the other hand, absolutely will not germinate unless the nighttime temps are in the fifties. If the weather is too cold, the seeds will just sit in the ground and rot! Parsley is another example. Folklore says that parsley must go to the devil seven times before it will germinate—that's because it takes so long and needs relatively warm soil to sprout.

> If you're unfamiliar with starting seeds, and you need only one plant, it may be easier to buy it— and it's definitely quicker!

Let's Simplify Things

So far, all I've done is confuse you, right? Let's break the whole thing down into categories: Herbs you *must* buy as plants; herbs that are better as plants, but that you can try to seed; seeds that really need to be started indoors under lights; and seeds that can be sown directly in the ground.

HERBS YOU MUST BUY AS PLANTS
- bay laurel
- Cuban oregano
- curry plant
- dittany of Crete
- eucalyptus
- French tarragon
- hen and chickens
- lemon grass
- lemon verbena
- passion flower
- roses
- santolina
- Silver King, Silver Queen, Silver Mound, etc.
- southernwood
- sweet myrtle
- vicks plant

NAMED VARIETIES OF:
- hyssop
- lavender
- marjoram
- mint, including peppermint
- oregano
- rosemary
- sage
- scented geranium
- thyme

Why? Because even though the species, or most common, basic version of the plant will set seed, named cultivars have been specially developed and will not set true seed. And some are sterile, not even setting viable seed at all. The same goes for variegated plants—most don't set true seed. These must all be propagated by cuttings (more about cuttings later).

STRATIFICATION

Certain seeds must be given special treatment to mimic the cold winter, or they will not break dormancy and germinate. This "fake winter" is called *stratification*; it involves planting the seeds in a container with damp starting medium (like sphagnum moss) and putting the container in the fridge for one to four months.

HERBS THAT ARE BETTER AS PLANTS, BUT YOU CAN TRY SEEDS

For these plants, the seed may have low germination rates. Or perhaps it must be very fresh or stratified. Or maybe its germination needs are too difficult to make it worth your while. These guys are not for beginners—go ahead and buy the plant! But if you love a challenge and already have some experience starting seeds, give 'em a try.

- angelica (seed must be very fresh)
- black cohosh
- bulbs like garlic, shallots, or Egyptian onion
- caper bush (possible but really not worth it)
- costmary (alecost)
- echinacea (can be done, but some varieties have low germination rates)
- ginkgo (can take twelve months to germinate)
- ginseng

- goldenseal (can take two years!)
- hops (better to start with rhizomes than seed)
- lungwort
- monkshood (aconite)
- sweet woodruff
- valerian (germinates poorly)
- wild binger

Woody herbs, like common rosemary, sage, thyme, and lavender, can all be started relatively easily from seed, but the plant takes much longer to mature and may not give a usable harvest in the first season. Perennial herbal flowers can also be started from seed, but they usually don't flower the first year.

SEEDS THAT NEED TO BE STARTED INDOORS, UNDER LIGHTS

Because they need a long growing season, these herb seeds need to be started indoors under lights—or must be started early if you want flowers. However, if you live in the far South, you may be able to sow some of these directly outdoors with good results. This is the largest group, consisting of both annuals and perennials.

- anise hyssop (will flower the same year if started early)
- arnica
- basil (better started early indoors in cold climates)
- beebalm (can also be direct seeded outside)

- calendula (for earlier bloom, sow inside; can also be direct seeded)
- chives (sow in clumps, not individually)
- clary sage (for earlier bloom, sow inside; can also be direct seeded)
- fennel (needs long growing season to get mature seeds)
- feverfew (best started indoors)
- Greek oregano (can also be direct seeded outside)
- horehound (can also be direct seeded outside)
- hyssop (can also be direct seeded outside)
- lavender (species only)
- lemon balm (can also be direct seeded outside)
- lovage (can also be direct seeded outside)
- pansy (sow outdoors in fall, or inside in January for May blooms)
- pennyroyal (can also be direct seeded outside)
- rosemary (species only)
- rue (can also be direct seeded outside)
- sage (species only)
- savory (can also be direct seeded outside)
- sweet marjoram (can also be direct seeded outside)
- thyme (species only)

HERB SEEDS THAT SHOULD BE SOWN DIRECTLY IN THE GROUND

Any of these herbs can be sown directly in the ground with good results. For those gardeners in areas with shorter growing seasons, you can still sow them outside—just expect a later harvest. Many are also suitable for starting inside under lights, later in spring.

Most annual herbs fit in this category; annual members of the Umbelliferae family are usually best sown this way (dill, chervil, anise, cilantro, cumin, etc.).

- borage
- chamomile
- foxglove (will not bloom until second year)
- milk thistle
- nasturtium
- Saint-John's-wort
- sweet Annie
- yarrow

> Sowing an herb seed in situ, or "on site," means to sow it where you want it to grow (rather than transplanting it from another location).

What to Look for in Plants at the Nursery

Many of the same rules for picking out herbs at a nursery apply for any garden plant. Find a reputable nursery; sometimes the huge chains don't care for the plants as well as they should. Ditto for grocery stores and non-garden stores. If you can find decent-looking plants in these places, grab them;

I've rescued many herbs from the certain death of the grocery store floral display! But the best places to buy herbs are greenhouses that grow most of their own stock and have a knowledgeable staff who can answer your questions. Many times, smaller can be better. Owner-operated nurseries may not be able to offer the bargain basement prices that the chains and grocery stores can, but you'll usually get considerably higher quality. And don't be scared off if the small places don't grow one hundred percent of what they sell; it's very difficult to propagate the hundreds of varieties they usually carry.

I always look for organic growers, but sometimes it's really hard to find them. If you *must* buy from non-organic sources, it's a good idea to repot or transplant into the garden quickly. Also, rinse the leaves very well before harvesting to remove any chemical pesticide residue.

WHAT TO LOOK FOR AT THE NURSERY
- healthy, vigorous plants
- compact, bushy plants
- bright green, new shoots
- no sign of pests or diseases

WHAT TO AVOID
- yellow or wilted leaves (can indicate disease)
- legginess, or tall spindly plants (a sign of neglect)
- potbound roots (roots coming out of the drainage holes, or completely encircling the pot)
- pests (check under the leaves)
- plants in bloom (I know they're prettier, but try to choose plants that are budded but not yet blooming)

One caveat: sometimes in the heat of summer, the plants will wilt in need of water, especially in a very hot greenhouse—a good drink of water will often perk them right back up.

At the end of the season, sometimes nurseries will have sales on plants that have outgrown their containers and are rootbound. If the plant still looks pretty healthy, go ahead and buy it—just cut the rootball open in several places before planting it in the ground.

CHAPTER 17

How to Sow Seeds: Indoors and Out

This chapter will cover everything you need to know about starting seeds—well, almost. Starting seeds is like watching little miracles happen right before your eyes. And if you decide to start them inside, you can watch their progress—from tiny, seemingly lifeless dry specks to healthy (hopefully) vigorous, real live plants that you can put in your garden.

How Do They Do It?

Talk about the miracle of life. A seed is just sitting there in the soil, waiting for the right conditions to come along. And then, all of a sudden, it happens—the temperature, light, and moisture elements all come together to produce the ideal conditions, and the seed bursts into life! First, the seed begins to swell, taking in moisture from the soil. (In some seeds, like basil, this is obvious; in others, like chamomile, you can't really see it.) Then the seed coat bursts, and a little tiny root shoots out, looking for soil to anchor itself into. Next, the cotyledons, or seed leaves, emerge. These leaves, which don't look at all like the leaves of the mature plant, provide food for a few days until the now seedling is ready to send out its first true leaves, which look more like the adult plant. This is the most critical time of the little plant's short life—making the journey from seedling to maturity.

You can help nurture it through this journey to becoming a beautiful garden plant by giving the best growing conditions you can. Here's how.

Getting Started: Inside or Out?

OK, you've read the previous chapter and know which herbs you'd like to start from seed. Now it's time to actually sow them. But already it's time for a decision: in the ground or in the house? Like I said before, it depends on where you live (warm climate or cold; long gardening season or short). In warmer climates, nearly any herb that is good to sow in general can be sown directly in the ground outside. (See list on page 197.) Or look on the back of the seed packet—does it recommend sowing outside? If so, do it and save yourself some time and work. But if the packet recommends starting indoors at least four to eight weeks before last frost, you'll get a significant jump on the growing season if you do it inside.

Equipment You'll Need for Sowing Seeds Inside

Starting seeds indoors doesn't have to be an expensive or complicated proposition, but you'll need to have a few things on hand before you start.

LOW-TECH VS. HIGH-TECH

Not to be a smartypants, but to begin with, you'll need to have your seeds. You'll also need containers, soilless starting mix, labels, and access to water, warmth, and light. These are things you'll need, whether you go low or high tech. The big difference is whether you want everything to be homemade or not.

VERY LOW-TECH

For the ultimate in homemade seed-starting setups, you can use old margarine or cottage cheese tubs (small ones, not the huge tubs), yogurt containers, paper cups, old Tupperware trays, or cut-up milk cartons. This is "reduce, reuse, recycle" at its best! Just make sure you punch a few drainage holes in the bottoms. If you only have a few seeds to start, this method will be fine. For the heat, you can use the top of your refrigerator or television—just make sure you don't overwater! The light requirements will be a little trickier to satisfy, but south-facing windowsills have been working for home seed starters for years. For your labels, you can use popsicle sticks, disposable plastic knife and fork handles, or tongue depressors. Make sure you use a waterproof marker!

You'll need to cover your containers with clear plastic bags or Saran Wrap until germination occurs. You can also use dampened newspaper for this, but most people use plastic wrap.

VERY HIGH-TECH

If you're planning on starting a lot of seeds, you may want to think about upgrading your milk carton system. Now that professional seed starting flats and equipment are widely available from garden centers and mail order catalogs, it's easier than ever to play (herb) nursery in your own home.

LIGHTS, HEAT MATS, ETC.

Oh, you wouldn't believe all the stuff you can acquire for seed starting. To begin with, there are the containers. For indoor use, there are basic open flats without drainage holes. (You want the drainage holes in a greenhouse, but indoors, all that water leaking out can make a real mess!) These can accommodate seedling trays, four or six packs, or larger containers. As far as the seedling trays, you can get them with tiny little compartments, ranging in size from 288 to twenty-four "plugs" in a single tray, or with little pre-formed rows that make seeding in rows easier. To cover your seeds, there are clear plastic domes available to keep moisture and heat in.

Which brings me to the source of heat—you can buy heating mats made especially for this purpose in a wide variety of sizes and prices. The best are heavy-duty rubber mats with the heating cable thermostatically controlled. You can also make your own out of old electric blankets or heating pads protected by plastic sheeting, but please, please, PLEASE, be careful about mixing electricity and water!

The next consideration is the light source. Even in the sunny south, February sunlight on most windowsills is pretty weak and may not produce the stocky seedlings you want. Unless you have a greenhouse or sunroom that gets at least ten hours of direct sun a day, think about using fluorescent lights. For just a few seedlings, a single Gro-Light may be fine, but if you have several large flats of plants, a shop light fixture with two bulbs will be a better choice. To add to the high-tech atmosphere, you can hook the lights up to a timer and set it for sixteen hours a day. But regular incandescent lights won't work for this; you really need to use fluorescents.

> Many growers recommend the use of "full-spectrum" grow-light type bulbs, but I've found that plain old (cheap!) cool fluorescents work just fine.

In my own seed-starting setup, in what should be my dining room, I have a long plywood tabletop set up on a sawhorse that accommodates a large rubber heat mat that holds five flats. Over that, I have two shop-light fixtures, which are almost exactly as long as the heat mat. By using "288s" (shop talk for plug trays with 288 cells) I can start 1,440 seeds at one time. Eventually I will outgrow this system, but for now it works great. If only I could find somebody to transplant all those seedlings for me!

How to Do It: The Easiest Methods

Whether you choose to go high- or low-tech, the actual work is pretty much the same.

STEP ONE

The first step is to make sure your containers are clean. If they're brand new, you're all set, but if you are reusing flats from last year, you need to sanitize them. You can do that in one of two ways: Either dip them in boiling water for a few minutes, or rinse them in a weak bleach solution (one part bleach to nine parts hot water) to kill any disease organisms that might be waiting for your seedlings. If there is old soil clinging to the sides, add a little dish detergent to the solution.

STEP TWO

The next step is to moisten your potting mix. You want it about the consistency of crumbly chocolate cake—not too dry, but not soggy, either. If you have a lot of mix to prepare, a bucket might come in handy for this step. Using warm water makes it easier for the mix to absorb, and it also makes it more pleasant to work with afterward. If you are using peat pots, moisten them according to package directions.

Don't use regular garden soil to start your seeds indoors—it may contain diseases, and its texture is too heavy. A better choice is "soil-less mix," a special blend of peat moss, perlite, and vermiculite that's available at garden centers. You can also make your own mix out of equal parts finely sifted compost and vermiculite.

Seeds contain enough of their own food to nourish themselves through sprouting, so seed-starting mix doesn't need to contain nutrients.

GOOD SEED-STARTING MEDIUMS: USE ALONE OR IN ANY COMBINATION

- compost (hot method)
- milled sphagnum moss
- peat moss
- perlite
- vermiculite

STEP THREE

Spread the moistened mix lightly into your containers, making sure you get it into the corners. If you're using cell flats, make sure you get the mix into the bottoms or the roots will be hanging in midair when you transplant—Voice of Experience talking here! Don't pack the mix too tightly, because the roots also need air circulation. Smooth the surface level with your hand.

Smaller, individual containers (including cell flats) dry out faster than large, open flats.

STEP FOUR

Now it's time to sow the seeds! There are a million different ways to do this, and every gardener has different preferences. Since seeds come in all shapes and sizes, there are different ways to sow them. Large seeds, like nasturtium, are the easiest to deal with. Just poke a little hole in the mix with your finger, drop the seed in, and cover it up. Not too deep, mind you, just below the soil surface.

A little trickier are the small seeds, like chamomile and sweet marjoram, because some people have less dexterity in their fingers. Every gardening book has different recommendations, so here are mine:

If you're only sowing a few seeds, try to pick up individual seeds with your fingertips and place them evenly. If they're too small, grab a tiny pinch of seeds and gently rotate your thumb and forefinger to slowly release the seeds onto the mix. This is called cluster sowing. It's the method that works best for me, but I have really small fingers; it doesn't work as well for my husband.

Other methods to try include:

- tapping the seeds out of the packet individually
- scattering the seeds from a spoon
- using a special "seed starting" device
- mixing the seeds with clean sand and scattering—but how much clean sand do you have on hand in February?

The general rule of thumb is to cover seeds to a depth of three times their thickness, but for the life of me, it always seems that the one granule of soil that falls onto a seed is already bigger than that! So for relatively large seeds, like basil, I just cover them lightly, which means sprinkling a little mix on top. For the tiniest seeds, I tamp them into the mix and don't cover them at all. The important point here is that the seed—whatever its size—needs constant contact with damp soil to germinate.

> *Tamping* seeds in means pressing the seeds lightly into the soil.

STEP FIVE

Next, water your newly sown seeds. Using a mister is a good idea at this point, so you don't wash away all those carefully spaced seeds with a big glop of water. Other people recommend watering from the bottom, using capillary action for the water to get soaked up through the mix. There are even capillary mats on the market for just this purpose. I haven't tried them yet; I still use a watering can with a seedling rose on the end. Once the seedlings are up, I also use a regular houseplant watering can with the long, thin nozzle to water whichever cell needs it.

STEP SIX

Cover your containers with plastic wrap, glass, damp newspaper, or plastic domes (I love those things!) and put them in a warm place like on a heat mat, on top of the fridge, or on a warm—*not hot!*—radiator. The point of this is to make a little mini-greenhouse to keep in warmth and humidity and optimize the conditions for germination. It really does make a difference.

> Most herb seeds germinate best when kept between sixty-five and seventy-five degrees, both day and night. On a heat mat this is easy, but it's trickier in most houses. That's why we recommend the top of the fridge.

PRETREATING SEEDS

I guess now is as good a time as any to talk about pretreating seeds. As we discussed in the previous chapter, some seeds need stratification in order to germinate. There are actually a couple of different ways to pretreat seeds:

Scarification: scraping or nicking the hard seed coat to enable faster water penetration. Be careful not to damage the seed inside. For very large seeds you can use a knife, or for smaller ones you can use a rough file or sandpaper. (Note: everyone has been saying for years that you need to nick the seeds of morning glory before planting, but I tried just sowing the seed on the heating mat and they were among the first to germinate! It really does pay to experiment!)

Stratification: exposing seeds to a period of moist cold in order to break dormancy. To stratify seeds, sow them in damp starting mix, cover with plastic, and put them in a cold place for one to four months. Some seeds need to actually freeze; others just need sustained cold of 34 to 40 degrees. Check the seed packet to know for sure. In some cases, the seeds will actually sprout in the cold place. Others will sprout when brought out of the cold and exposed to warmer temps.

Presoaking and presprouting: very few herb seeds need this type of pretreatment, but here's the definition anyway. Presoaking is fairly self-explanatory—it means to soak the seed in warm water for a few hours before sowing. Presprouting takes this one step further, by placing the seeds in a damp paper towel, rolling it up, and putting it in a warm place. Check back in a couple of days to see if germination has happened. When it does, handle the fragile seedlings carefully and put them in their own containers.

Like I said in the previous chapter, some seeds are so difficult to germinate that it can be better to let someone else do the hard part. You just go buy the plant at the nursery!

DARK VS. LIGHT

Much has been said about which seeds need light to germinate and which need dark. For years I agonized about which seeds to sow together in a flat so I could keep them apart in a dark place. Then I decided to experiment with not keeping the dark ones dark, and guess what? Same germination rate as before!

So now, I sow dark and light seeds together and I've had no problem. The exception to that is that some seeds do germinate slower in the dark than in the light (I once forgot that angelica needed light and covered with too much soil, and it took an extra week to emerge, but it did finally come up!) So my advice is if it makes you feel better to follow the directions on the packet on this one, go right ahead. It certainly won't hurt anything. But if you have limited space and a lot of different seeds to start, don't panic or worry about separating the light from the dark seeds. They'll figure it out and come up on their own!

STEP SEVEN

Last but not least, label your seeds! Once you have a little forest of seedlings growing in a flat, it can be very easy to forget what you planted. Many look alike, especially different varieties of the same species. So trust me: label, label, label! Another helpful habit to get into is to keep notes on what you planted, what combination of starting mix you used, the temperature, how many days to germination, and the rate of germination (Did you sow very thickly, but have only a few come up?). These notes, no matter how sure you are, you'll remember all this a year from now, will be invaluable to you next spring when you're racking your brain to figure out how you did so well with the basil starts this year.

The Vigil Begins . . .

So you've sown your seeds, covered them, and put them in a warm place—now what? Basically, all you have to do is keep an eye on them every day until they come up, at which point a new set of responsibilities comes along.

Make sure you keep the soil surface evenly moist, and when the surface does dry out, water it gently. If you've used a soil-less mix like I've recommended, the color will turn light brown, so it's easy to tell when you need to water. For obvious reasons, containers kept on a heating mat will dry out sooner than containers kept at room temperature. Water with a mister if possible, or from the bottom, and use room temperature or lukewarm water. (You don't like ice cold showers in the morning, do you? Well, neither do your seeds!)

Germination will take anywhere from two days to several weeks, depending on the type of seed, moisture, and heat levels. The heat mat method will speed up germination time considerably. For exam-

Common Germination Times (at 70°):	
anise hyssop	6 days
chamomile (German)	4 days
cilantro	6 days
dill	5 days
Greek oregano	4 days
lemon balm	7 days
parsley	8 days
sage	9 days
summer savory	6 days
sweet basil	4 days
sweet marjoram	5 days

ple, parsley takes at least three weeks to sprout outside, but only one week on heat.

Many annual herbs take less time to germinate; perennials may take a little longer. These times are not etched in stone—your own experience may be quite different.

Sprouting

Hooray! Those lifeless little specs have sprouted and have their first set of leaves! Congratulations—you're the proud parent of bouncing baby herb seedlings!

The first thing you need to do is take the plastic

cover off, because the new seedlings will need fresh air circulation. If only one or two have sprouted, and you're waiting for the rest, it's OK to leave the plastic on a little while longer, but make sure the seedling's leaves don't touch the plastic, or the leaf will rot away.

You probably won't need to water quite yet, but do keep an eye on everything, because you don't want your newly sprouted treasures to dry out now. Once they've dried out, there's no getting them back. I'll discuss watering in more detail in a minute.

SEEDS THAT DRY OUT, DIE OUT

The next thing you need to do is make sure the seedlings get sun—at least six hours a day, remember? Now's the time for the high-tech folks to turn on their shop lights for sixteen hours a day.

If you use shop lights, make sure your seedlings are no more than four inches below the light bulbs. Using a chain on the lights makes it easy to adjust the height for growing seedlings.

Seaweed Tea, Anyone?

Earlier in the chapter I mentioned that seed-starting mix doesn't need to contain nutrients because seeds have enough food within them to get through the sprouting process. Well, time's up! Now that your seedlings are up and have their leaves, it's time to give them a little boost of food. You can wait until they have their first true leaves for this step, but you can get a jump on the process by watering your seedlings with diluted liquid seaweed or compost tea. Giving them a good start like this makes for nice, stocky seedlings that grow very quickly.

Thinning Out and Potting Up

Consider this next step like graduation from pre-school to kindergarten: It's time for the seedlings to go out on their own, sort of. Once they've got their second set of leaves (the true leaves we talked about earlier), you can safely transplant them into their own little pots. I'll warn you right now—if you have a lot of seedlings, this step can get *very* tedious, but it has to be done. If you let it go, they'll get too leggy and weak to transplant properly into the garden. They'll also probably get too tangled up to take apart later on. Here's how to do it. First, have everything ready to go. You'll need:

- pots
- transplanting mix
- seedlings (duh!)
- labels
- water

Make sure your pots are clean (just like for seed-starting), and pre-moisten your mix. At this point, you can use compost (sifted), the same mix you used for starting the seeds, or a combination of both. Loosely fill the new pots with the mix, leaving some room at the top.

I like to use the pointy end of a plastic label to gently dig the seedlings out of the original container. If you've sown very thickly, gently tease the delicate roots apart into natural groupings of three to five, which you can then put into the new pot. For individual seedlings, you can skip this step.

Poke a little hole (dibble) in the soil in the new pot with your finger, then put the seedling in the hole. I always put the seedling into the new pot a little deeper than it was in the original container—usually up to the seed leaves. Then gently tamp the soil around the plant, adding a little more if necessary. Remember to leave a little room from the soil surface to the top of the pot for watering (¼ inch should do it.) The plant should stand up on its own in the pot, propped up enough by the surrounding soil to not flop over, even after watering.

> *Dibbling* means to poke a hole in soil with your finger, pencil, or other instrument, to make a space for the transplant.

The key to this whole process is gently, gently, gently! The roots and stems of these little guys are incredibly delicate, and this is a very traumatic experience for them. Try not to disturb the roots if at all possible, and grasp the top by the leaves, not the stem, which can break very easily. It takes practice, so be prepared. You'll feel like a brain surgeon after doing this a few times!

Water your newly transplanted seedlings with diluted seaweed, and put them back under the lights, raising the chain if necessary to accommodate the new pots. Or just stick them back on the windowsill.

The potted-up seedlings will quickly recover from their first transplant shock in a day or two, and they'll resume growing. Continue to water and fertilize, and in three to six weeks they should be ready for the garden. If you find there are still too many seedlings in the pot, you can further thin them out by snipping the weakest off with small scissors. (If the roots aren't too intertwined, you may be able to gently pull the unwanted seedling out of the soil, but you risk damaging the roots of the plants you want to keep.)

Once the seedlings have a few sets of leaves, they'll be ready for the next big step: the transition to the garden! We'll talk about how to get them ready for that in the next chapter.

Problems to Watch For

As great as starting seeds indoors is, there are still a few pitfalls to be on the lookout for. Even though you're trying to give your seedlings the most favorable conditions possible, lots of things can happen to ruin all your efforts. Here are a few of them.

No Germination at All

If a week or two has passed and you haven't seen the slightest sign of emergence, look for one of these problems.

TOO COOL

If the soil stays too cool, your seeds will just sit there and rot. Most seeds germinate best when soil temperatures are between 55 and 75 degrees, with 70 being optimum.

TOO HOT

I've baked my share of seedling flats by putting them in the greenhouse and forgetting to take off the plastic cover on sunny days. Because the temp of the greenhouse is already eighty to 90 degrees (even in chilly April), the temps under the domes can reach 20 degrees higher than that! If you're lucky, the seeds will just remain dormant until the temperature goes back down to a reasonable level, but the embryo inside the seed can die if the temps are way too high.

TOO DRY

Seeds need constant contact with evenly moist soil to absorb enough water to break the seed coat. If the soil dries out before germination, you may lose the seed.

TOO WET

This is the same principle as the soil being too cool; if the soil is sopping wet, the seed may rot before it has a chance to sprout.

OLD SEED

Some seeds have a long shelf life; others are only viable for a short time after they ripen on the plant. If you have low germination rates, check the date on the back of the package. If it's more than a year old, it may be past its prime. Old seeds that do germinate often result in weak, puny plants that don't do as well in the garden as they should. If you do decide to sow older seeds, do it fairly thickly to compensate for the reduced germination rate.

One way to extend the life of your unused seeds is to store them in the freezer. Even angelica, a notoriously short-lived seed, can sprout a year later if kept in the freezer. The fridge is usually too humid and not quite cold enough.

SEEDS BURIED TOO DEEP

If you sow your seeds too deep, they may not have the energy to push their way up through all that extra soil to get to the light.

Problems after Germination

OK, your seedlings are up and growing; the next most critical time is at hand. Here are the problems to look out for.

THE HEARTBREAK OF DAMPING OFF

I've gone on and on about not letting your seeds dry out, but one of the biggest problems for seedlings that do sprout is damping off, where the seedling just flops over at soil level. It's caused by soil organisms that thrive when the soil is too moist—the stem basically rots. Damping off spreads from seed to seed, and can wipe out an entire tray of seedlings before you know it!

There are several things you can do to prevent this problem. One is to use sphagnum peat moss in your starting mix. Something in it inhibits the growth of the organisms. Another is to not overwater. Seems like a no-brainer, but it can be difficult for beginners to get the hang of watering seedlings. Another preventative is to spray periodically with chamomile tea, a great tonic for plants. Chamomile tea can even stop the damping-off fungus after it starts!

I've also been able to save seedlings that have just flopped over by mounding fresh soil up around them. This doesn't always work, but if you only have a few seedlings and you've used up all your seed, give it a shot; it can work.

Seedlings that have collapsed in a slimy, moldy heap cannot be saved, and they must be removed from the flat as soon as possible to avoid contaminating the rest of your seedlings. And don't water so much!

DRYING OUT

From one extreme to the other, huh? But it's true, if you let your seedlings dry out to the point that they collapse, you've lost them. They can take a very short drought, just enough that they wilt slightly, but it's a trauma that they really don't need. So keep an eye on the flat, and don't let it completely dry out.

WATERING TOO HARD

This is a common problem that takes a little practice to overcome. You water with a big watering can and the water comes out in a big glop and knocks over all the seedlings, burying them in the mix. You can't just leave them like that, you know. You have to go through with a pencil or something similar, and lift each seedling so that it stands back up. If you don't, the leaves will rot in the soil.

One good way to avoid this problem in the first place is to get a watering can that has a seedling rose. It distributes the water in a nice, gentle stream. Another possibility is misting with a spray bottle, but if you have a lot of seedlings, your hand will get pretty tired with all that pumping. You also need to make sure the water is getting to the roots, not just the top of the soil.

Another option is to use a houseplant watering

can with a long, tapered spout. With practice, you can really control the stream of water that comes out of it.

LEGGY GROWTH

This is when the seedling stretches and gets too tall and spindly. A real problem for windowsill gardeners, it comes from too little sun (or other light). The solution: Either put the seedlings in a place where they'll get more sun, or move the lights closer to the flat.

Sowing Seeds Outside

Sowing seeds inside is too much trouble, you say? Don't care about getting a jump on the growing season? That's OK, you can grow them outside, too, just like Mother Nature has been managing to do for a few million years without benefit of heating mats and grow lights.

You, however, are not Mother Nature, and sowing outside doesn't have all the control that inside sowing has. Not to worry, though, going outside has its own benefits—like saving several steps of work.

Keep in mind: If you're sowing seed of frost-tender annuals, you'll need to wait until the last frost date, paying attention to weather reports and noting how cold night-time temps are getting.

We talked at length about how to prepare garden beds in Chapter 15, so I won't repeat myself. However, seedbeds need even more TLC in their preparation than regular beds do. Basically, you need to make sure every single, solitary weed scrap is long gone, and that the soil is of a finer consistency. Be sure to add plenty of compost, and rake the surface until it's super-smooth, getting as many pebbles and stray pieces of garden debris out of there.

Unless you're making a special "nursery bed" for holding plants before they go into the garden, herbs are usually cluster-sown on site. After you've raked your area smooth, scatter the seeds and cover with about a half-inch of soil, tamping down the surface slightly to ensure good soil contact. Water them in with a gentle spray, label, and you're done.

When the seedlings emerge, thin them if necessary—if you do it carefully enough, you may be able to transplant them to a different location. Then sit back and wait for the harvest. Of course, you'll still have to do all the weeding, watering, and feeding, but you'll have saved a few steps.

By the way, the hungry bugs of spring just love the tender new shoots of herb seedlings. Watch out for slugs and cutworms, which can mow down a patch of seedlings before you know what's happening. More about those unwanted guests in Chapter 23.

CHAPTER 18

Transplanting Your Little Treasures into Their New Beds

We're really moving along here now, aren't we? We've spent some cozy winter evenings by the fire, designing the herb garden and perusing catalogs; we've chosen the plants and decided which to start as seeds and which to buy from the nursery; we've done the ugliest job, preparing the ground and amending the soil; and finally, we've got a windowsill full of seedlings that are just itching to get outside and play. But *is it time yet?*

If you're finding yourself asking this question once the weather warms and you've got a house full of seedlings, then keep reading! In this chapter we'll cover everything you need to know about actually moving your seedlings into their permanent spots in the garden.

Yes, It's Time!

Well, actually, it might not be. As I write this, it's a spectacular May afternoon, sunny and comfortably warm. People have been coming by for two weeks now, wanting to plant. But here in Vermont, we're still two to three weeks away from the average last frost date, and these folks seem to have forgotten the week of frosty nights that just passed. If they were to put that little basil seedling in the ground right now, I'd be seeing them again very soon, needing a replacement.

OK, so when is it safe to put your plants in the ground? Well, there are a few correct answers here. Super-hardy annuals and perennials can go in the ground earlier than tender ones, sometimes by several weeks. It's not safe to put anything out when the temperatures are plunging into the twenties at night—even if other perennials have started pok-

ing their heads out of the ground. Once frosts have become rare, it's probably safe to put out the hardiest plants (after a proper hardening-off period, which we'll cover in a moment). You can compare this to planting peas in earliest spring.

For herbs that are frost tender, you really have to wait until that magic date—the last average frost. Your county extension office can help you out in determining when this is for your area. Of course, microclimates (remember Chapter 5?) will affect frost, too, so areas closer to water will be safe sooner than areas at the bottom of a hill. In my own town, which has both big hills and a big river, people on one side of town have a good two weeks of safety that the folks on the other side of town would kill for. And even in my own yard, I can put out plants in my protected dooryard garden weeks sooner than I would dare in other parts of the property.

What this all boils down to is that for anything remotely tender, wait until nighttime temperatures in your area are settled in the fifties. And even then, be prepared for a freak cold night now and then.

Hardening Off

Hardening off—the process by which you gradually expose the seedling to outdoor conditions—is key to the whole transplanting process. No matter how hardy a plant is supposed to be, if you transplant it into the garden while it's too tender for outdoor conditions, it's probably going to die. So what does this mean? Most growers recommend taking a week or so and putting the plant outside in a protected, shady area—first for just an hour or two, then slowly working up to 24 hours. Make sure you watch the weather forecasts and keep a close eye on your little babies. Too much sun at this point can be just as deadly as freezing temps, so don't let them dry out, or all your hard work will be lost. Also, cut back on the fertilizer.

I'll let you in on a little secret I discovered: You can also harden off if you're sure you'll have several consecutive days of cool, misty, dreary weather. This still means no freezing temperatures at night, but the absence of hot sun during the day makes it possible to leave your treasures outside overnight from the beginning. Keep in mind that this is a very risky way to do it. I'm just letting you know about an alternative to the two-week in-and-out process.

One last point about hardening off: Even plants that come from a greenhouse need to be acclimated to the great outdoors. Sometimes plants will be on display outside, and those will probably be OK, but ask a greenhouse staff person just to be on the safe side.

Talking about the Weather

So, it's a beautiful, sunny day—but not quite hot. There's a good stiff breeze blowing, just enough to keep the bugs away. That's a perfect gardening day, right? WRONG! Maybe for pulling weeds or preparing the soil, but definitely *not* for transplanting! I know it's hard to resist, but you have to!

The ideal day for transplanting is cloudy and cool, with no wind, preferably after a soaking rain, and better yet, when more rain is expected. Think England in the spring—misty, foggy, cool. Your plants will love you for it! This is not to say that planting in a torrential downpour or thunderstorm is what you want, either. In fact, if very heavy rain is in the forecast, you may want to put it off until the weather breaks.

If the weather just doesn't act like England where you live, try to do your transplanting in the cool of the morning (before eleven a.m.) or in the early evening. You want to avoid the hottest part of the day.

The Big Day!

The weather is perfect, your garden is ready, your plants are ready, let's go plant!

First, make sure you have everything you need on hand before you get started. There's nothing more frustrating than having to run back into the house fifty times to get something you forgot. Here's a checklist to help you out:

Make sure your garden is really ready the day *before* you plant. The moment you're taking the plants outside is not the time to discover a big patch of weeds you forgot to remove, or to remember to put on the compost.

Keep your plants in a shady place while they're waiting to go in the ground; water them well several hours ahead of time. If you've ordered plants from a mail-order source, make sure you unpack them well ahead of time. They won't appreciate going straight from a dark cool box to the great outdoors!

Got your tools? All you'll really need is a trowel or hand fork for transplanting. Sometimes a dibber can come in handy too. You'll also need labels and a marking pen, gloves if you use them, and a water source, either a watering can or your garden hose.

Got your garden plan? After all we went through in Chapters 7 and 8, I should hope you have a gorgeous map all done up in parchment, maybe laminated. OK, back to the real world. If you did draw up a real plan on graph paper with the plants already positioned, congratulations! If you're like the rest of us, and have something scribbled on a cocktail napkin, that's OK too. It'll just take a little more time to space out the plants. And please don't decide at the last minute to change the whole plan!

> Take a picture of the bare garden before you start. Having before and after pictures can really help in working out problems and designing next year's beds. And they're great for bragging, too!

Spacing and Placing

I find it helpful to actually place the plants, containers and all, throughout the bed to confirm spacing and colors before I dig the first hole. Knowing ahead of time how big each plant gets is crucial to making this easier and your garden bed better; check out the plant profiles in the back of the book. Don't forget that the tiny little plant that you have in your hand may reach over your head before the season is out.

Give these guys room to spread. A tiny little tansy in a three-inch pot already has dreams of world domination, and will totally shade out anything smaller that grows too close. So the basic rule of thumb is the smaller the mature plant, the closer you can space. See why you needed that garden plan?

Are You Ready to Plant?

All of which brings us to the actual planting of the herbs. This is actually the easy part. All you need to do is make a small hole in the soil with your trowel or fork (or your hand, if you can) a little larger than the pot size.

> It's nice if you don't even need a trowel because your soil is so friable and humusy.

Next, gently knock the plant out of the pot. Never pull the plant out by its stem, which could rip it right off its rootball. Next, spread the roots out gently, especially if they encircle the pot. Actually,

Make sure you wait to transplant your seedlings in the ground when they're nice and stocky, and have several sets of true leaves. Don't do it when they are too tiny to handle, or if they flop over at the gentlest watering.

you can use a little more force than you could when the seedlings were really tiny. If those roots are a total root-bound mess, feel free to either cut them in a couple of places with your pruners or rip them apart. I know, I've been harping on being gentle with the root systems and now I say the exact opposite, but otherwise the roots will never spread out into the ground, continuing to circle around in the same place. This makes for a less healthy plant, more prone to dry spells because it can't find its own water.

Plant Depth

Plant your seedling slightly deeper than it was in the container, if it's nice and stocky. Now's a good time to correct leggy seedlings that have been needing more sunlight—plant them deeper, up to their first set of true leaves. Fill in the soil around your newly planted seedling, making a little depression for water to collect in. Firm the soil well, making sure there are no air pockets to dry out the plant's roots.

Watering In

After your plants are in the ground, water them in deeply. It's a good idea to use fish emulsion or compost tea when watering for the first time, but it's not absolutely necessary. It just gets them off to a better start.

Now's also a good time to pinch the plants back. It encourages new growth and branching out. Pinching means to remove the growing tips—the top sets of leaves from a plant. It's usually done with your fingers, although small scissors will work just fine.

Label, Label, Label!

I've said it before and I'll say it again—label your plants, especially now that they're in the ground. This is really important for beginning gardeners, because you'd hate to rip up that herb plant thinking it is a weed, wouldn't you? Until you've gardened for a while and are confident of how each plant looks (at each stage of growth), keep your little guys labeled!

Once you've got your garden planted, watered, and labeled, check on it at least once a day, and more frequently in warm, dry, or windy weather. If any of the plants show signs of wilting, water them immediately! It takes a while for roots to get acclimated and to start looking for their own water. Remember, they've been pampered up to now, and they'll have to get used to living on their own.

CHAPTER 19

Propagation

Propagation—it sounds so intimidating, doesn't it? Well, it's not, really. It just means making new plants from ones you've already got. Some herbs take to it easier than others, and I'll help you sort it all out.

How to Make Plants from Plants

Remember in Chapter 16 how we talked about which plants are better to start from seed and which are usually grown from cuttings? Some plants are just too difficult to start from seed, while others are named varieties that don't come true from seed and can only be propagated vegetatively.

There are several different methods to use, depending on how the plant grows—cuttings (sometimes called slips), division (crown, root, and rhizomes), and layering.

Cuttings

Nearly everyone has a childhood memory of Mom or Grandma with a windowsill full of cuttings in jars of water. This is probably the easiest way to get plants from plants, and it works for all kinds of herbs and flowers, not just houseplants. You can easily take cuttings of dozens of herbs, both perennial and annual.

WATER VS. SOIL
The main consideration is whether to do your rooting in water or soil. Again, different plants react differently. Water is a perfectly good rooting medium, according to many herb growers.

Most of these herbs will root fairly quickly in water, some as soon as one week. Others might take two weeks or more.

STICKING CUTTINGS
Some herbs prefer being rooted in a soilless mix to water. This method can be slightly more difficult

HERBS THAT ROOT EASILY
IN WATER

- basil
- lemon verbena
- mints and close family members like lemon balm and beebalm
- patchouli
- pineapple sage
- rosemary

HERBS THAT ROOT EASILY
IN GROWING MEDIUM

- bay
- beebalm
- catnip
- French tarragon
- Greek oregano
- hyssop
- lavender
- lemon balm
- lemon verbena
- mints
- sage
- santolina
- scented geraniums
- southernwood
- thyme
- winter savory

and have a higher failure rate, but it is the preferred method in most commercial greenhouses.

The cuttings must have just the right conditions to strike roots, or they'll just sit there and eventually die. Don't be scared off, though, because "the right conditions" are very similar to seed germination: lots of moisture, light, and a rooting medium that allows in plenty of oxygen.

Good rooting mediums include vermiculite, perlite, sphagnum peat, rockwool, and oasis floral foam. I personally don't care for the way some plants root in the foam, but some growers love the stuff. An old-fashioned way is clean sand, but it doesn't hold water as well as the other media and has lost its popularity. You can also root cuttings in the same combination of vermiculite, perlite, and sphagnum peat moss that you use for your potting mix.

How to Take Cuttings

These tips apply to all cuttings, whether rooted in water or in other media:

- Take your cuttings from energetically growing outdoor plants. Spring is the best time, but you can root stems cut anytime during the growing season.
- Choose stems that do not yet have woody growth, but are still green and pliable. Avoid flowering stems.
- Choose healthy, disease and pest-free plants.
- Take more than one cutting of a plant, just in case of failure.
- Cut three to five inches from the tip with sharp pruners, scissors, or a knife—just be sure it's a clean cut. Try to cut just below a leaf node. Some plants will root anywhere on the stem; others root only at the nodes.
- Remove the bottom leaves, but make sure there are at least a few sets of leaves left on the stem to feed it through this rather traumatic time.

> **THE VOICE OF EXPERIENCE**
>
> Don't let the roots grow into a tangled mess, or they will be impossible to separate when you do get around to transplanting them.

> Don't take cuttings in the fall, when plants are beginning to go dormant, or from indoor plants with soft thin stems.

Rooting cuttings in water is really simple, but there are a couple of things to take into consideration to ensure success. Here's how to do it:

After you've followed the guidelines mentioned above, just group the stems in a short, clean glass of water (you can also use Styrofoam cups). Try not to let any foliage be underwater, or it will rot. If you have several different cuttings, label them (If I've said it once, I've said it a hundred times!). Put the container on a bright windowsill, avoiding direct sun.

Change the water frequently, and make sure you don't let the cuttings dry out. When the cuttings have roots about half an inch long, they are ready to transplant, using the same method as for seedlings.

The method for rooting cuttings in growing medium is slightly different. To begin with, make sure your medium is pre-moistened and ready to go—don't wait until you've got a handful of cut stems to do it. Then follow the guidelines above. When your cuttings are ready, stick them into the growing medium, making sure there is contact with the moist mix all around the stem. The stem should stand up on its own.

You can use a commercially prepared "rooting hormone" to try to speed up the rooting process, or go the natural route: dip the cutting in liquid seaweed, fish emulsion, or willow bark tea.

The big difference between this and water rooting is that the stem needs a constant supply of moisture when it's stuck in the soilless mix. The leaves are the only way for a newly stuck cutting to get water, even though you're keeping the mix nice and damp. The best way to provide needed moisture is with a spray bottle of regular water. You can also use liquid seaweed, to speed up the rooting process. It's important to keep a close eye on them, because if the cuttings dry out too much, they won't strike roots at all, but will die.

Next, cover the container with a plastic bag, an upside-down glass jar, or, if you're using a flat, a humidity dome to maintain humidity. Keep the container in a bright spot, out of direct sunlight. Now the vigil begins. It can take as long as four to six weeks for cuttings to root this way. A good way to tell if rooting has begun is if there is brand new top growth, but sometimes that can begin before rooting does. Most growers give the cutting a gentle tug to see if there's any resistance; if so, that means you've got some roots!

As with water rooting, wait until the roots are at least half an inch long before transplanting into individual containers. And if you're putting them directly into the garden, put them in the shade for a few days beforehand.

Layering

Nature's way of rooting is called layering, and it's really easy to do. In nature, if a stem touches moist ground, it will send out roots and anchor itself to the ground. In the garden, you can prompt Mother Nature along.

Start by selecting a long, flexible, young growing branch near the ground. Strip the leaves off the area you'll be burying, then bend it over and bury in the ground about two to three inches deep. Mound soil over the top of the buried stem. You

HERBS THAT ROOT EASILY BY STEM LAYERING

- chamomile
- pennyroyal
- rosemary
- sage
- santolina
- southernwood
- tarragon
- thyme

may need to secure very stiff stems with bent wire pins or sticks.

> Wounding the stem before burying it can help speed up the rooting process. Just scrape away a couple of inches of the thin green bark on the section you're planning to bury.

Keep the layered area well watered but not soggy. Roots should form in three to four weeks, but the timing will vary depending on soil and weather conditions. The great thing about layering is that you can do it and forget it, coming back to check occasionally. There's no daily (or hourly) misting or other pampering. The drawback is that there are a limited number of transplants you will end up with this way, so if you need twenty-five rosemary starts, this is *not* the way to do it.

When a good mass of roots has formed, the rooted stem is ready to be separated from the parent plant. Just snip the new plant free, gently lift it out of the soil—be careful of the new roots!—and transplant in its new location.

Dividing Plants

Some herbs are more suitable to propagate from division than from other methods. It's a down-and-

HERBS THAT DIVIDE EASILY

- artemisias
- beebalm
- chives
- germander
- Greek oregano
- horehound
- lemongrass
- marjoram
- mints
- sorrel
- sweet woodruff
- tansy
- tarragon
- thyme (creeping varieties)

dirty way to go, with only a couple of tools needed. You're basically digging up plants and ripping them apart. It doesn't have to be so, well, violent, but some herbs may take some serious coaxing to be pulled apart.

In the group of herbs that benefit from division, there are different types of growth. Chives, for instance, multiply into many little bulblets, and are extremely easy to divide. Tarragon, on the other hand, gets its name from the French "little dragon," a reference to its tangled mass of roots. You may need brute force with this one.

Division is also a way to keep your garden in check. Every few years it may become necessary to divide your perennial herbs to make sure they behave and don't take up too much space. Division also helps rejuvenate older plants that are beginning to decline. Finally, division helps discourage disease by thinning foliage and increasing air circulation.

The cool, damp conditions of early spring are the best time to divide your herbs; after the plants get too large, they may suffer from the rough treatment. The best plants to choose for this surgery are herbaceous perennials that die back to the ground every year, coming back from spreading root systems.

All you'll need are a sharp spade, shovel, or garden fork, pruners or a knife, and a trowel. To begin, dig around the clump, staying just outside the plant's root system. Lift the whole clump, roots and all, out and onto the ground. Shake as much soil off as you can (or hose it off) and begin the surgery. Try to keep as large a root system as you can for each new clump. Mints and other spreaders will yield many more new clumps than herbs with only a few new shoots in their crowns, like sorrel. Slice especially tightly bound root systems apart with your pruners or knife. Don't feel guilty; it has to be done. If you leave enough root attached to the parent plant, it will recover quickly.

Once you've completed your surgery, it's time to replant in a hole lined with compost to reduce transplant shock. Firm in and water well, just like any other transplant.

> Plants that grow by runners, like mint, can be divided without digging up the whole plant. Just grab a stem end and gently pull it up, following the underground stems. Then cut it off and replant in a new spot.

Saving Seed

Saving your own seed to replant next season is an ancient and time-honored agricultural practice. A few hundred years ago, farmers and gardeners didn't pad down to the local garden center and pick up a few packets of seeds. No, they had to save their own from year to year, or go without.

We're fortunate that we have the option today of choosing from hundreds of seed and plant vendors, but there is still a strong connection to the past that makes today's gardeners save their own seed.

GATHERING SEEDHEADS

Saving ripe seedheads can be tricky for the beginning gardener—and even the experienced!—because flowers mature at different times and look different when the seedpods are ready. You may want to go through a growing season, carefully observing the different herbs before jumping into seed saving.

That said, seed saving isn't all that complicated. You just need to wait until the seeds have matured on the plant before collecting them. They usually dry up and turn tan, brown, or black when they're ripe. You can hold the seedheads over a container and tap the dry seeds into it, or cut off the seedheads and hang them in paper bags to dry. Make sure the seeds are completely dry before storing them in airtight containers, or they'll get moldy and go bad before next season. Just to be on the safe side, I store my seeds in the fridge, or better yet, the freezer. This is especially important for seeds that have a very short "shelf-life," like angelica.

CALLING ALL VOLUNTEERS!

The other way to save seeds is much less complicated—let them sow themselves! I love all my little "volunteers" in the garden; they save me lots of extra planting. Many annuals and biennials will reseed themselves. The only tool you'll need is patience: for resisting the urge to cultivate the bare ground where you know seeds fell, and for waiting the following spring to see who's coming up where. If you're lucky, the seeds will fall and germinate right where you want them. If you're like everyone else, the seeds will go every which way and you'll have to move the seedlings back to their proper place. You'll no doubt have some extras popping up in the pathways and in other beds; pot them up and give them away to your friends.

HERBS THAT SELF-SOW

- anise hyssop
- bachelor buttons
- borage
- calendula
- chervil
- chives
- clary sage
- coriander
- dill
- fennel
- foxglove
- German chamomile
- Johnny-jump-up
- lemon balm
- valerian

From Seedlings to Mature Plants: The Care and Feeding of Your Herb Garden

6

Hooray! You've got the garden all planted—but now what? In this section we'll discuss the easiest ways to take care of your new garden, from fertilizers to pest control to mulch.

CHAPTER 20

Fertilizers

In this chapter I'll try to explain the theories behind organics, why they're the best method for growing herbs (and everything else!), and how you can use organic fertilizers to feed your herb garden.

Why Organic? A Primer

Chapter 5 discussed the basics of soil fertility and Chapter 12 already covered the mechanics of making your own compost, but here's the theory behind organic gardening in general.

> According to *Webster's Dictionary*, organic means "relating to, produced with, or based on the use of fertilizer of plant or animal origin without employment of chemically formulated fertilizers or pesticides."

IT WASN'T ALWAYS THIS WAY

Even as recently as the end of the last century, synthetic chemicals were unheard of in gardening and farming. Anyone who tended the soil went about it the same way people had been doing it for centuries: amending the soil with manure and compost, and then depending on that well-fed soil to produce a plentiful harvest. Because of the healthy soil, plants were not as susceptible to insect pests. And when there were a few pests, they were tolerated, while bad infestations were treated with homemade concoctions.

These people weren't gardening organically because it was fashionable, but because it worked.

As agriculture became a bigger business and larger farms were needed to produce more food, farmers turned to the new technology of chemically produced fertilizers and pesticides. Scientists became involved in farming, and they considered the soil just a sterile anchor in which to hold the crops in place, while asserting that the use of chemicals to feed those plants was the only acceptable "modern" method.

Not everyone agreed, however, and soon other scientists were studying the organisms in soil that work together as a living system that required the recycling of organic wastes back into the soil.

In this more holistic view of the relationship between soil and plants, they realized the importance of returning nutrients to the soil in the form of organic matter like manure and compost. A few farmers followed this "new" theory—which was really just the good farming practices of the past! These farmers believed the synthetic chemicals to be not just unhealthy, but actually dangerous for the environment and for wildlife. For many years this "organic method" was considered weird or radical, but the emergence of new information on pollution caused by pesticides, herbicides, and synthetic fertilizers, as well as the publication of books like *Silent Spring* by Rachel Carson, had a direct impact on how the general public felt about the chemicals they were using on their food.

MODERN TIMES

Today's organic gardeners realize they don't have to resort to "chemical warfare" to have healthy crops of food. All that's needed is to understand the natural processes that keep the cycles going. Nature makes its own fertilizers—in the decay of plant and animal matter, the organisms that feed on that decay release nutrients back into the soil to feed the next generation of plants. In nature, biological diversity uses natural predators to help keep pests in check. Organic gardening works in much the same way.

The mantra of organics today is "feed the soil, not the plant."

> According to the FDA, homeowners are responsible for more pesticide abuse than any other group.

Here's a quick wrap-up on the pitfalls of chemicals:

- They pollute the environment, both the groundwater and the soil.
- Chemicals actually deplete the soil of its natural nutrients, and they can destroy soil structure. This is why long-time chemically farmed fields can look almost white—there's no organic matter remaining in the depleted soil.
- Chemicals make the plants they are used on dependent on those chemicals to thrive. Non-organic crops have been compared to heroin addicts because of their addiction to chemical fertilizers.
- Pests can develop resistance to the very pesticides that are supposed to kill them; herbicides accumulate in the water supply.
- Chemical pesticides kill non-selectively, which means they kill not just the bad guys, but also the good guys who might be perfectly willing to eat the bad guys for you (for free, even!). This includes birds, frogs, bees, and other beneficial wildlife.

- All those chemicals are expensive! Proponents of the non-organic way claim that using organic methods are much more expensive, but most of the things you can do to keep your garden chemical-free are either free or much less expensive than store-bought chemicals. Compare the cost of washing aphids off a plant with your garden hose to Malathion, or feeding your herbs with homemade compost to buying a bottle of Miracle-Gro.

> It was recently discovered that the spraying of orchards was responsible for the decline in robin populations. The trees were being sprayed at the same time the baby birds were hatching, killing them.

OK, I get the impression I've brought you down. Actually, growing organically can make you feel really good, because you know that you're being a good steward of the environment, and that you have a much closer relationship with not just the plants in your garden, but the whole ecosystem of plants, soil, and wildlife that lives in it. And you don't have to worry about using poisons on the herbs that will be going on your plate.

Even if I didn't feel so strongly about the benefits of gardening organically, the fact remains that there are no chemical pesticides approved for use on herbs. What does *that* tell you?

Here are some of the principles of organics:

"Feed the Soil, Not the Plant." This just means adding organic matter to your soil to enrich it every season. Use a long-term approach to build healthy soil that will feed your herbs on its own, rather than looking at short-term goals of high yields *right now*. Another corollary follows: Leave your garden soil in better shape at the end of every season than when you began.

Your hands aren't tied when it comes to fertilizers. There are many perfectly acceptable organic fertilizers available to you, including animal manures and crushed mineral rock. These will be discussed in detail later in this chapter.

Pest control is still in your control, too. Start by keeping a close eye on your plants, so you'll know when to take action. Keeping your plants healthy also goes a long way in keeping pests and diseases in check—it's the stressed-out plants that usually get munched first!

Prevent problems from the start by having a diverse ecosystem that encourages the good guys to come and eat the bad guys before they get out of hand. And don't panic if you see a single bug! There are many beneficial insects out there ready to devour garden pests (for free, even!), so learn which are which (see section "Good Bugs vs. Bad Bugs: How to Tell the Difference" on page 226).

Other organic pest control methods include the following:

Physical: barriers like row covers to exclude pests; hand-picking (especially effective on larger pests like Japanese beetles); traps and lures; cutworm collars, copper strips, etc.

Biological: using both beneficial insects to get the bad guys, as well as items like Bt (*Bacillus thuringiensis*) and milky spore.

Sprays: insecticidal soaps and horticultural oils, homemade concoctions like hot peppers and dish soap; and as a last resort, botanical insecticides, which are natural but still toxic. See Chapter 23 for more details.

Weed control doesn't have to mean RoundUp! Heavy mulching, green manures in pathways, and mechanical cultivation—as well as plain, old-fashioned hand weeding—are very effective.

Other organic practices include crop rotation, cultivation, selecting well-adapted cultivars, companion planting, and good garden sanitation (keeping it clean).

The best news of all is that herbs are especially well suited to organic methods. They're remarkably pest-resistant, and respond enthusiastically to compost and animal manure. You'll get your high yields and not even need to think about going chemical shopping!

Popular Organic Fertilizers

Now that I've convinced you (I *have* convinced you, haven't I?), here are some of the organic fertilizers available. If you've done a good job of enriching your soil, you probably won't even need to use these products, but it's still a good idea to know what's out there.

> The main difference between organic and chemical fertilizers is that the organic materials serve both to feed plants and act as soil conditioners, whereas chemicals have mineral salts that tend to acidify the soil and make soil structure decline over time, increasing the need for even more chemical fertilizers.

MAKING THE SWITCH

Oh, man, you say, this is going to be complicated and probably expensive! To the contrary! Of the store-bought items, most are just as easy to mix with water as their chemical counterparts. And while it's true that you can get very specific with the different mineral additives, it's not necessary unless you want to do it. Like I said before, herbs aren't picky!

We talked about soil fertility in Chapter 5, and how NPK affects the overall health of your garden. Just to recap:

N=Nitrogen: for leaf and stem growth, and to maintain the plant's green color

P=Phosphorus: for flowers, seed, fruit, and roots

K=Potassium: for overall healthy growth

Animal Manures		
TYPE	**NPK RATIO**	**BENEFITS AND COMMENTS**
Cow	0.6-0.2-0.5	Lower in nutrients than other manures, but is balanced and does add organic matter to soil.
Horse	0.7-0.3-0.6	High in nitrogen—always compost before use. Can vary widely in quality, depending on type of bedding it is mixed with.
Chicken	1.1-0.8-0.5	Very high in nitrogen—must be composted. Has strong smell.
Duck	0.6-1.4-0.5	
Pig	0.5-0.3-0.5	
Rabbit	2.4-1.4-0.6	Very high in nitrogen.
Sheep	0.7-0.3-0.9	
Bat Guano	10-3-1	Extremely high in nitrogen; a little goes a long way. Available from organic specialty catalogs.
ZooDoo	varies	Manures of various zoo animals—reputed to also help keep animal pests out of gardens.
Worm Castings	0.5-0.5-0.3	Good all-around soil amendment, adding organic matter as well as 11 trace minerals to soil. Large amounts are difficult to come by, but are available through mail order catalogs.

Different kinds of organic fertilizers can supply differing amounts of these nutrients, along with various other minor but necessary nutrients, like calcium, magnesium, and sulfur. And remember, get your soil analyzed so you know beforehand if you even *need* fertilizers!

ANIMAL MANURES

When most of us think of organic fertilizer, we think animal manure. It has been in use for thousands of years, and with good reason. Animal manures not only add organic matter to the soil, they also nourish it with a variety of nutrients.

I told you earlier about how whatever animal manure you can get your hands on is the best kind for you to use, but if you have access to many types and want to know the differences between them, you've come to the right place.

> Keep in mind that you need to let most manures sit (or better yet, compost!) for at least six months to a year before using them, because fresh manure can burn your plants and release ammonia into the soil, and it's frequently full of weed seeds. Composting solves those problems.

Most of the livestock manures mentioned above are available at local farms either for free or for a small fee. You're usually responsible for hauling it yourself, but sometimes you can get them to deliver it to you. Some garden centers sell dried, bagged horse, cow, and chicken manure.

FISH EMULSION AND KELP MEAL

Native Americans used to put a fish head in the bottom of the hole as they were planting their crops. Sounds a little weird, but they knew the value of their harvests from seas, rivers, and lakes. Today, you can still take advantage of the benefits that fish and seaweed have to offer. There are many different forms this stuff can take, powder or liquid, and they offer a range of nutrients. Here's a quick rundown.

If you live close to the shore, you may be able to find fresh versions of these items. I've heard of people harvesting seaweed at low tide for their seaside gardens (they wash off the salt before using it). Fish processing plants may also be a source. The rest of us have to buy it pre-packaged from garden centers and catalogs that specialize in organic products.

The foliar sprays are especially good for con-

Fish Emulsion and Kelp Meal

TYPE	NPK RATIO	BENEFITS AND COMMENTS
Fish Meal	5-3-3	Good source of nitrogen, phosphorus, potassium, and micronutrients. Has strong odor; best used outdoors.
Fish Emulsion	4-1-1	Liquid form of fish meal that makes a great foliar (leaf) feeder. Spray on leaves or add when you water. Also has strong odor.
Kelp Meal	1.5-0.5-2.5	Made from dried, ground seaweed. Good source of potassium, as well as calcium, sodium, sulfur, and many trace elements. Not as strong an odor as fish products, so can be used indoors. Makes a great compost addition!
Liquid Kelp (Liquid Seaweed)	1-0.5-2.5	Liquid form of kelp meal, can be used like fish emulsion. Good for houseplants.

Bone Meal and Other Animal Byproducts

TYPE	NPK RATIO	BENEFITS AND COMMENTS
Blood Meal	11-0-0	Slaughterhouse byproduct; dried, ground animal blood adds a very quick boost of nitrogen to plants. Don't add too close to plant stems as it can burn. Expensive.
Bone Meal	1-11-0	Slaughterhouse byproduct that adds phosphorus and calcium to the soil more quickly than rock phosphate. More expensive than rock phosphate, too. One application lasts about 6 to 12 months; gradually raises soil pH.

tainer plants that aren't able to search around in the ground for their nutrients. The sprays provide a quick pick-me-up of nitrogen and phosphorus and usually must be reapplied every so often.

Liquid seaweed and fish emulsion are the only products I use on the plants in my greenhouse, by the way. I've never needed to use anything else, and people always comment on how healthy the plants are in early spring.

> Beware of any store-bought product whose NPK ratio adds up to more than fifteen, or has a single ingredient whose number is larger than ten; it may not be organic.

The use of these products is a little controversial—especially if you're a vegetarian! While they are of natural animal origin, they are nonetheless slaughterhouse byproducts and, to some people, getting pretty close to the line with organic. It's up to you to decide whether to use them in your own garden.

Tips on Using Compost as Fertilizer

As I've said many times before, regular compost is the best food for your herb garden. When you add it, you're not just building up the soil; you're also adding nutrients that will feed the plants.

Here are some tips on using compost in your garden:

- Add a trowel-full to the bottom of each planting hole when you are transplanting.
- Make a compost "tea" to water in your transplants after planting.
- To feed perennials, simply add the compost on top of the soil, mixing it in lightly. This is called "side-dressing."

- If you have a lot of compost, you can use it as a mulch, spreading it evenly on top of your whole garden bed. It will help retain moisture, and it will feed your garden a little bit every time it rains. Then next season, you can turn it into the soil.
- You can work compost into your garden soil at any time during the growing season. It won't burn your plants, and you can't "overfertilize" with it. One exception: Don't add it right at the end of the summer because you may stimulate growth that will soon be killed by frost.

HERBAL HELPERS

Did you know that there are several herbal fertilizers you can grow and make yourself? Comfrey is famous for providing nitrogen, phosphorus, and potash, as well as trace minerals and elements. Here's the basic recipe:

Pour four cups of boiling water over a good-sized handful of fresh herb. (You can substitute two tablespoons of dried herb.) Cover and steep for ten minutes minimum. Strain through cheesecloth and use as foliar spray or add to your watering can.

Nettles are also great herbal helpers, not just for people but also for your herb plants. Make a tea using the above recipe, but let steep for three weeks. Nettles add iron, nitrogen, and trace minerals.

Other herbal fertilizers to choose from include:

- dandelion: adds copper
- dill: minerals, potassium, sulfur and sodium
- horsetail: rich in silica
- yarrow: good general fertilizer; adds copper

Finally, chamomile is such a great food as well as fungus-fighter for seedlings, it's known as "the plants' physician." Make a cup of chamomile tea and use it on seedlings to prevent damping off—and to stop it from getting worse!

CHAPTER 21

To Mulch or Not to Mulch

In this chapter I'll explain the different types of mulches available to you as an organic herb gardener, and why using them is a good idea.

> *Mulching* simply means covering the surface of your herb garden soil with a layer of material like shredded bark, straw, or pine needles.

Why Mulch?

There are many reasons to mulch your garden, both during the growing season and over the winter. Once you start using mulches, you'll wonder how you ever got along without them. I feel like my gardens aren't finished in the spring until they've got that finishing touch a nice mulch provides.

Summer Mulches

WEED CONTROL

A nice, thick layer of mulch discourages weed seeds from germinating in the soil, and those that do germinate are usually very easy to pull out of the loose layer of mulch.

MOISTURE RETENTION AND TEMPERATURE CONTROL

In the summer, that same thick layer of mulch can help keep moisture in and heat out, reducing the need for watering.

CONTROLLING DIRT SPLASH

Mulch is especially important in the herb garden, where you really want the foliage on your herbs to be pretty clean. It can nearly eliminate the dirt splash caused by heavy rains, keeping your herbs nice and neat!

ADDING ORGANIC MATTER AND EROSION CONTROL

Organic mulches break down over time, adding valuable organic matter to the soil. At the same time, covering the soil surface helps discourage erosion.

GOOD LOOKS

Most mulches really improve the looks of the floor of the garden—especially in new gardens, where the plants are still small.

BLACK PLASTIC AND LANDSCAPE FABRIC

These types of mulches are non-organic. In this context, that means they aren't made from natural materials—not that they aren't allowed in organic gardens! These are very good at keeping weeds down, but black plastic can also be a barrier to rainwater, meaning you'll have to water the beds yourself.

Landscape fabric, on the other hand, is more like netting, preventing weeds from coming through, but allowing air and water to penetrate.

A very good use in the herb garden for these types of mulches is as weed control for pathways. Lay the plastic or fabric down in the pathway, then cover it with a traditional organic mulch like shredded bark or sawdust to hide it. These materials can be a little on the pricey side, but if you take care of them, they should last through several seasons of use.

Winter Mulches

Mulching in the winter is a whole different philosophy. Here, you're protecting your garden from the elements—especially important in Northern climates!—not from weeds and drought. A thick enough mulch can even provide enough protection to safeguard plants that aren't usually hardy in your zone.

This is not to say that you can grow basil year-round in Minnesota with just a covering of hay. But you can certainly experiment with different types of "almost-hardy" plants that would not survive without any protection at all.

There are two main reasons to mulch during the winter. First, for protection from freezing and thawing; applying your mulch *after* the ground has frozen in late fall can help keep the soil from alternate freezing and thawing, which can be a real killer to many plants. Second, it can also prevent "heaving" caused by frost.

> *Heaving* is when the ground is frozen and then thaws. It moves upward, or "heaves." It can push newly planted or shallow-rooted plants right out of the ground, killing them. A thick winter mulch can help prevent this problem.

PROTECTION FROM DRYING WINDS

I always tell people that April—or March, depending on where you are—can kill a plant faster than the bitterest low temps in February. That's because the drying winds of early spring can injure and even kill plants that have survived all winter long under an insulating blanket of snow. A layer of mulch can help perennials acclimate better to the stark contrasts of spring, where one day will be sunny and warm, and the next can be brutally windy and cold. So, leave the blanket of winter mulch on your plants until the weather has settled down a bit.

The Difference between Summer and Winter Mulches

So there you have it: the good reasons to mulch your herb garden. But not every mulch is appropriate to use in both seasons. It would be very difficult to use cocoa shells as a winter protection, just as straw, a very good winter protector, is not particularly attractive in the formal herb garden.

Summer mulches are more for weed and moisture control; they only cover the ground underneath your plants. Winter mulches are more for temperature and wind protection, and they go on top of the plants themselves—especially woody herbs like lavender and roses. You can also cover herbaceous perennials like mint and oregano, but know in advance that you'll have to remove the mulch in spring to allow warmth to get in and spur new growth. Most winter mulches need to be removed in mid spring (not too early!), so the sun can warm the ground underneath; summer mulches can be left in place year-round.

Mulching

To mulch in summer:

Weed the area first: You don't want to be protecting weeds, now do you? If the soil is already beginning to dry out due to dry weather, water the bed first.

Lay down a nice, thick layer of material, between one and four inches to be really effective. Make sure you actually cover all the soil surface. A scrap here and there does no good; it just wastes your mulch. Keep in mind, though, that shady areas may need a little less, while hot, dry areas may need more.

Wait to mulch until seedlings and transplants are big enough to hold their own and not get smothered by the material.

Don't bring mulch right up to stems: It could harbor pests like slugs and cutworms, and it could also promote rot when wet.

A QUICK RULE OF THUMB

Light mulch: keeps soil cool for plants that prefer cooler temps (like mint).
Dark mulch: keeps soil warmer; good for plants that like it hot (like basil).

"Juicy" mulch (like grass clippings, leaf mold, and compost) breaks down faster than chunky mulch (like bark nuggets).

Wait until the ground warms up in spring to

Characteristics of Popular Mulches

MATERIAL	TYPE	COMMENTS
Compost	Summer	One of the best mulches for herbs. Apply at least 1" thick as top-dressing or along rows. Tends to break down quickly.
Shredded Leaves	Summer/ Winter	A very attractive mulch for ornamental gardens. Gather leaves in the fall and run them through a shredder or chop up with a lawnmower with a bag attachment. Apply in 3 to 4" layers. Adds nutrients as it breaks down. For winter protection, make the layers 6" thick.
Leaf Mold	Summer	Not as attractive as shredded leaves, leaf mold is really just broken down leaves. It takes quite a while to make leaf mold, but if you have access to woods you can get it from the forest floor. You can also make it yourself.
Straw/Hay	Summer/ Winter	As a summer mulch for vegetable gardens and utilitarian herb beds, straw and hay are great mulches if looks aren't important. The difference between the two is that straw consists of coarse stalks of grain, usually free of weed seeds, and it takes longer to break down. Hay is just bound, cut meadow grass, and it can frequently be full of weed seeds. You may want to compost it first. Salt hay is a wonderful weed-free alternative, but it's expensive and hard to come by. Both straw and hay are excellent winter mulches for roses and other perennials. Apply it very thickly (up to 2'!) for the best protection. By the way, spoiled hay is just as good for mulch as fresh hay—and it's a lot cheaper! Ask for "mulch hay" at the end of the summer from local farmers.
Grass Clippings	Summer	Not the most attractive mulch for formal herb gardens, grass clippings are still a great summer mulch to retain moisture and keep weeds down. Don't apply too thickly, or it could mat down and mold. Also, make sure clippings are herbicide-free. Apply 1" layers of fresh clippings, keeping the mulch away from plant stems. Double the thickness for dried clippings.
Shredded Bark	Summer	An attractive mulch for herb gardens, shredded bark can also be used to cover up less attractive materials like plastic, landscape fabric, and leaf mold. Can be used both on garden beds and in pathways. Apply in 3 to 4" layers. The small pieces break down faster than other types of bark mulches.
Bark Chunks	Summer	A very attractive, more permanent mulch than shredded bark, chunks are great for weed control, and they stay in place through the season. Spread to a depth of 3 to 4".
Wood Chips	Summer	Longer lasting than shredded bark, but not as long lasting as bark chunks, wood chips come from entire chipped trees, not just the bark. Chips make a decorative, weed-suppressing mulch. Good for both perennial beds and pathways. Apply to a depth of 3 to 4". Fresh chips may tie up nitrogen in soil, affecting plant growth, so you may want to let them sit for a few months before using them.

continued

Characteristics of Popular Mulches *(continued)*

MATERIAL	TYPE	COMMENTS
Cocoa Bean Shells	Summer	One of the most decorative mulches, cocoa shells (AKA cocoa hulls or cocoa mulch) smell like chocolate when first applied. The shells are lightweight, easy to handle, clean, and weed-free. Better for perennial beds than pathways. Can be expensive, unless you have a chocolate factory nearby.
Newspaper	Summer	Not the prettiest mulch, but it works well to suppress weeds, while allowing rain in. Lay down whole sections of paper at least six layers thick—on a calm day, please!—using stones or bricks to hold them down. It's a good idea to cover the paper with a more decorative mulch to keep it from blowing around. Newspaper adds organic matter to the soil as it slowly breaks down. Don't use colored newspaper because the inks may be toxic.
Pine Needles (Pine Straw)	Summer/ Winter	Attractive, lightweight, clean, weed-free mulch. Tends to acidify the soil, so don't use it around plants like lavender that prefer sweet soil. A good winter mulch for low-growing acid lovers.
Sawdust	Summer	A good choice for both garden beds and pathways. Nice to mix with other mulches like compost. Spread 1 to 2" on soil surface. Fresh sawdust is too high in carbon to use directly on beds, so it's best to let it age a year or two, which also leaches out any toxic materials in the wood. Breaks down quickly and must be reapplied every season.
Evergreen boughs	Winter	Instead of throwing away your Christmas tree in January, cut off the boughs and use them to cover the taller, woodier herbs in your garden, like sage and lavender. Remove them in spring.

apply summer mulches; in the fall, apply right after planting. For winter mulches, wait until the ground freezes or you'll end up creating a lovely rodent bed and breakfast. Where the ground doesn't freeze, wait until early winter—or don't winter mulch at all.

Apply the mulch at the rates suggested below, and keep an eye on the depth over the course of the season; you may need to reapply if it breaks down very quickly.

You may have noticed that peat moss wasn't on my list. That's because I don't find it to be a good mulch; I save it for potting mixes. It's too dry, too acidic, and too expensive for use in the herb garden.

CHAPTER 22

Keeping Things Tidy

Ah, summer. Your garden is in, the mulch is down, the herbs are starting to take off. Your work is done, right? Well, the hard part is over, but you're not totally off the hook. You still have to do a little housekeeping in the garden. This means keeping things neat by deadheading your perennials and doing a little weeding here and there. But don't despair; many gardeners find the time they spend doing this kind of work to be the most enjoyable of all!

How to Pinch, Trim, and Deadhead

It's said that the best gardeners spend a little time in their gardens every single day, pulling weeds as soon as they see them and snipping off dead leaves right as they appear. Yeah, whatever, good for them. The rest of us have lives to live! Most people who work for a living can't necessarily spend a couple of hours in their gardens every night after work—unless you *like* gardening by flashlight!

But, if you've taken the time to put down the mulch we discussed in the previous chapter, you'll save yourself a huge chunk of time in the weed department, leaving yourself time to do the other necessary housekeeping: pinching and deadheading.

> *Pinching* is a form of pruning that keeps plants from getting leggy by "pinching" off the growing tip, encouraging branching.

PINCHING

Pinching is a necessary part of early summer gardening. It's a good way to help plants stay bushy, rather than leggy, in the garden. It can also help taller plants stand up on their own, reducing the need for staking (don't worry, I'm getting to that!).

When should you pinch? When the plant is still young enough to develop a full shape. That means, when it's still in the pot, if you've started it

from seed. You should always pinch before flower buds develop, so you don't lose that season's bloom. Depending on the size of the stem you're pinching, you generally want to remove the growing tips an inch or two down to just above a leaf or bud. Keep in mind that pinching does set back flowering by a week or two.

One last thing: I don't find it necessary to pinch the big patches of herbs like beebalm, mints, tansy, etc. On the other hand, large, stalked, individual plants usually benefit from pinching.

There's a whole tray of bachelor's buttons in my greenhouse that I forgot to pinch early in the season, and now they are each just one long stem with a flower on the end, not the healthy, branching plant you normally think of.

CUTTING

Cutting back is a more drastic form of pruning that keeps your garden tidy. Think of it as a great big haircut! It has several benefits, including improving air circulation, controlling insects and diseases, and encouraging a fresh flush of healthy new foliage. It is especially good for controlling powdery mildew on beebalm, and to eliminate the sprawling of large plants like comfrey, which tends to flop over from the center. It's also a way to keep plants looking tidy after flowering, especially large, floppy, flowering perennials.

You may want to wait to do a drastic cut until after flowering, depending on the plant.

When I say cutting back, I mean *way back*, like to the ground, or at least a third to half of the stem. You should cut diseased stems to the ground—and don't put the scraps in the compost, or you'll just spread the disease around.

Cutting back early in the season also helps keep bully herbs like tansy a little more under control. You may lose a flower or two, but you'll have a much better-behaved plant.

Thinning is similar to cutting back, but not quite as dramatic. When a mature clump of perennial herbs sends up *too* many stems in the spring, they may crowd and shade each other, resulting in overall poor growth and flowering, and increased susceptibility to disease. Thinning solves these problems by removing one-third to half of the weaker stems to improve air circulation, giving the stronger stems a chance to really shine. This practice will encourage strong new growth.

STAKING

Staking, or using a support of some kind to prevent tall plants from flopping over, is another kind of housekeeping task you should do pretty early in the season. It's also one of those things you can do high-tech (lots of money) or low-tech (no money), depending on your personal style.

Don't wait to stake until the plant has done its flopping; you could break the stems. Try to remember to do it early in the season, when the plants are just emerging from the soil, or when you first set the plants out in the garden.

High-Tech vs. Low-Tech, Revisited

Just like in seed starting, you can choose to spend lots or no money on this venture. The high-tech way is to buy those green metal plant stakes you see in mail order catalogs; some garden centers sell them, too. There are many different types, from grow-through rings to individual metal stakes with a hoop on the end for supporting individual blooms. They're very nice, and certainly effective, and I use them for plants like peonies that are not part of the regular garden.

In the middle ground are bamboo sticks, tomato stakes, string, and chicken wire you fabricate yourself into supports. Use your own ingenuity to make supports for plants in the least conspicuous way for your garden.

The low-tech—my favorite, of course!—is to use branches and twigs to hold plants up. Another option is to plant sturdy, shorter plants thickly in front of the tall ones, letting everyone hold each other up. These methods are much more natural looking, and ultimately easier, than the other ways.

> *Deadheading* means to keep the spent flowers pulled off your perennials in an effort to keep them blooming a little longer. It also keeps seedheads from forming, which gives the herb more strength for flower production and plant growth. And it makes the garden look neater, to boot!

DEADHEADING

Many herbal flowers will rebloom if you deadhead the first flush of flowers when they fade: beebalm, chives, pinks, yarrows, foxgloves, feverfew, delphiniums, red valerian, calendula, lavender, and echinacea. These are the ones you're probably growing for the flowers in the first place.

There are other herbs you'll want to remove the flowers from to keep the foliage coming: basil, lemon balm, horehound, parsley (in its second season), chervil (to prevent a whole garden of chervil!), mints, catnip, salad burnet, summer savory, and sorrel are examples.

> Since the flowers of some of these plants are so lovely (like the variegated basils), you might want to have more than one so you can let one flower and keep the other for the foliage.

For still others, you *want* to let the flowers go to seed, because that's the whole point of growing them: for example, caraway, anise, dill, coriander, and fennel. (The last three you may want for foliage only, in which case you'll need to cut off the flower stalks when they form.)

For soft-stemmed flowers, it may be easiest to pinch off the spent flowers with your fingers, but others will need to be clipped with your pruners or a sharp knife—this is where my Felcos get a real workout! Sometimes new flower buds will be right next to the old ones, so use care when snipping them off. In most cases, you'll want to cut off to a leaf, bud, or another stem. No one wants to look at a garden full of stubble!

Cut flowers on long stems back to the next set of buds; if there are no more, cut the whole stalk back to the ground.

How to Keep Unwanted Plants from Joining the Party

There's an old saying in gardening: "a weed is just a plant out of place." I really believe it's true. My neighbor considers the Johnny-jump-ups that cover her yard in early spring to be noxious weeds; I love them because they're so eager to bloom anywhere and everywhere. But my husband hates them growing on the floor of the greenhouse, and I must admit I get annoyed with them when they crowd out the thyme plants in the garden.

So are they a weed? No, just a misplaced plant. Same with dandelions and motherwort. I don't mind

the dandelions when they're blooming, but if I wait too long to mow and the puffballs duck under the blade of the lawnmower, that's annoying. And the motherwort and catnip that grow everywhere on my property I don't mind at all *if* they find their way into my apothecary garden, saving me from having to transplant them into it.

But sooner or later, no matter how laid back you are about the volunteers who move into the garden neighborhood, you'll need to weed. Like I said earlier, if you did your homework and laid down a nice thick layer of mulch both on your beds *and* in your paths, your work is half over. A few weeds will probably germinate or root their way in, but the majority will be eliminated.

> Be careful of using animal manure as your only mulch. There are probably more than a few weeds seeds lurking in it.

Nature Abhors a Vacuum

It's true, nature can't stand to see a bare patch of soil; it sends weedy warriors to fill it in. That can be a big problem if you have other plans for the spot! But believe it or not, weeds have a role to play in the grand scheme of things. They deter erosion, aerate and break up compacted soil, conserve nutrients that would otherwise leach out of bare soil, feed beneficial insects, and in some cases, fix nitrogen in the soil. And some weeds have only come to be considered weeds in our era of perfect lawns. Dandelions, purslane, and chickweed are actually very healthy additions to salads!

But that's beside the point, you say. I want that stuff out of my formal herb garden! Now!

OK, you don't have to take them under your wing and nurture them if you don't want to. Here are a few easy tips on getting rid of the less desirable additions to your garden.

First, learn to identify weed seedlings. Ragweed can look like feverfew to the untrained eye, and you don't want to pull up the plants you want to keep. It's also important to learn which ones are annual, and spread by prolific seeding, and which are perennials, spreading by runners or roots.

Make sure you pull out annual weeds before they set seed.

If you pull out perennial weeds by the roots, make sure you get the whole white root, otherwise any remaining bits will become whole new plants. For the same reason, *do not rototill* quack or witch grass—these grasses will make a new plant from each little piece of root!

For weeds with long taproots, like dandelions, use a long forked dandelion weeder to get the whole root, or leaves will just re-sprout from what little chunk is left in the ground.

Prevent problems to begin with by planting

thickly. This will hopefully crowd out the weeds, preventing them from taking root in the first place.

Lawn grass can be one of the worst weed pests in the garden, creeping in around the edges and popping up in the middle of beds. There are two things you can try: Get a tool called an "edger" to use around (what else?) the edges of the garden. This tool will slice the roots and keep them from coming in. The other thing you can do is install permanent edging at the border between the garden bed and the lawn. You can use old bricks, stones, or plastic edging from the hardware store. Just make sure you go down at least four to six inches to keep the grass stolons from coming underneath.

Try to hoe, scrape, or pull weeds at least once a week; this will go a long way in preventing them from taking over. You can use any number of tools created for just this purpose (see Chapter 13). Two tips: The younger the weed, the easier it is to remove, and if the soil is damp, the roots release a little easier than if the soil is bone dry.

Starting Over

Things got away from you, huh? What started as a formal herb garden has become a giant witch grass/ chickweed field? It will probably be easier to just start from scratch if it's really that bad. Dig up what valuable herbs you can still find, and set them aside where they won't dry out. Don't underestimate the amount of time this may take you—you might want to replant them in a holding bed!

If the garden is small enough, dig up the whole thing (see Chapter 15 for a refresher course on starting a new garden bed), making sure you get every last fleshy weed root. And I mean EVERY one! You do *not* want to go through this again, do you?

If the area is too big for you to dig by hand, try solarization. This takes a whole growing season, but it can really work. After you've removed your valuable plants, do a "scalp" mowing, as close to the ground as possible. Then lay a sheet of clear plastic (available at hardware stores) over the whole area, covering the edges with a layer of soil or rocks. Make sure the soil underneath is moist, so weed seeds will germinate and then fry under the hot plastic. The top layer of soil under the plastic will get so hot that not only weed seeds, but also roots, diseases, and insects will be killed. This only works in hot, sunny weather, so you'll have to wait until summer to do it. Give it a minimum of four to six weeks if the weather cooperates, eight to twelve if it's been cooler (75 degrees or cloudy). Because this process will also kill soil organisms, you may need to add compost or fertilize with seaweed after you replant.

> Some weed seeds can remain dormant in your garden for as long as one hundred years!

When Friend Becomes Foe

I really hate to tell you this, but some of our favorite herbs can become our least favorite weeds if given half a chance. There are some real bullies out there, and I feel it's my duty to at least warn you.

You could be like me, though, and say, "I really want this plant, so let's give it a try." But I really wish someone had warned me about common yarrow.

And I wish I'd listened to the well-meaning neighbor who said, "Whatever you do, *don't* plant Jerusalem artichoke in a small garden!"

Well, all I can do is give you the information. What you do with it is totally up to you. I must point out, though, that some of the plants that I'm about to malign may *not* try to take over your garden. It all depends on where you live, and the growing conditions there. The same English daisies that drive lawn owners insane in some areas may need to be pampered just to get through a winter in others.

Reseeders, Climbers, and Just Plain Brutes

Different herbs become unruly in different ways. Some are prolific (and I mean *prolific!)* seeders, while others climb all over their neighbors, shading them out. Still others just get bigger and bigger every year. Here's a rundown of some of the worst offenders.

- Prolific self-seeders: angelica, borage, catnip, chamomile, chives, clary sage, dill, echinacea, fennel, feverfew, foxglove, Fuller's teasel, garlic chives, horehound, Johnny-jump-up, lady's mantle, lemon balm, lovage, milk thistle, motherwort, nigella, perilla, poppy, Queen Anne's lace, rose campion, rue, silver tansy, sweet Annie, violets.
- Herbs that take over from underground (runners and roots): achillea "The Pearl," beebalm, ground ivy, lady's bedstraw, lamb's ears (also reseeds), medicinal yarrows, mints, mugwort, Roman wormwood, Silver King artemisia, soapwort, sweet goldenrod, sweet woodruff.
- Herbs that grow bigger and bigger—and bigger!: angelica, comfrey, costmary, horseradish, tansy, valerian, viper's bugloss, wormwood.

Keep in mind that I'm *not* telling you that you can't or shouldn't grow these guys—most of them are mainstays of all herb gardens! What I'm saying is that given the optimum conditions, they run the risk of getting out of control. Now go plant some comfrey!

CHAPTER 23

The Nasties: When Problems Strike

All your hard work is finally paying off! You've got all your herbs in the ground and they're looking great. And just when you're ready to take a little of the harvest for yourself, you discover to your horror: bugs! Don't panic, there are lots of things you can do to keep a small infestation from getting out of hand.

An Ounce of Prevention

Most herbs are naturally resistant to pests of all kinds because of their pungent essential oils, and some herbs actually poison pests! Keeping your herbs healthy, including good housekeeping techniques like picking off dead or yellow leaves, pinching back leggy plants, deadheading, proper watering, and regular baths, goes a long way toward keeping your herbs pest and disease free.

Help! I've Got a Problem!

Ok, you know your plants look a little sickly, but what's the problem? Is it caused by bugs, disease, or not being in the right spot? Not enough sun? Too much? What about water? Has it been raining enough?

Yellow leaves are the number one symptom of plants' problems, but they can be caused by many different things, including overwatering, underwatering, bugs, and nitrogen deficiency. How do you tell the difference?

The first thing you should do is familiarize yourself with what's normal so you can tell when things aren't. But first time gardeners sometimes have a hard time knowing what's normal—should those nasturtium leaves really be the size of dinner plates? But a healthy plant looks just that: healthy. They have strong stems, deep green color, and compact, bushy growth.

Check on your plants frequently, so you'll know whether they're growing quickly or not, and also so

you'll spot anything amiss before it becomes a huge problem.

Also, check the severity of the problem; take a look to see if it's on just one plant, or spreading through the entire bed. Sometimes a bug infestation will be very brief—just a blink in the life cycle of the bug—causing you little or no damage.

How to Tell the Difference Between Disease and Bug Infestation

BUG INFESTATION

Well, actually, bug infestation is pretty easy to differentiate from cultural problems or diseases: There's usually a bug or two nearby! Check underneath the leaves and at the axils, where the leaf joins the stem. That's where bugs usually hide. If you see little clusters of bugs (or eggs) under there, you've got your culprit. But sometimes bugs do their damage at night and hide out during the day. These are the ones that chew big holes in the leaves or mow the stems down entirely. That's another big clue—if the leaves and stems have been chewed, it's definitely *not* a disease problem!

Other signs of insect damage:

- shiny slime trails
- webs on stems or leaves
- tiny eggs under leaves
- leaves rolled with webbing

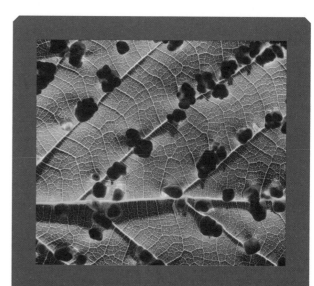

Insects usually strike inside houses and greenhouses because of poor air circulation and the lack of predators. Plants grown outside have fresh air and rain to wash their leaves.

- tiny holes in leaves
- leaves spotted, tunneled, or speckled
- stems and leaves sticky, frothy, puckered

And guess what? Bug infestation can *cause* disease problems! When a plant gets an infestation of creepy-crawlers, the bugs can carry fungal or other diseases with them, transmitting them to the plant.

DISEASE

Diseases, on the other hand, usually manifest themselves in distorted leaves, strange colorings, and furry growths. Once they get a foothold, they're very difficult to control, so you really need to stop them as early as possible.

Signs of disease include:

- leaves curled, distorted, spotted
- stems or roots with swelling or galls
- powder, fuzz, or furry growth on leaves
- leaves and stems with "off" colors
- seedling stems collapsed at soil line

SIGNS OF CULTURAL FACTORS

These are signs of nutrient deficiencies, water, light, or heat problems, or plain old gardener error.

- wilted stems, rotted roots
- pale leaves
- leaf scorch
- leaf or bud drop
- spindly, leggy growth

How Much to Tolerate before You Bring in the Big Guns

A few bugs are generally not going to destroy your plants, but in this age of picture-perfect gardens, gardeners have been taught a zero-tolerance rule. Well, try to forget that rule if you can. Unless the bugs are decimating your garden, you can learn to share a little with them. Some gardeners even plant extra for them!

It's easy to trot down to the chemical store and pick up some deadly concoctions that will kill everything in sight, but you can't use most of that stuff on culinary herbs. Besides, we've already had the organics discussion (see Chapter 20 for a refresher course). In the organic garden, the life cycles of the bad guys are usually synced up with the life cycles of the good, so when the pests increase, so do their predators.

So, in early spring, if you notice a few aphids chowing down on the brand new growth you've been waiting for all winter, hang on for a while. Chances are it's a passing phase in their life cycle. But if a couple of bugs become a horde, then reach for the organic solutions listed on page 233.

Good Bugs vs. Bad Bugs: How to Tell the Difference

All bugs in your garden are not bad! Really! There are lots of beneficial insects out there ready to do battle in honor of your herb garden. They eat the bad guys, but you have to give them a chance. This means don't spray every single bug you see without learning first whose side it's on.

FAMOUS BENEFICIALS

Most people know that ladybugs aren't garden pests, but did you know they *love* aphids? It's one of the mainstays of their diet! And their larvae love aphids even more! Ladybug larvae, though, look like red and black alligators, and I bet you've squished more than a few if you've seen them. Learn to identify them!

Other garden beneficials include praying mantids, lacewings, dragonflies, assassin bugs, big-eyed bugs, and soldier bugs; centipedes and millipedes; ground and rove beetles; predatory wasps (Don't worry, they don't sting people!); and even a few species of flies.

You can attract beneficials to your garden by providing them with access to food, water and shelter.

By the way, we consider honeybees, bumblebees, and other wasps to be good guys because they're so crucial to pollination. As a once-terrified avoider of these flying sting machines, I've since learned that a policy of mutual avoidance can be effective. Maybe we just have some really tame wasps, but we've decided not to look at them as enemies who must die, maintaining a healthy respect to their right to pollinate our flowers. Do be careful and certainly don't antagonize them, but don't kill every one you see, either.

Herb vs. Vegetable Pests

Not every pest of the vegetable garden is going to attack your herb garden, so that narrows down the enemy list a bit.

SUCKERS!

The sucking insects usually hide on the underside of leaves and suck the plant's juice out, weakening it. They'll spend their whole lives under there, eating, raising their young, going to PTA meetings . . . Uncontrolled, large infestations can kill plants.

Aphids: tiny, soft-bodied insects (also called plant lice), clustered on growing tips. The damage they cause includes pale green leaves, wilting and new leaves curled and sticky from honeydew (aphid doo), which supports the growth of sooty mold. If there are only a few, just wash them off in the sink; otherwise spray with insecticidal soap. (Don't spray if you see ladybugs or their larvae eating the aphids—give them a chance to clean the plant up for you!)

Ants tend to congregate on aphid-infested plants. They are "farming" the aphids because they love the sweet honeydew they produce!

Spider mites: Talk about the itsy-bitsy spider! These microscopic spiders prefer hot, dry conditions. You may not notice an infestation until the whole tip of a plant is covered with a very fine webbing that's filled with tiny moving red dots. They can seriously weaken a plant if left unchecked, but a simple spray with a hose or a quick dip in the sink will get rid of them. Keep the plants misted regularly to prevent further problems. You can also release predatory mites, or spray insecticidal soap.

Whiteflies: You can always tell when you have whiteflies—they fly up like ashes whenever you disturb the plant. They're annoying, especially in greenhouses, and once established can be a little tougher to control. If you catch them early, you may be able to control them with regular soap and water baths. For more severe infestations, spray with insecticidal soap, summer oil, or garlic oil. In the greenhouse, you can release parasitic wasps.

Mealybugs: Mostly a problem in the southern US and in greenhouses, mealybugs are small, white, "fluffy" insects that feed on ornamental herbs. Control is the same as for aphids.

Leafminers: larvae of a small fly that tunnels its way around ornamentals, leaving winding mines. They're mostly a nuisance, but they can damage young plants. Handpick and destroy the mined leaves.

Scale: Usually only a problem on woody herbs like bay and rosemary, scale can go unnoticed until the plant is weakened. These guys are bumps that latch on to new leaves and stems and look very much like part of the bark. One of the signs of infestation is shiny, sticky drops of liquid on the large leaves of bay. You can scrape small infestations off with your fingernail (pretty fast), swap the insects with alcohol (not as fast), or try to rub them off with a cloth and soapy water (slow).

CHOMPERS

The damage from chomping insects is much easier to detect, because it's usually more severe. These are the culprits when you have big holes chewed in the leaves—or no leaves left!

Flea beetles: very small, black or brown beetles that jump around like fleas when disturbed. They chew tiny holes in leaves. Young plants may die, but older plants usually survive. Since they're an early spring pest, try to plant as late as possible. Cover seedlings with floating row covers or mesh. As a last resort, spray with rotenone or pyrethrum.

Japanese beetles: What a scourge! Especially bad in areas with vast expanses of lawn—near golf courses, for example—these blue-green metallic-looking beetles can skeletonize the leaves of entire plants in a matter of days, chewing off your flowers, and devastating a garden. Large populations may completely defoliate plants. And their young are the nasty little grubs you see in turf. To prevent, let your lawn dry out in midsummer to kill off the eggs and grubs, or apply Bt (milky spore disease) to kill grubs. Handpick the adults in early morning, when they are sluggish, and drown them in pails of soapy water. *Do not* use Japanese beetle traps, or you will lure them into your yard from your neighbor's!

Slugs and Snails: When you see that slimy trail, you know the slugs are here. These mollusks are relatively small in some areas of the country, and frighteningly huge in others. They can completely demolish seedlings and seriously damage older plants. They're especially prevalent during wet times. Try to prevent them with a healthy population of toads and snakes (not what you wanted to hear?). Trap them under flowerpots and boards laid across the ground, destroying the catch every morning. Repel them with copper strips, which carry a mild electric current that kills them. Sprinkle diatomaceous earth or fireplace ashes around plants to repel them. Salt kills them, too, but be careful about using salt in the garden—you may damage your plants. Everybody talks about using beer or yeast traps in the garden, but I didn't find them as effective as other methods. Feel free to give it a try; it may work better for you.

Cutworms: Largish gray or brown caterpillars that live in the soil, ready to sever your newly planted seedlings overnight. Sometimes you'll find the plant lying on the ground; sometimes it will be completely gone. Make cutworm collars out of toilet paper and paper towel rolls cut into three-inch pieces; plant your seedlings inside. If you find the worms while planting or cultivating, handpick and squish them.

TRY TO LOOK THE OTHER WAY

There are a few bugs that, while they may be unsightly, or may actually eat some of your herbs, aren't worth killing—or may be worth saving.

Parsley Worm: The caterpillar of the black swallowtail butterfly is striped black and chartreuse, and loves members of the Umbelliferae family—some of our favorite herbs are their favorites, too. You'll see them for just a few weeks in early summer on parsley, dill, fennel, and the like. The butterflies are so beautiful that most herb gardeners welcome the caterpillars, and even plant a little extra for them. They don't do too much damage, unless you only have one or two plants that they seem to favor. In my own garden, I pick them off the more valuable plants and carry them over to the huge patch of Queen Anne's lace at the edge of the yard.

Spittlebugs (froghoppers): Yes, seeing a big frothy glop of "spit" on your plants can be unnerving, and sometimes a large population of these guys can actually do some damage. But for the most part, spittlebugs are just unsightly. Hose the spit off the plant, or ignore it.

Earwigs: I'll probably get some mail on this one, but I don't worry about earwigs. No, they don't crawl up in your ears while you sleep (unless you sleep on the ground regularly), and I've never seen them do any damage. They like to hide under just about anything: garden ornaments, bee skeps (I started calling my bee skep an earwig skep during one really bad summer!), trays in the greenhouse, whatever. They look quite ferocious with their little pincers, but those are for fending off ant attacks. If you do notice that they are damaging your plants, spray with insecticidal soap.

How to Handle Fungal, Viral, and Bacterial Infections

Diseases are much more difficult to diagnose than bug problems, and they're more frustrating to deal with.

Here's the lowdown on the worst offenders in the herb garden.

Damping off: We talked about this one in the section on seed starting. Caused by too much moisture, the stems of seedlings flop over and die. This disease can wipe out a whole flat of seedlings in no time. To prevent it, don't keep your seedlings too moist. Provide good air circulation, and water with chamomile tea regularly. Chamomile tea is also the best treatment for damping off in the early stages—if you have any seedlings left!

Powdery mildew: One of the most unsightly problems in herb gardens, especially in humid areas, powdery mildew can also be a problem in greenhouses. It's a grayish-white, powdery substance on the leaves and flowers of many plants, including beebalm, valerian, roses, tansy, lemon balm, calendula, and tarragon. While it won't kill established plants in the garden, it can cause severe damage to potted plants. Prevent it by giving your plants good air circulation, giving them full sun instead of moist and shady spots, and keeping the area weed free. When mildew does strike, spray with a mixture of one teaspoon baking soda mixed with one quart water. (This mix also kills black spot on roses.) If that doesn't work, cut the plants back to the ground; healthy new growth should appear.

Rust: One of the few problems to plague mints, rusty-looking orange spots appear on the leaves. Immediately cut the plants back to the ground, and burn the cuttings. *But don't add it to the compost pile!* You'll just spread the disease. If the rust reappears, you'll have to dig up and discard your whole mint bed and start over with new plants in a whole new spot. To prevent this disaster from happening in the first place, never put fresh manure on your mint bed—it's the leading cause of rust. Rust also affects beebalm, germander, roses, and yarrow.

Crown rot: If your herbs are planted too deeply (especially ones with taproots and shallow crowns), the crown of the plant won't get enough air and will rot away, killing the plant. You may see a red or light brown crust on the soil surface around the plants; the plants yellow, wilt, and die. Prevent by not planting too deeply; if it strikes, dig up and burn the plant.

"Melting Out": The dog days of summer also bring heat and humidity, which can bring on a variety of foliar diseases that can turn herbs to black mush. Take care not to overwater if you see the beginnings of rot; cut out the affected foliage and discard. Increase air circulation and mulch with material that drains well, like gravel. Especially susceptible herbs include sweet woodruff, southernwood, thymes, lamb's ears, artemisias and yarrows.

There are many other diseases that can affect herb plants; often there is no treatment except promptly pulling up and burning the plant. Don't compost them because many disease organisms can survive even hot compost piles. Keep your garden clean and free of debris; try not to water in the evening—foliar diseases spread in damp, cool conditions, like on wet plants at night; don't cultivate or weed when plants are wet; remove diseased leaves early on—don't let the disease spread; keep pests under control, because they can spread these diseases; mulch with compost, which contains organisms that help keep diseases at bay; and thoroughly clean up your garden each fall.

Nutrient Deficiencies and Cultural Problems

Not all problems can be blamed on pests or diseases. Sometimes plants can have nutrient deficiencies or simple lack of water or sun. Many nutrition and cultural problems look just like diseases or pest problems. Here are a few common problems.

Nitrogen deficiency: Older, lower leaves are affected first; they become pale green to yellow, and later the entire plant is lighter than normal. Veins may be brown or purple on the underside of the leaf. Leaves eventually turn yellow and drop. Top dressing with compost may be sufficient to fix the problem; for a quick fix, spray with liquid seaweed or fish emulsion. For severe deficiencies, dig in bloodmeal around roots.

Phosphorus deficiency: This is one of the easier nutrition problems to identify. The leaves turn purplish to blue-green, especially along veins, stems, and twigs. Plants are spindly, slow-growing, and produce few or no flowers. This can be caused by too-low pH in acid soils; add lime or bonemeal when planting. Amend with plenty of compost; compost tea is a quick fix.

Potassium deficiency: One of the more difficult problems to diagnose, potassium deficiency can look like many other fungal diseases. Older leaves develop yellow patches, with brown tips and brown spots near the margins. Leaves can appear scorched. General growth is poor, with small leaves, thin shoots, and weak roots. Amend the soil with compost or rotted manure; if a soil test indicates it's needed, add kelp meal, granite dust, greensand, or wood ashes, which also raise the soil's pH.

Iron deficiency: More of a problem for acid-loving plants, this occurs when the soil pH is too high (too alkaline) for their needs. First affected are youngest leaves on upper shoots, which become light yellow between the veins. The veins themselves remain normal green. To control, add aged manure, compost, or peat moss into soil around plants. Add sulfur to soil to reduce pH if necessary.

Too little water: This is mostly a problem in drought-prone areas, but it can strike anywhere a plant doesn't get enough water. Wilting is an obvious symptom—water ASAP! But lack of water can also cause stunted growth and pale leaves. Water soon, and mulch to retain moisture.

Too much water: Believe it or not, one of the symptoms of overwatering is wilted leaves! The difference is that the soil is obviously moist. Yellow leaves are another common symptom, because the roots aren't getting any oxygen. Fungus gnats may thrive in these conditions. Houseplants that get "too much love" are especially susceptible. Let the soil dry out between waterings, and repot if necessary.

Not enough sun: Are your plants tall and spindly, reaching for the light? Well, that means they need more light! Move them to a sunnier spot.

Too much sun: On the other hand, if certain plants that need partial shade are getting too much sun, they also may show signs of stunted growth, and the leaves may appear scorched. Move them to a shadier spot.

Frost damage/winter kill: Late frosts (or planting too early!) can cause damage to tender new growth, even killing it. Leaves may turn black, especially on basil. If the frost was not too severe, new growth may replace the old, but the plant will be set back.

Winter kill has many causes: Winter temps going lower than normal can kill marginally hardy plants; frost heaves can toss plants out of the ground, exposing the roots to freezing temperatures; and ice can cover the stems of woody perennials and cause tip dieback. Mulch well in fall after the ground freezes; pray for snow.

Organically Acceptable Pesticides and Fungicides

Here's a quick rundown of the natural pesticides and fungicides that are considered acceptable in organic gardening. Keep in mind that even some of these can be harmful if not used correctly, so please follow the label directions.

Characteristics of Popular Mulches

PRODUCT	ACTION
Bt (*bacillus thuringiensis*)	Several varieties available—specific to target pests (e.g. caterpillars, mosquitoes); not harmful to humans, pets, or beneficial insects.
Milky Spore (*Bacillus popilliae*)	Type of Bt specific to Japanese beetles and their relatives.
Summer Oil (Superior Oil)	Controls aphids, spider mites, scales, mealybugs by smothering them. Can be used on fully leafed plants. Use only at temps below 85°F. Test for leaf damage before widespread use.
Diatomaceous earth	Nontoxic mineral powder that pierces soft bodied insects like slugs.
Insecticidal Soap	Available as liquid concentrate; formulated from fatty acids that kill aphids, whiteflies, spider mites. Spray every 2 to 3 days for bad infestations. May cause damage if plants are drought or heat stressed.
Pyrethrums	Plant-based insecticides that are effective on suckers, chompers, and flies and mosquitoes. Toxic to mammals and fish; don't apply around ponds or waterways.
Rotenone	Nonselective poison effective against most chompers and many suckers, but highly toxic to animals, birds, and fish, and can cause allergic reactions in some people. Wear a face mask and rubber gloves when using.
Hot Pepper Spray	Use as a repellent for chewing insects. Blend ½ cup hot peppers with 2 cups water. Strain and spray. (Use caution—hot peppers can burn skin and eyes.)
Bug Juice	It takes bugs to beat bugs! Collect ½ cup of the bug that's bugging you and in an old blender, mix with 2 cups water. Strain, add a few drops of soap, then mix ¼ cup of this mixture with 2 cups water, and spray.
Copper	Controls many diseases; available as dust, sprayable solution, or wettable powder. Toxic to people and animals, skin irritant. Use carefully.
Fungicidal Soap	To control powdery mildew, black spot, leaf spot, and rust; available as liquid concentrate. Nontoxic to humans and mammals.

CHAPTER 24

When Summer Ends

It seems like just yesterday you put your garden in, but summer has already sped by! The days are getting shorter, and the air has that familiar crispness to it. Before you know it, it's fall again. And while that may signal an end to gardening for many people, it doesn't have to be the end for the herb gardener. A windowsill herb garden is a wonderful way to enjoy the cheer of gardening even in the snowy winter.

Bringing in Your Garden for the Winter

Not every herb in your garden is a perfect candidate for the move indoors, but many make terrific houseplants. And many herbs that wouldn't make it through their first frosty night outdoors can live for years in a container. Unless you'd like to buy new ones every year, it makes sense to pot up and bring in bay laurel, rosemary, lemon verbena, tricolor sage, sweet marjoram, French lavender, and scented gera-niums in the fall. An even better solution is to leave it in a pot year round, repotting to a larger size every spring or fall. This latter method is much easier on the plant because of the reduced transplant shock. Let them spend the summer outdoors, on the patio or in the garden, and just bring the pot inside for winter.

Of course, our friends in toasty zones 8 through 10 don't have to worry much about this part; their herb gardens are productive year round. But for the rest of us, here are the facts.

How to Decide What to Bring in, When, and How to Do It

When deciding what to bring in and what to leave outside, keep these pointers in mind:

- Is the herb an annual, whose useful life is about over anyway, or is it a perennial you'd like to keep for years? You'll probably want to keep

Herbs that *must* be brought inside if they are to survive in most areas include bay laurel, lemon verbena, eucalyptus, curry plant, lemon grass, dittany of Crete, pennyroyal, vicks plant, Cuban oregano, sweet marjoram, French thyme, pineapple sage, fringed and French lavenders, heliotrope, curry plant, rosemary (north of zone 6), and scented geraniums.

those with sentimental value, those that you've pampered through the summer, and any that were expensive, such as bay laurel or scented geraniums.

- Is the plant huge in the garden? If so, it may be better to try to take cuttings rather than bringing in the whole plant. On the other hand, prostrate rosemary, dittany of Crete, and eucalyptus look great as houseplants.
- How much window space do you have? If your only sunny windowsill is in the upstairs bath, it

may not be worthwhile for you to bring in dozens of pots of kitchen herbs.

- Is the plant diseased or pest-ridden? It's better to replace these next spring than to have a houseful of bugs.

Two Indoor Heavy Hitters

Two of the most familiar herbal houseplants are rosemary and bay. They make wonderful houseplants, but there are a couple of things you should keep in mind about their care.

ROSEMARY

Some people grow rosemary as an annual. But, properly cared for, a rosemary plant can live for many years, reaching up to six feet even in a container. Rosemary can live outdoors all year long as far north as zone 6, but it generally can't take the harsh temperatures of northern winters. The most important thing to remember about growing rosemary indoors is not to let the pot dry out completely. The reasons so many people lose their plants during the winter are one, underwatering them, and two, placing them in too warm an area. Keep the soil evenly moist, and when the days start getting longer, make sure they're getting enough water. Rosemarys also appreciate occasional misting.

Rosemary goes through a period of dormancy in early winter—usually between Christmas and Valentine's Day—when you should not feed it at all, and only give it enough water to keep it from drying out. But keep an eye on it, because as the light begins to increase in February, rosemary will "wake up" and begin needing more water. You'll know dormancy is over when a little new growth appears. Make sure you water the plant enough, because it's easy to get used to the lower watering schedule of dormancy.

BAY LAUREL

In their native habitat of the Mediterranean, bay trees are full-sized trees. Grown in containers they won't reach their full potential, but they're quite long-lived and can attain a height of five to six feet. This can take years, though, because bays are slow growers and really should stay in their pots year round. This herb can get by with a little less light; allow the soil to dry between waterings. If the plant is attacked by scale, scrape the insects off with your fingernail, then wash the plant off in the sink.

Rosemary and bay are two of the essentials of the windowsill herb garden; thyme and sage are two more that make delightful additions to the kitchen. With the exception of tricolor sage, most varieties of thyme and sage are hardy up north, but they are so easy to grow indoors that it would be a shame to live without them all winter. Unless the plants are huge, they're easily popped into a container and brought inside. If they *are* huge, you can either take cuttings or divide them in late summer.

Of course, some herbs are too large, or must go through a dormancy period. It's really not worth it

to bring these in: dill, fennel, beebalm, lovage, tarragon, lemon balm, chamomile, and borage.

And finally, there are herbs that need the dormancy period. Some are tender annuals or somewhat tricky to keep inside, but they're worth the effort: chives, garlic chives, mints, cilantro, parsley, basil, and oregano.

> The *dormancy period* refers to the need for some plants to go through an annual freezing as part of their cycle. These include chives and tarragon. Pot them up first and leave them outside. They lose their foliage after frost, but put out a fresh growth when brought inside.

With all this in mind, remember that it's your herb garden, and if you want to try something different than what I recommend here, go for it! Some people have great luck with everything they bring in, and some don't. If there's any doubt about the winter hardiness or indoor suitability of a certain plant, try taking cuttings rather than potting up the whole thing.

When and How to Bring Your Herbs In

At least two weeks before the expected first frost, prepare a porous potting mix that will be well drained. A combination of equal parts peat moss, coarse vermiculite, and compost will usually give good results.

Dig the plants *gently*, shaking some but not all of the soil from the roots. Make sure your pots are large enough to accommodate the whole root system. This is also a good time to divide large clumps, either for replanting or sharing with friends. Place the herb in the pot, water thoroughly, and set in a shady outdoor spot for at least three days. Also at this time, check for any "hitchhikers" you'll need to get rid of before bringing the plant in. A good (but gentle) hosing off is probably a good idea, too, but for some insect pests you may need to spray with insecticidal soap. *Never* use chemical pesticides on any herb you will be using for food.

The preparation for the winter should mirror the hardening-off process in the spring: Bring the plants inside on cool nights, and let them stay out during the day. You only need to do this for a few days before bringing them in for good. They should all be safely indoors by the first frost.

> The key is to not let them get too acclimated to cool temperatures before they come inside to the warm, stale air of the typical home in winter.

Taking Cuttings for Indoors

When a tender plant is just too big for your kitchen window, the best way to save it for next year's garden is to keep root cuttings. Good candidates for cuttings for the winter windowsill include mints, pineapple sage, scented geraniums, and any other plant that has gotten so large that digging up the whole thing would be too difficult and space consuming. You might also want to take cuttings of certain plants that you *think* can make it through a winter outdoors, but you'd like to be sure you'll have some for next spring, just in case.

For a more detailed discussion of taking cuttings see Chapter 19, but for now, here's a quick recap. Take a five-inch cutting from the end of a vigorously growing, but not yet woody, stem. Strip the lower leaves from the stem to encourage rooting and to prevent rot.

The rooting medium should consist of equal parts peat moss, vermiculite, perlite, and compost, although many people just use plain sharp sand or vermiculite only. Some people also dip the cutting, either in a rooting hormone (try to find an organic one), a "tea" made from willow bark, or a very weak solution of liquid seaweed. I use the latter method. Stick the stem into the rooting medium and firm the soil around the stem. To conserve moisture, place a plastic bag loosely over the cutting in the pot. Do *not* allow the plastic to touch the plant! Place out of direct sun. An alternative to the tent is hand misting several times a day.

Different herbs have different rooting times, ranging from two to more than six weeks. New growth indicates that roots have formed. Remove the tent and gradually introduce more sunlight and water to your new plant.

Caring for Your Windowsill Herbs

Once your newly potted herbs are inside, there are just a few things to keep in mind:

First and foremost, you'll need a sunny window. Most herbs need at least five hours of direct sun a day. A south-facing window is by far the best, with east- and west-facing windows the next choice. Most herbs won't tolerate a north-facing or mostly shaded window. And whichever direction your window faces, any foliage that touches a freezing pane of glass will freeze and die.

Second is water. Keep the soil evenly moist—not soggy, which promotes root rot, especially in thymes, but not dry, either. Feel the soil surface with your fingers before you water. Your herbs will appreciate an occasional misting, especially if you heat with wood and the humidity levels in your home are very low. If possible, place the pots in trays filled with pebbles and water to increase the humidity right around the plants.

Third is temperature. Most herbs prefer slightly cooler temperatures than other houseplants, ranging from daytime low seventies to nighttime fifties, although some can take forties.

Fourth is fertilizing. When you first pot them up, you may want to give them all a little diluted fish emulsion or liquid seaweed for a boost before the winter. As light levels diminish, growth will slow down or stop. Don't feed at all until late winter, when you start to see some new growth.

Fifth is pests. Sometimes if the plants are stressed (and just being indoors is stressful for them), they become fair game to insect pests. The easiest and cheapest method I've found to get rid of most pests, including aphids, spider mites, and whiteflies, is a bath in the kitchen sink. The bugs wash right down the drain! Just be sure to wash the undersides of leaves, where the bugs lay their eggs. For larger pots, put them in the bathtub or shower. The other winter problem is powdery mildew on rosemary. You can wash this off, too—or snip it, if the plant is big enough—but for a severe infestation, use the baking soda spray recipe in Chapter 23. This formula really works, although you may need to repeat it every couple of weeks.

Putting the Beds to Bed

You've got your indoor herbs all taken care of; now what about the rest of the outdoor gardens? Fall cleanup can be as easy as ignoring the whole thing after the harvest or as complicated as cutting back all perennials, pulling spent annuals up, adding compost or manure, and finally, mulching.

You can even tackle large projects, like creating and planting new beds—making sure you aren't planting tender herbs too late in the season, of course. Let's just plunge in, shall we?

THE LAZY WAY OUT

After your first frosts, there will be a lot of dead stuff. If that doesn't bother you, leave it. Not everything will succumb to the very first frost, though, so you can still harvest some of the cold, hardy herbs like mint, thyme, sage, and chervil. The cheerful blooms of calendula will continue far into autumn, as will Johnny-jump-ups. Enjoy this time in your garden, and try not to think about all the work you're leaving yourself in the spring . . .

What I mean by that is that if you leave the tall stalks of the mints, comfrey, tansy, wormwood, etc. for the winter, they are still going to be there to greet you in the spring. It just depends on how much energy you have left to cut them down, and whether you want it to be now or later.

The one big benefit of leaving everything standing now is that the seedheads of flowers like echinacea, calendula, and many others can become a cheap and easy birdfeeder, providing not just food but protection for birds.

Another benefit in the snow belt is that the standing tops can catch the snow and hold it in place. And of course, snow is the best winter insulator of all!

LATE FALL CLEANING

Some people, on the other hand, can't stand a messy-looking garden at any time of year, win-ter included. That's fine, too. It can also be a great excuse to get outside in the cool crisp weather.

Late fall garden cleanup for the inspired includes cutting back all herbaceous perennials to about an inch from the ground, gathering up the clippings, and composting them. Don't cut back your woody perennials like sage or lavender by more than a third; the plant needs its wood to get it through the winter. For tips on how to use what you do cut, see Chapter 25.

> If you have a problem with diseases or pests, a thorough fall cleanup is essential for keeping them under control.

Now is also a good time to gather seeds from both annuals and perennials. Dry them thoroughly, and store them in an airtight container in the freezer.

After the tender annuals have given up the ghost to frosts, pull them up and compost them, too. This is a good time to add manure or compost to your newly manicured beds and to top-dress the perennials. The timing can be a little tricky on this part. You'll want to wait until things have gone dormant, or you may spur some new growth that will be quickly killed by frost. This can weaken even established perennials—and it's just not very nice!

Early autumn is a great time to divide overgrown perennials, move things that need moving, and even put in new perennial herbs. Don't wait until too late in the season, though, because they need some time for their root systems to get settled in before the cold nights put them to sleep. I've put in new plants as late as daffodil-planting time, with only a few casualties.

Winter Protection

In mulching for winter protection, you mainly want to defend your plants against alternate freezing and thawing, frost heaves, and drying winds. You can do this with layers of straw or hay—salt hay is best, but hard to find and expensive—evergreen boughs, or both. Some people push back the tops of the plants to place the straw on the ground, then cover the tops with evergreen boughs. For more information on mulching, see Chapter 21.

> Do not mulch until several frosts have frozen the top inch or two of soil. Otherwise you'll end up with a lovely haven for rodents, who will eat the very plants you're trying to protect!

Some hardy herbaceous perennials don't need any winter protection at all; others need a moderate covering, and still others need a very thick blanket—it all depends on where you live. For guidance in your own region, ask other gardeners, your local herb nursery, or your local extension office. Compare the hardiness zone given for the individual plants to your own zone. If the plant is close or a zone higher, the more protection it needs. If you are in a warmer zone than is listed, no protection at all may be necessary. For example, if you live in Arkansas (zone 7), you won't need to mulch your chives at all—they're hardy to zone 3! But you'll still need to be careful with bay, rosemary, and lemon verbena (zones 8 and 9).

Harvest Time!

Well, you've done it! You planned, planted, and tended your herb garden all summer, and now the bounty is coming in. Here are some easy ways to handle your harvest.

7

CHAPTER 25

What to Do with All These Herbs!

Summertime is the best time to begin your herbal harvest, so I hope you read this chapter before the first frost! You should actually begin to think about your harvest as early as June (earlier in warmer areas) to get the highest levels of essential oils. Don't wait until they're all gone to start picking.

General Picking Tips for Culinary, Medicinal, and Crafts

Here are some basic guidelines for you to follow, whether you're picking basil for tonight's pesto or gathering your large, end-of-season harvest.

- The general rule of thumb is to harvest just before flowering. That's when the essentials oils are most concentrated and the leaves tender and sweet. After flowering, the foliage diminishes; it becomes smaller, tougher, and sometimes changes color.
- Reserve your first cutting for cooking, tea, and medicinal uses. Use your second cutting for crafts—except flowers!
- Cut with your pruners, sharp scissors, or a garden knife; don't pull.
- Choose a dry day, in the morning after the dew has dried but before the hot sun evaporates the oils. Dew doesn't actually hurt anything, but it makes your drying time longer—same with rain.

But, you should pick edible flowers while they are still dewy; choose perfect blossoms when they have just opened—not yesterday's bloom, if you can help it.

For large harvests, cut annuals when they're about five inches high. Take no more than the top half of a plant at any one time. Cut perennials when they're four to six inches high, taking up to two-thirds of the foliage at once. This is different from the end of season amounts—see below.

On the other hand, you can take snippets of leaves and flowers continuously if they're just for tonight's recipe.

Herbaceous perennials can be cut back to ground at the end of the season *only* (right before killing frost).

Cut first year plants sparingly; they need time to get established.

> You should stop cutting a month before first frost in cold climates because the plants use their foliage to manufacture food to subsist through the winter, which they store in their roots.

Try to harvest clean foliage; if it's dirty, hose it off first and wait until it's dry to cut it. Avoid washing if at all possible (except in obvious cases like pine pollen time, if you live on a dusty road, etc.).

By the way, mulching helps keep plants so clean you may not need to wash at all!

- Don't pick bug-infested or diseased foliage, obviously.
- Cut only what you can deal with right now. If it wilts before you can clean it and dry it, it will be ruined.
- Label! This goes hand in hand with the previous tip; don't cut so much that you can't remember what you've got, and if you're doing a large harvest, process (cut, gather, bunch) each herb all at once so you can label it correctly.

Harvesting Culinary Herbs

Since most people grow herbs primarily for culinary uses, that's where we'll start.

FRESH IS BEST

Once you've cooked with fresh herbs, you'll never go back to that ageless stuff on supermarket shelves. Most commercially packaged herbs are imported from foreign countries, shipped here in huge bales, fumigated and sprayed, then processed into little glass jars that sit for who knows how long? No thanks, I'll just pop out to the garden, thank you.

Using fresh herbs is also the reason I suggested way back in Chapter 4 that you place your herb garden right by the kitchen door—so you can run out and get a snip of this and a pinch of that. And there's nothing like pesto made from your own fresh basil!

> There are some herbs that are better suited to fresh use. Some don't dry well, or they may lose their texture and flavor. Among these are:
>
> - angelica
> - chervil
> - cilantro
> - good King Henry
> - salad burnet
> - sorrel
> - all edible flowers
> - most salad herbs

Regular cutting from your herb plants also encourages new growth.

Fresh herbs can be used in a multitude of ways: sprinkled on salads, as herb blossoms for garnish, or rubbed on meat or fish before grilling.

Use the guidelines above in picking your fresh herbs for cooking. You can store most herbs in a glass of water in the fridge until you're ready to use them, or wrap them up in a damp paper towel. Of course, if you've been at work all day and you didn't have a chance to pop home at ten a.m. to pick your herbs, it's not that big a deal. You can really pick any time for fresh use; it's just not at its peak of perfection after noon.

You should plan to use fresh herbs for culinary projects like herb butters, vinegars, oils, jellies, and honeys, as well as candied herb flowers.

How much to pick? Consult your recipe first. If it calls for dried herbs, you'll need to double that amount for fresh herbs. And remember that you won't be using the stems of most herbs, just the leaves, so take that into account when picking. If you have leftovers, you can always use them for garnish!

FREEZING YOUR HARVEST

If you have a larger harvest, a great option is to freeze it. This works very well for things that don't dry very attractively, like basil. It still isn't beautiful, but it sure works well. You can use frozen herbs much as you would fresh.

To freeze your harvest, use only freshly gathered herbs. Strip the foliage from the stems of basil,

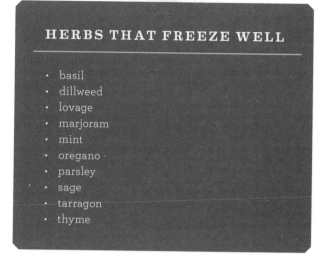

HERBS THAT FREEZE WELL

- basil
- dillweed
- lovage
- marjoram
- mint
- oregano
- parsley
- sage
- tarragon
- thyme

tarragon, sage, and rosemary; more delicate sprigs like thyme, parsley, and dill can be frozen whole.

The leaves should be clean; use a paintbrush to clean them off rather than washing them in the sink. If you must wash, make sure the foliage is completely dry before freezing—it can be damaged by residual water.

There's an ongoing debate about whether or not you should blanch herbs before freezing. The color may stay greener, but you'll lose some flavor. I don't blanch, and I haven't had a problem, but your experience may be different. If you'd like to blanch your herbs, just pour boiling water over them for one second. *Don't* plunge them into cold water to cool; it may dilute the flavors.

Spread out the herbs on a cookie sheet one layer thick, and freeze for a few hours. Once they're frozen you can put them in freezer bags. Be sure to label them! You can also mince fresh herbs (by hand or with a food processor) then freeze them on cookie sheets or in ice cube trays.

> Don't leave your frozen herbs unsealed for too long in the freezer; they could get freezer burn and become useless as seasonings.

Another neat trick for freezing is to make an herb paste. This works especially well with basil. In a food processor, mince the herb, adding a little olive or other vegetable oil at a time until the mixture forms a paste. Freeze in ice cube trays, then pop into freezer bags. The cubes can be used in sauces, soups, and stews, and they will taste very close to fresh!

> Whether chives freeze well or not depends on whom you ask. I've had very good luck freezing chives. I cut them up first, then freeze them using a cookie sheet, putting it all in containers after it's thoroughly frozen. Give it a try and see if it works for you.

DRIED HERBS

Dried herbs are probably the most familiar to most of us, and drying is still the most common way to preserve the harvest for culinary, medicinal, and craft purposes. There are a couple of things to keep in mind when drying any herbs; we'll get to the specifics of each type in a moment.

You want to dry your herbs as soon as possible after picking to maintain aroma and color. Make sure you start with dry foliage—I mean no moisture *on* the leaves!

During the drying process, keep the herbs out of light; it will fade their color. The best place is warm, dry, and dark, with good ventilation.

High humidity is your worst enemy. If it's too high, your herbs won't dry but will turn moldy instead. If you must, choose an air conditioned or dehumidified room over a room with high humidity. And did you know that dried herbs can even *reabsorb* moisture in very humid weather?

Maintain good air circulation. Use a fan on low speed if you have to!

If you're drying on screens, turning the herbs regularly will speed drying times.

Your herbs are ready when they are crispy dry. There should be no flexibility left in the leaves; check the stem attachment to be sure.

Drying Culinary Herbs

Most herbs are suitable for drying, but some, like bay and tarragon, are even better dried than fresh! Quick drying is preferable to slow, to retain flavors. Listed below are some of the tried-and-true methods.

CULINARY HERBS THAT DRY WELL

- dill
- lemon balm
- lemon verbena
- mints
- oregano
- parsley
- rosemary
- sage
- savory
- sweet marjoram
- thyme

There are quite a few effective methods for drying herbs, some better than others. Each has its advantages and disadvantages.

HANGING TOUGH

This is the romantic, old-fashioned way to dry your herbs—and the easiest! Gather your herbs into bunches (about one-inch diameter; no more or the center won't dry properly), and tie the stems with rubber bands. Hang them up on rafters, out of the direct sun. Depending on the weather conditions (warmth, humidity, etc.) and the type of herb, they can be dry within a week or two. While this is a very decorative way to go, if your house is dusty, or your bunches are hanging in the kitchen where there is lots of humidity and grease in the air, you'll want to remove the bunches as soon as they're dry. Please don't let them hang so long they get cobwebs!

The best herbs for hanging include lemon balm, mints, marjoram, oregano, sage, and savory.

SCREEN TEST

Here's a cool idea: Use an old window screen to dry your herbs! It's a great way to dry herbs with short stems and small leaves, loose blossoms, or delicate herbs that might not hold up to hanging. Put a layer of paper towels underneath if the plants are already falling apart. Just spread out the herb one layer thick on the screen and place in a warm, dark, dry place—preferably one where the cat/dog/baby won't get in and tip over the screen! If you have an unused room, a well-ventilated barn, or an attic, those are all good choices. Turn the herbs every once in a while to speed the process up. Some people even put the screen in their hot car for a few hours!

The main disadvantage to screen drying is the mess it can make if it tips over.

OVEN DRYING

I think oven drying is one of the best methods, since it's quick and even.

Get the cookie sheets out again, and spread the herbs one layer deep on a sheet or two of paper towels. If you have a gas oven, the pilot light may provide enough heat to dry on its own; in electric ovens, set the temperature between 80 and 100 degrees. Place the herbs inside, and leave the door ajar to let the moisture escape. Stir every half hour, and in three to six hours, the herbs should be all dry. Keep in mind that fleshy leaves (basil) will dry more slowly than thin leaves (dill). Make sure you remove the herbs from the oven before they turn brown; remember—you're drying them, not cooking them!

MICROWAVING

This is a great, quick method for drying if you have a limited amount of harvest. If you have baskets and baskets, think twice before using the microwave.

To do it, first strip the herbs off the stems, and place them between sheets of paper towels on a microwave-safe plate. Put a cup of water in the back of the oven. Nuke for one minute on defrost or low, watching constantly. Don't put too much in at once, or it won't dry evenly. Check to see if it needs more time; after the initial minute, only go for fifteen to twenty seconds. This can really go quickly!

The two disadvantages to nuking are the limitations of how much you can do at once; and the fact that on some herbs like basil, if the leaf stem gets too hot, it could catch the paper towel on fire! This has happened to me twice; it may have been that I forgot to put in the cup of water.

FOOD DEHYDRATORS

This is one of my favorite methods for drying herbs. It takes less energy than using the oven, and even though it takes a little longer, you can mix different herbs in a batch—on separate trays, of course! It gives terrific results, especially with basil. I have found other methods of drying basil end up giving you blackened leaves, but the dehydrator always retains the green.

There are many dehydrators on the market, in a variety of price ranges, but my favorite for home use is one with a fan. It really makes a difference if the air is well-circulated. If you are seriously into drying large harvests, consider investing in one of the commercial types. They are expensive but worth it.

The directions are much the same as for oven drying: Strip large leaves off the stems; spread one layer thick; stir occasionally; check frequently. It can take as little as three hours or as long as twelve hours to complete drying. Rearranging the trays can help speed things up, moving the tray that needs the most drying to the bottom where the heat is.

> Did you know that dried herbs should be replaced every year? So, that twenty-five-year-old jar of thyme from your grandmother's kitchen is safe to throw away—it won't season anything any more!

SALT OR SUGAR PACK

Here's a neat, old-fashioned way to preserve herbs, and it's incredibly easy! This method works especially well with basil, chives, dill, garlic, marjoram, oregano, rosemary, savory, tarragon, and thyme, but nearly any culinary herb will work.

HERBS FOR SUGAR PACK

- anise hyssop
- beebalm
- borage
- lemon verbena
- mints
- pineapple sage
- scented geraniums

SEEDS TO DRY

- anise
- caraway
- coriander
- cumin
- dill
- fennel

HERE'S HOW

1. Pour a layer of salt (or sugar) into an airtight container.
2. Alternate layers of fresh (clean and dry) herbs and salt or sugar, making the bottom and top layers of salt a little thicker.
3. Cover tightly and store on a cool, dry shelf.

See? I told you it was easy! You'll end up with two products here; the actual dried herbs, and the herb-flavored salt or sugar, both of which can be used in cooking. You may find that you'll use less salt in cooking by using the flavored version.

You need to watch the plants carefully after flowering, or the seeds will fall onto the ground and be lost. Harvest the seeds as they turn brown, but keep in mind that they won't all ripen at the same time.

Cut off the whole seed head and place it in a paper bag to catch the seeds as they fall off. Hang up the bag and wait a couple of weeks. (You may want to poke holes in the sides of the bag for ventilation, but I generally don't bother.) Once they're all dry, strip any remaining seeds from the stems and discard any chaff. Store them in an airtight container.

If you see any insect hitchhikers on your seeds, heat the seeds in the oven at 350 degrees for one minute, or blanch them in a cheesecloth bag in boiling water for one minute. You need only do this for seeds for the kitchen, because these methods will kill the seed embryo as well, permanently preventing germination.

DRYING HERB SEEDS

There are quite a few herbs that are grown specifically for the seeds.

Drying Medicinals

Drying herbs you plan to use for medicinal purposes is pretty much the same process as for culinary herbs. You want to choose healthy looking foliage and flowers, harvest on a dry day after the dew has dried, and dry the harvest quickly.

As with culinary herbs, you need to know which part of the plant you will be using (foliage, flowers, seeds, etc.) in order to harvest and dry it properly.

Many herbs can be used to make teas (*infusions*), so how they look is not particularly important; what's important is the quality of the essential oils.

If you're really interested in using herbs medicinally, I suggest doing further reading. There are many excellent books on the subject of medicinal herbs. What we're going to cover in *this* book is mainly for "dabblers": those who want to soothe a tummy ache or relax with a cup of chamomile tea before bed.

Drying Ornamentals

The methods for drying ornamentals are similar to those used for culinary and medicinal herbs, but you have a few new options that aren't appropriate for the latter two.

For craft uses such as dried arrangements, wreaths, and tussie mussies, looks are the number one concern, so harvest accordingly. Choose only perfect blossoms and leaves, with no spots. Make sure the blossoms are newly opened so they won't wilt too quickly. For other uses like catnip toys or sachets, you can choose less perfect flowers and leaves to use.

> You should pick these flowers while they're budded but not fully open. Some of them have a tendency to keep growing and developing past their prime, even after being cut. Picking earlier prevents this.

> ## LET SEED HEADS FORM AND DRY ON PLANT
>
> These can be picked and will probably already be dry enough to just stand up in a vase or basket: nigella, poppies, rue, teasel

SILICA GEL: FOR CRAFTS ONLY

While the drying methods we talked about for culinary and medicinal also work for crafting purposes, one of your new options is the use of silica gel. In the old days, people used borax powder or kitty litter to do this, but with the advent of reusable, clean silica in recent years, the earlier materials have become

FLOWER	BEST DRYING METHODS
delphinium (spike half open/half in bud)	hang
globe thistle	hang
goldenrod	hang
lavender	hang
peony	hang
sweet Joe-Pye weed	hang

obsolete. (Of course that doesn't mean you can't try them!)

Silica is a good method for very small or very large buds that don't do well with traditional methods, like hanging. Among the flowers to try are roses, pinks, bachelor's buttons, and flat flowers like pansies.

Most silica gels come with detailed instructions, but here's a rundown of how it's done:

1. Pour a layer of silica gel into an airtight container.

2. Carefully layer your flowers onto the gel. Make sure you like the placement—that's how they'll dry!

3. Cover the flowers carefully with gel. Some people even spoon it in.

Flowers to Pick Open or at Prime	
FLOWER	BEST DRYING METHODS
artemisia	hang
bachelors buttons	silica gel/microwave
beebalm	hang/screen
calendula	hang/screen
celosia	hang
chives (before seeds form)	hang
feverfew	hang/screen
lady's mantle	hang
lamb's ears (flower spikes)	hang
larkspur	hang
marigolds	hang
pinks	silica gel/microwave
roses	silica gel/microwave
sweet marjoram	hang
tansy	hang
thyme	hang
violets, Johnny-jump-ups, pansies	silica gel/microwave
wild marjoram (AKA common oregano—pink flowering type)	hang
yarrows	hang

4. Seal the container. Check every few days for dryness. Remove as soon as they are dry. Don't wait too long, or they'll get too dry and crumble when you remove them.

5. Store the flowers in an airtight container until they're ready to use.

After a few uses, put the silica gel in the oven on low to dry it out for its next use.

> Don't EVER use the silica method on herbs you plan to eat!

PRESSING

When employing flowers and foliage for crafts, pressing is another old-time drying method. It's been used for centuries to preserve the harvest, though not in any large quantities. The specimens will usually retain their shapes, colors, and even aromas for years if properly stored.

Good choices for pressing include:

- costmary
- hyssop
- lady's bedstraw
- lady's mantle
- lamb's ears (leaves)
- lavender
- mint
- pennyroyal
- rosemary
- rue
- sage
- scented geranium (cut leaf forms are especially nice)
- thyme
- yarrow

You can use any heavy book to do your pressing; in the old days they always used the Bible, but nowadays you can use telephone books—if you're in a big enough city! Flower presses come with thick pads of cardboard and blotting paper, making them very good choices, too.

Once your herbs are pressed and fairly dry, they can be used in a variety of ways: as bookmarks (by themselves or laminated); découpaged onto notepaper, cards, as Christmas decorations or jewelry; arranged onto velvet backing and framed—this was a wonderful childhood pastime I remember doing with my grandmother!—or carefully painted and printed onto watercolor paper to make herb prints.

FOR PROFESSIONAL DRYERS ONLY: FREEZE DRYING

Roses, peonies, and fruit are popular materials for dried arrangements, swags, etc., but the process of freeze drying these flowers is dramatically different from our home method of freezing chives. It involves *very* expensive equipment that only professional flower processors have access to. It's best to just spend the extra bucks and splurge on the store-bought ones.

Storage

You've gone to all this trouble to dry your herbs for cooking, medicinal, and craft use, now you need to store them properly or they'll fade to uselessness.

There are a few rules that apply to everything you've dried:

- Store in an airtight container. It can be Tupperware, a tightly sealed tin, screw-top jars, or Ziploc bags, but it must be airtight.
- Store in a dark place; light will fade the color right out of dried material.
- No heat, no steam. This is a rule that applies mainly to kitchen herbs, because the most obvious place to store herbs is right over the stove, right? Well, it's a really bad choice. The steam and grease that cooking generates quickly deteriorates even herbs that are stored in airtight jars. Do us all a favor, and find another spot.
- Specifically for culinary and medicinal herbs: Once the herb is crispy dry, your natural inclination will be to crumble it before you package it. Resist this urge! Try to leave the foliage as intact as possible to retain the flavor. You can strip them off their stems, but leave the leaves intact.
- Same with seeds: Store them whole until they're ready to use, in order to keep the flavor at its best.

Glass jars are a good storage container for your herbs because you can check them for moisture. If moisture appears on the inside of the glass, remove the herb from the jar immediately and dry, dry, again. Otherwise it'll all get moldy and your efforts will be down the drain.

When you're ready to use the herbs, you have several choices: You can pulverize them with your fingers (only good for small amounts); grind them in an old-fashioned mortar and pestle; or grind them in a newfangled coffee or spice grinder. We have two grinders, one for coffee and one for herbs. It's a really good idea to keep them separated.

Replace the leafy herbs every year—that'll be easy with such a bountiful harvest, right? The herb seeds can last as long as three years.

Bremness, Leslie. *The Complete Book of Herbs*. New York: Penguin Group, 1988.

Brown, Deni. *Encyclopedia of Herbs and Their Uses*. New York: DK Publishing Inc., 1995.

Damrosch, Barbara. *The Garden Primer*. New York: Workman Publishing, 1988.

DeBaggio, Thomas. *Growing Herbs From Seed, Cutting and Root*. Loveland, CO: Interweave Press, 1994.

Foster, Steven. *Herbal Renaissance*. Salt Lake City, UT: Gibbs-Smith, 1995.

Hynes, Erin. *Rodale's Successful Organic Gardening: Controlling Weeds*. Emmaus, PA: Rodale Press, 1993.

Hynes, Erin. *Rodale's Successful Organic Gardening: Improving the Soil*. Emmaus, PA: Rodale Press, 1994.

Michalak, Patricia S. *Rodale's Successful Organic Gardening: Herbs*. Emmaus, PA: Rodale Press, 1993.

Michalak, Patricia S. *Rodale's Successful Organic Gardening: Controlling Pests and Diseases*. Emmaus, PA: Rodale Press, 1994.

Mornis, Risa. *An Herbal Feast*. New Canaan, CT: Keats Publishing, 1998.

Rodale's Illustrated Encyclopedia of Herbs. Emmaus, PA: Rodale Press, 1987.

Rodale's All-New Encyclopedia of Organic Gardening. Emmaus, PA: Rodale Press, 1992.

Shaudys, Phyllis V. *Herbal Treasures*. Pownal, VT: Storey Communications, 1990.

Simmons, Adelma Grenier. *Herb Gardening in Five Seasons*. New York: Plume (Penguin Group), 1964.

ACKNOWLEDGMENTS

I want to begin by thanking my literary agent, Jeanne Fredericks, for never giving up on this book or on me. She believed in this project long before I did, and it was by her sheer dogged determination that all these years later, this book is finally seeing the light of day. There are no words to express my appreciation to her. She's been called "the best literary agent in the world," and I wholeheartedly agree! Thanks also to my publisher Countryman Press for taking a chance on a new writer; Editorial Director Ann Treistman for working with Jeanne to breathe new life into this project when no one else would; the incredible Editorial Associate Sarah Bennett for her endless patience while we searched for manuscripts and dealt with family crises during the entire process. She is truly a miracle worker! Thanks to Natalie Eilbert and Devon Zahn and all the copyeditors and designers who transformed the bare manuscript into a work of art; Publicity & Marketing Manager, Devorah Backman; and a huge thank you to all those at W. W. Norton who supported and helped market this book.

Special thanks go to all the authors ancient and modern who paved the way and taught me so much through the years—Hildegard of Bingen, Maude Grieve, Adelma Grenier Simmons, Tasha Tudor, Sharon Lovejoy, Lesley Bremness, Risa Mornis, Barbara Damrosch, Phyllis Shaudys, Steven Foster, Sal Gilbertie, Emelie Tolley, Chris Mead, and countless others who inspired and taught me along the garden path.

And last but certainly not least, I can't forget the love and encouragement of my husband Steve, who taught me to believe in myself, and my children Ian and Virginia, who have shown great patience in the years it has taken to finally see this book in print. When I first finished the very first draft of this manuscript, I was pregnant with my first child. Today, he's about to get his driver's license. This book has truly been a lesson in "Never say never!

A heartfelt thanks to you all!

INDEX

herbs. *See also* culinary
    herbs; seeds (*continued*)
    that root easily in growing
        medium, 191
    that root easily in water, 191
hilltops, 49
hoes, 134–35
hollyhock, 108
honeybees, 227
hops, 113
horehound, 112
horsetail spray, 231
hose fenders, 137
hose reels, 136
hoses, 54, 136–38
hot composting, 148
house architectural style, 62
house drip lines, 65
houseplants, 55, 235–39
hummingbird garden, 81–82
humus, 57, 145. *See also*
    organic matter
hybrids, indication of, 32

I

Indian healing traditions,
    19–21
Industrial Revolution, 27
informal garden designs, 62
informal garden styles, 80–83
insects
    beneficial, types of, 226–27
    chomping, types of, 228–29
    sucking, types of, 227–28
invasive herbs, 69
iron deficiencies, 232
irrigation systems, 54–55,
    137–38
island beds, 65–66
ivy, ground, 119

J

Japanese beetles, 228
Jefferson, Thomas, 26

jewelweed, 117–18
Josselyn, John, 26, 35
journals, 44–45

K

kelp meal, 206–7
kitchen gardens, 85–86
knot gardens, 79, 86

L

Labiatae family, 30–31
ladybugs, 226–27
lady's mantle, 108
lakes, and microclimates, 50
lamb's ear, 16
landscape fabric, 211
landscaping with herbs, 93–97
Latin names, 29–33
Latin words, pronouncing, 33
lavender, 13–14, 107, 114
lawn mowers, 140
lawns, herbal, 94–95
layering (rooting), 193–94
leach fields, 42
leafminers, 228
leaves, of herbs, 36
lemon balm, 104
light
    full sun, 51
    for growing seeds, 173
    lack of (full shade), 51
    and microclimates, 50
    not enough sunlight, signs
        of, 232
    partial sun, 51
    photosynthesis process, 51
    too much sunlight, signs of,
        232
    for windowsill herbs, 239
Liliaceae family, 30
lily family, 30
Linné, Carl von, 29
loam, 56
loppers, 136

lovage, 106
lungwort, 108

M

Malvaceae family, 30
manure, 151–52, 205–6
manure forks, 134
marjoram, 104
mealybugs, 228
medicinal garden, 76
medicinal herbs
    drying, 252
    top ten list of, 111–14
medieval gardens, 24, 78
"melting out," 230
microclimates, 49–50
microwaving herbs, 250
Middle Ages and monaster-
    ies, 22–24
mildew, 230, 231
millefolium, meaning of, 31
mint
    about, 103
    family, 30–31
    growing, 16–17
mold, 231
Monasteries, 22–24
monastery garden, 78
money, budgeting, 43
motherwort, 118
mulches
    benefits of, 209
    dark, about, 212
    light, about, 212
    mulching, defined, 209
    popular, list of, 213–14
    summer, 54, 209–11, 212–14
    winter, 211–12, 214, 241
Myrtaceae family, 30

N

nasturtiums, 16
native plants, garden of,
    80–81

neighbors, 42
nettles, 118, 208
nigra, meaning of, 31
nitrogen, 57–58, 231
node, defined, 124
nozzles, 137
NPK meters, 59
nutmeg, 16
nutrients
    insufficient, common prob-
        lems, 231–32
    insufficient, signs of, 226,
        231
    needed for soil fertility, 57–58

O

obelisks, 98
oceans, and microclimate, 50
odorata, meaning of, 31
officinale, meaning of, 31
oregano, Greek, 102–3
organic fertilizers, 204–8
organic gardening, 201–2,
    203–4
organic matter, 56–57, 143–45.
    See also compost
ornamental herbs
    drying, 252–55
    top ten list of, 106–9
ornaments, garden, 97–99
orris root, 115
ovary, 36
oven drying herbs, 249–50
ovules, 36

P

parsley, 103
parsley worm, 229
pathways, 63, 66
pennyroyal, English, 116
peppermint, 111–12
perennials
    cutting back at end of sea-
        son, 246